QUILTS FOR BABIES & CHILDREN

A (detail)

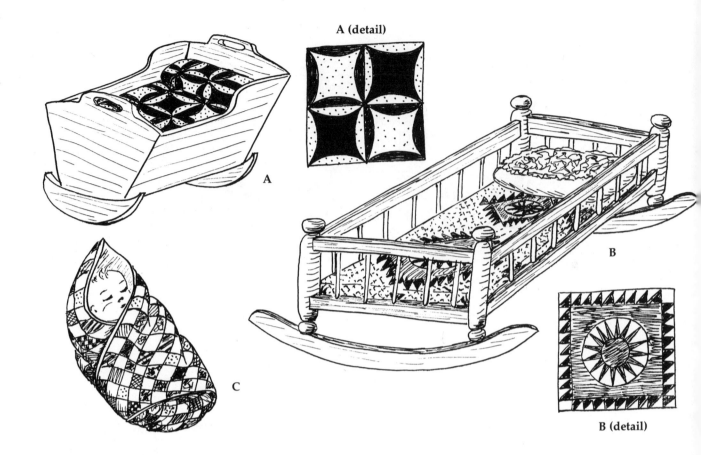

A

B

B (detail)

C

D

E

QUILTS FOR BABIES & CHILDREN

DOLORES A. HINSON

ARCO PUBLISHING, INC.
NEW YORK

To all grandparents and the babies they love:
This book is dedicated to the proposition
that you cannot quilt without adding love
to your stitches.

Published by Arco Publishing, Inc.
215 Park Avenue South, New York, N.Y. 10003

Library of Congress Cataloging in Publication Data

Hinson, Dolores A.
  Quilts for babies and children.

  Includes index.
  1. Quilting. 2. Children's paraphernalia.
3. Infants' supplies. I. Title.
TT835.H515 1983   746.9'7   83-8778
  ISBN 0-668-05475-1 (Cloth Edition)
  ISBN 0-668-05986-9 (Paper Edition)

Printed in the United States of America

10 9 8 7 6 5 4 3 2 1

Contents

Introduction

The fall before I began writing this book, I received word from four very good friends that each was about to become a grandparent for the very first time. (As it turned out, one friend's sixth child and her first grandchild arrived almost simultaneously!) With five babies arriving within a few months of one another, I combed my quilt pattern collection for motifs that would appeal to babies and children. The results were patterns of every description and from every design era of the past 200 years. As I sorted through the patterns from my collection and in books I had not read in many years, as well as patterns sent by friends (Mary Schafter, Cuesta Benberry, and others), it became apparent to me that this was a field of patterns loved by quilters. But—much loved as such patterns are—there is little information in any of the quilt magazines or books about these quilt patterns as a special subject. I therefore decided to compile a book of patterns and the short history of children's quilts that follows.

My line of investigation led me into some strange byways; the librarians at the Austin Public Library, Central Branch, helped me find librarians' research books on the topics needed. Several friends, including those mentioned above, lent patterns. My son, Trey Hinson, allowed me to use the patterns I had designed just for him. My mother, Iris Codling, helped with questions and an untiring ear. Everyone was needed, and to all go my heartfelt thanks—especially to new little Charles, Dru, Sally Ann, George III, and Dhana Dhu. I couldn't have done it without you.

Note to the Reader

It is recommended that you test your patterns before cutting any cloth. Do this by tracing the pattern pieces, in the exact arrangement in which they will be sewn, onto a piece of paper the size of the finished block. Make sure that all the pattern pieces fit together properly; use a pencil and ruler to make any minor adjustments. If you alter any pattern pieces, retrace the entire block on another piece of paper to double-check the arrangement. After making any necessary adjustments, cut the final cardboard cutting patterns and begin tracing your patterns on cloth.

1

A Short History of Children's Quilts

Bunnies, puppy dogs, kitty cats, and baby birds are the traditional motifs for baby quilts. Right? —Wrong. The baby animals of our modern baby quilts, even the motifs of toys, fairy-tale figures, clowns, and so on, considered necessary elements of today's quilts for children, are all less than 100 years old.

It seems that every 60 to 150 years, adults' perceptions of their own children undergo a drastic revision. We now call these revisions "advances in child psychology," but they were taking place long before the word or even the concept of "psychology" emerged. These changes in conceptions and idealizations of children and childhood concern the student of American quilt history and lore from about 1650 on.

The following brief summary depends on generalizations. Nothing in the study of human behavior and fads is perfectly true for 100 percent of any population, or even for any fraction of that population. Things are only *generally* true for 51 percent to about 95 percent of any group.

Before 1780, children were thought of as "small, rather stupid adults" (to paraphrase the conclusions of books on the subject) who should have been born knowing all the things adults did. The primary evidence for this is that children wore the same clothing fashions—in smaller sizes—as their parents, no matter how unsuitable those fashions were for free movement and play. Corsets were laced onto two-year-olds, both boys and girls. Ribbons, laces, multiple buttons and buttonholes, high-heeled shoes, petticoats, farthingales, and basket hoops tortured both mother and daughter, while sons were forced to be careful of silk stockings or wigs if fashion decreed them for their fathers. Of course, there were also *dishabille*, or casual, costumes. These were cut down from outmoded or adult clothing and worn when children were not in public. But since people had to work, and children were considered working members of the family and town, there was little playtime allowed even for the children of the wealthy. If poor children had to do manual labor, rich children had to learn their lessons in order to take their places as leaders of society quickly. As children's fashions of this period mirrored those of the adult world, so did their other possessions, including the quilts used on their beds.

This idea—that the child is a small adult who possesses knowledge, but lacks the discipline to follow it—started during the Middle Ages. It was not seriously challenged until the rise of Protestantism and the formulation of the theory of predestination. The idea of Original Sin combined with the idea of the "small adult" led many people to believe that since children were conceived and born in sin, they must be naturally evil. Therefore, a child did not make mistakes out of ignorance or laziness, but out of willful disobedience to God's Law. And God's Law covered everything from sitting still in church and keeping clothing neat and clean to finishing a task before suppertime. After all, the Bible stated firmly that children must obey their parents or guardians. Cold baths, restricted menus (the eating of meat by a person with an undeveloped body would overheat the blood, causing wicked thoughts, leading to wicked deeds, reasoned the great minds of the day), and regular times for beatings were also instituted on authority found in the scriptures. Some fine baby quilts were made in this period, but they do not show much wear.

You must remember that while this harsh and strict treatment of children was the generally accepted model for child rearing, many parents then—as they always have—reasoned that the prevailing child psychology methods did not quite apply to their little Susie or Johnnie. In fact, most children manage to grow up without too much warping of their personalities in spite of too harsh (or too lenient) periods of child management.

The work of Jean Jacques Rousseau, a French philosopher, provided the impetus for the next change, which occurred over the last decades of the eighteenth century. Rousseau's theory was founded

1

upon the basic equality of all men; he has been blamed or congratulated, according to point of view, for indirectly contributing to the American and French Revolutions as well as to the social revolution in Western society that happened about the same time. One of his ideas was that society and education changed humans from "Children of Nature" and "Noble Savages" into civilized—and hence evil—people. Parents and educators who wished to be up-to-date in their approach to children abandoned the idea of Original Sin. Instead, the phrase "children are born without knowledge of evil until civilization teaches them to sin" expressed the popular viewpoint. In other words, if the child did something wrong, it was the fault of his or her training. This shifted the blame from the child to the parents and teachers; we have not altogether outgrown this attitude.

The first hint historical evidence offers us of this complete reversal is when, about 1780, children began to be depicted in drawings and portraits wearing loose, flowing dresses and one-piece, loose coveralls—clothes altogether different from the costumes of their parents. A few years later some of the adult styles changed slightly to imitate the children's fashions, while keeping adult inconveniences and accessories.

Another sweeping change was in toys. Before this time, except for a handmade doll or similar item made by a relative or friend, children did not usually have any toys. Toys were made for wealthy adults and were too expensive or complicated for children. At first, the handmade toys—wooden dolls or animals, tin dishes or "kitchens," paper theaters and costumes—began to be ordered from central European peasants for distribution in the city marketplaces of France, Italy, and Great Britain. The toys were inexpensive enough that most children, except the very poor, could have at least one or two. From clothing and toys to special furniture, bedding, and other household goods was a short step. Therefore, this era of 1780-1830 marks the beginning of our survey of American children's quilts.

It took time for something as new as quilt pattern designs pleasing to small children to develop. At first, quilts for children followed the same processes of development as had children's dress; they were adult patterns used in smaller-sized quilts. Of course, only the favorite adult patterns were used. The finest materials the family could afford and the finest needlework the seamstress could manage often went into the quilts made for beloved children, especially baby quilts for the family's first child. Though these quilts should have been magnificent, they were often spoiled by the use of patterns that were too large and that overbalanced the quilts' small dimensions. Fashionable adult color schemes often dull or dark in tone, were also used. Some of the color combinations popular at this time were blue and brown, navy and cream (or brown), orange and blue. Red on yellow prints, bluish red on white, or blue on white chintz were imported from France and England and could be found only in the quilts of the wealthy. Even in these quilts such materials were often used rather sparingly.

During this same era it became customary for a betrothed girl to create a wedding quilt for special use on her marriage bed. These quilts started out rather simply at first, but as the turn of the century approached and then passed, they became more and more elaborate in design and execution. The quilts were displayed with the other wedding finery and were prime examples of the bride's expert needlework. After a time the recent bride, now about to become a mother for the first time, used the finest and fanciest pattern she had to make a baby quilt. Since this pattern was usually that of her wedding quilt, the baby quilt was made to match. Later on in the same period, brides-to-be obtained enough material for both quilts and then put away the portion to be used for the baby quilt until it was needed. The wedding quilt–baby quilt sets are very interesting. Some of the patterns make darling miniature quilts; others are designed with elements that are too large and are, perhaps, not as attractive.

Quilts B and D in the Frontispiece are of this type. President Wilson's Rising Sun pattern, B, was made in the 1850's and was used on the crib of the future President Woodrow Wilson. Two blocks of the adult-sized pattern were used with a similarly patterned border. Quilt D is an appliquéd Peony design. This was originally an elaborate wedding quilt with a Peony and Grapevine border. Its colors are red and green on white, typical of 1840-era quilts, although the red is almost a wine color. The wedding quilt was used for at least two generations, until it began to show signs of much wear. It was then cut down and pieced together to form this baby quilt, which has continued to serve later generations of the same family.

The all-white quilt, E, is a reconstruction of this same type, using adult-sized patterns on a miniature quilt. The Tulip, Star, Folk Flower, and Princess Feather patterns could be found on quilts made on the Eastern Seaboard from Boston to Baltimore from about 1750 through 1850.

Gradually, the patterns for baby and children's quilts were reduced in size to make more delicate designs. The designs themselves, though, remained those popular for adult quilts. The Melon Patch pattern, for instance, was designed and became very popular in Philadelphia in the 1820's; an example can be found in the Frontispiece, Picture A. This particular example was probably made in the 1850's or 1860's; from the color combination, I believe it was made by a Pennsylvania Dutch needlewoman. The block is probably either 6 or 8 inches square rather than the 12 inches square usual for an adult-sized pattern. The colors in the original are dark green with black and dark gold with red, both calico prints.

The remaining quilt pictured in the Frontispiece, C, is a simple design of alternating squares of white and print scrap material. This quilt was made in 1963, but the design is much older. Baby quilts made from squares in scrap designs were made on all of the American frontiers by women who did not have the time or the material for more elaborate patterns. They became fashionable again after 1900, when needlewomen rebelled against over-elaborate Victorian patterns. My Great-Aunt Emma, who made this quilt for my son, was a young woman at the turn of the twentieth century, and this remained one of her favorite quilt patterns. The squares in the original are 1½ inches on a side for a baby quilt and 4 inches on a side when used in adult-sized quilts.

To return to our history, after 1850 the Victorians sentimentalized their little ''Children of Nature'' into ''Mother's Darlings'' and ''Angels Unaware.'' They put children back into semi-adult clothing styles. The child's chores and lessons were cut back to give more playtime, and shops opened to sell a flood of newly invented toys. Lest it be thought that children of this era ''had it made,'' the Victorians also invented the idea that ''children should be seen and not heard,'' started the fashion of music lessons for almost all children (so the parents could show off before friends), and in general approved only of children who obeyed and did not try to think for themselves. Some people must have known real children, however, or the play *Peck's Bad Boy* and the novels *Tom Sawyer* and *Huckleberry Finn* would not have proved as popular as they did. Although these stories were considered adult fare when they first appeared, books and plays were being written and illustrated just for children. By the 1880's, women's magazines were putting a page of stories, paper dolls, or craft instructions for children into each issue. By the turn of the century several female illustrators were able to earn their livelihoods almost entirely from their work in the children's book field. Several of these illustrators are still well known, like Rose O'Neal for her Kewpies and Bertha Corbett for the Sunbonnet Babies. From these illustrations made just to please children, quilters drew inspiration for the first quilt patterns designed just for children. After the turn of the century, Peter Rabbit took his place on quilts; then, in turn, Grimm's fairy tale figures, Little Women, Tom Sawyer, and the many Disney characters. Recently Holly Hobbie and her cousins have jumped from various printed media to children's quilt tops. It would have been very nice to have included some of the early twentieth-century patterns in this collection, but many of the earliest are quite rare and I have only heard of them. Other patterns are copyrighted or held in company catalogs and are not available for reproduction. Also, some in my collection of pictures are just not clear enough to be copied correctly. The Alphabet pattern from a 1910 *Ladies Art* catalog (which is not in the company's current pattern list and has not been available for many years) is in this category. I have therefore worked out a set of substitute designs for the block patterns that were unclear or missing from my copy, since the idea for an Alphabet quilt was such a nice one.

2

General Directions

The patterns in this book have been chosen to give an assortment of old and new, easy and difficult patterns in a mixture of pieced, appliqué, embroidery, and combination patterns. Most of the patterns are given in two or more sizes or with two or more methods of execution. Pattern sizes range from plain piecing squares 1½ inches on a side and appliqué or embroidery patterns 6 inches square up to center designs that measure 24 or more inches wide by 30 inches long. Several patterns are given in sets containing center design, border, and quilting motifs. Other patterns can be mixed or matched so that the quilter can design her—or his—own original quilt.

The motifs in this book were chosen with children newborn to sixteen years of age in mind. There are more designs for younger children than for older ones because many so-called adult patterns are entirely suitable for teenaged boys and girls. Also, there are rather more designs that might appeal to boys than to girls, because almost any floral quilt looks good in a girl's bedroom but patterns of boyish interests are rare. However, if you have a tomboy who would like an airplane quilt rather than one with dolls on it, please indulge her—she will grow up all too soon, as children have a habit of doing.

The drawings show where dark, light, and medium colors should go in a pattern. They are deliberately drawn in black and white with cross-hatching because colored patterns have an influence on the viewer. Seeing blue and rose colors used in a certain pattern makes it difficult to envision that pattern afterward in yellow and brown. Conversely, if the bedroom you are making the quilt for is one that needs the yellow and brown color scheme, there will be a tendency to ignore the blue-and-rose-illustrated pattern when that may be the exact pattern that would suit the child best. By seeing the patterns in black and white, you can let your imagination supply any color scheme needed.

Carefully observe where light, dark, and medium colors are used in the pattern chosen. A design often depends on the placement of the tones of color, and if the placement is altered a different pattern emerges. This makes for confusion in design when more than

one of these tonal patterns is used in a single quilt.

In the directions for each pattern, any traditional color scheme will be noted. Such color schemes may be used or not as you choose. There are fashions in colors as in anything else. In America, from roughly 1840 to 1860, red and green motifs on white backgrounds were used in about 65 percent of all the quilts that have been preserved for us to see. By the end of the nineteenth century, browns, maroons, deep blues, and greens were fashionable—making the quilts very dark. As a reaction, in the 1920's and 1930's pastel colors were used everywhere. Meanwhile, back in the 1890's, cleanliness had become such a fashionable issue that white paint was used for everything in the kitchen and nursery. (Mothers began to brag that their children had never touched clothing or bedding of any other color before they started school at six or seven years of age.) In the 1940's, medium and darker colors again became fashionable for adults, but the dictum for white and pastels had become so ingrained that we are still a little worried when we see a baby or small child dressed in bright or dark colors. If you like pastels, use them—but if the child likes brighter colors, they will look fine in the bedroom, too. Colors should be chosen to look well in the child's room and to please the child.

Materials for a child's quilt should be chosen for softness and washability. Because of the nature of children and their tendency to catch colds and childhood illnesses easily, their bedding needs to be washed often; you should consider this before making a child's quilt. Cotton or cotton-acetate blends in a not-too-heavyweight cloth, not too sheer or stiff, are best.

It might be a good idea to take a quilting needle with you when you shop. Run the needle through a doubled section of the cloth to make sure the needle will not stick in the cloth. Some of the new synthetic fibers are so stiff that the needle of a sewing machine actually breaks a hole through the fibers. If you use a sewing machine to make your quilt top, these synthetic fibers are acceptable, but they are impossible to use in hand sewing or hand quilting. Do not use any of the stretch knit materials for hand sewing, and do not sew them with a straight stitch on your sewing machine. The only stitch that will hold stretch knit fabrics is a loose zigzag machine stitch.

The following chart gives the quilt dimensions needed to fit various bed sizes and the overall yardage estimates for quilt tops in each size, using material 36 inches wide. The yardage for the backing will be the same amount needed for the quilt top, plus another yard to provide an 8-inch overhang on all four sides for attachment to the quilting frame. For appliqué designs, allow at least ½-yard more than the estimate given.

Description	Size (feet)	Yardage
Small Carriage Quilt	3 × 4	1½ yards
Crib Quilt	4 × 4	2¼ yards
	or	or
	4 × 5	2¾ yards
Youth Bed Quilt	5 × 7	4½ yards
Twin Bed Quilt	6 × 8	5½ yards

"Overall yardage" is the estimate of *total* cloth needed for the top. It is the sum of the different pieces of cloth needed for each particular pattern. You would be wise to allow extra material for shrinkage and for layouts that may entail some waste.

For pieced quilts:
1. First sort out your pattern pieces into groups by color.
2. Find (or estimate as closely as possible) the area in square inches of each pattern piece within the group. For example, you can find the area of squares by multiplying the length of a side *plus* ½ inch by itself. (The ½ inch allows for ¼ inch seam allowance on each side.) The formula for triangles is ½ base × height; for rectangles, length × width. Remember to add ¼ inch per seam for seam allowances.
3. Then multiply the area of the pattern piece by the number of these pieces you'll need for the entire top.
4. When you've done this for every pattern piece in the color group, add the figures together to find the total amount in square inches of this color cloth that you will need for your top. Convert to yards. If you buy fabric from a shop that sells in meters, convert yards to meters by allowing 39 inches per meter. A meter is 3 inches longer than a yard.
5. Repeat the process for each color group.

Add some yardage to the amount of fabric for each color: This will allow for cutting between pieces whose edges do not touch, for nap, and so forth. How much you'll want to add depends on your estimate of how much waste your particular pattern will involve. Visualize your layout; if you'll want to position pattern pieces on the grain of the fabric in a certain way (for example, you may want to lay out triangles so that one of their short sides is on the grain of the fabric and their long sides are on the bias, or diagonally cross-grain), you'll have to allow extra material.

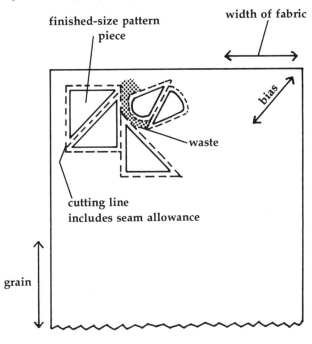

grain-lengthwise thread
direction - parallel
with selvage
bias - diagonally cross-grain

For appliqué quilts, you'll first have to figure the area of the background piece and the borders, again including seam allowances. Then follow the instructions for pieced patterns as well as you can to estimate the area of the appliquéd material, again sorting pieces by color and adding yardage at the end to allow for waste. Most shops will cut pieces of material as small as ¼-yard, but no smaller. In any case, it's better to have a bit more than you need than not to have enough.

This is the correct technical method of estimating yardage, but I have never found a quilter who uses it. After a mistake or two—getting too little and piecing with other cloth, or getting too much and making three quilts out of it—you *do* learn to estimate by eye and size of pattern. Then, too, in all my years of meeting quilters, I've discovered that we all love yard goods and have pieces of various sizes put away because we couldn't pass up a pretty length of cloth. I have two traveling trunks full of such pieces and a smaller one for doll's clothing, silks, velvets, and laces. Most of my friends have more.

The following is a list of the tools and materials that will be necessary or useful in making quilts from the patterns in this book.

Materials for Making the Cutting Patterns:
1. Scissors
2. Tissue paper or onionskin paper
3. Cardboard, sandpaper, or thin, stiff plastic
4. No. 2 soft pencil and sharpener
5. Ruler and compass for drawing

Materials for Marking Cloth:
1. No. 2 soft pencil for light-colored fabrics
2. White conté pencil for dark fabrics (available from art supply stores)

Sewing Needs:
1. Sharp scissors just for cloth
2. Thimble
3. No. 7 or 8 quilting needles. If quilting needles are not available, "betweens" are adequate.
4. A paper of straight pins and a pincushion
5. No. 40 or 50 thread, 500-yd. spool, in white or suitable colors

Extras:
These items are only needed for some quilts. Check the sewing directions given with the pattern to see which supplies in this list would be useful for a specific quilt.

Embroidery thread in several shades and colors and needles

Three-ply yarn in several shades and colors

Ribbons, lace, small buttons, and other accessories

Tapestry, yarn, and embroidery needles in suitable sizes

Embroidery hoops or frames

Fabric paints and accessories in assorted colors

Crayons and wax paper

Choosing a Pattern

Top Designs

The first step in making a quilt is to choose a pattern, then a color scheme, a border (if one is desired), and a design for combining these elements into a top. Pages 8 and 9 show new top designs that you might want to choose from, or you may prefer a traditional-style top like those on this page and page 7. The traditional top is made of blocks joined pattern block to pattern block, forming an overall design (diagram A). Tops can also be joined pattern block to plain block (diagram C), creating a checkerboard effect. Or, the pattern blocks can be separated by lattice strips (diagram D). Diagrams B and E and the drawings of the complete quilts given with many of the patterns in the book show other ideas for top designs. Among the many different designs that could give interesting effects with patterns other than the ones they are presented with here are Tumbling Blocks (page 60), Humpty Dumpty (page 72), and Ethnic Dolls (page 168).

Many magazine illustrations have recently shown quilts that are composed just of square scraps of material. Section Two contains several different ideas and pattern sizes for this fashionable style.

The top designs on pages 8 and 9 are marked with small squares that may be used as patterns for quilt tops with backgrounds composed of squares and other blank spaces, to be filled in with your choice of appliqué, embroidery, fabric paint, or crayoned motifs. The squares may also be viewed as graphs for computing the size of the different quilt areas if you do not wish to have the background spaces cut into small squares. Multiply the number of squares by the sizes given beneath the drawing to obtain the overall size of the quilt. If you would like the quilt size enlarged or made smaller, change the size of the squares.

The quilt top illustrated in diagram F, page 8, has squares 1½ inches on a side. The quilt made to this

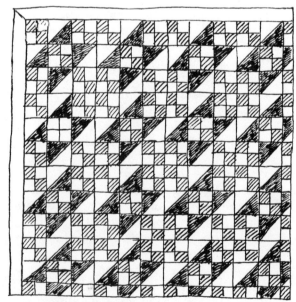

A. Block and Block

B. Plain and Block, diagonal

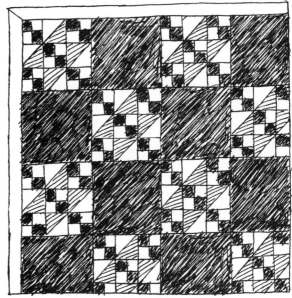

C. Plain and Block, straight

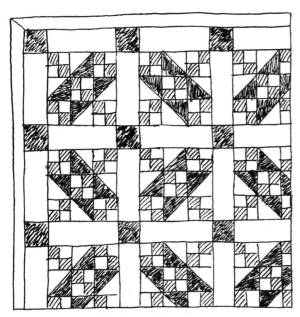

D. Block and Lattice with corner square

E. Diagonal blocks with lattices

design will thus be a 3½′ by 4½′ crib quilt. To make a twin bed quilt from this design, add 3 inches to the width of each border, making them each 6 inches wide. Then add two more blocks in pattern to each row (the rows across will now contain five blocks each) and three more rows of five blocks each to the bottom of the quilt for a depth of 7 blocks. The quilt top design in diagram G on page 8 is 3 feet 2 inches by 4 feet 10 inches without a border or edge. It could be changed to a twin bed size by enlarging the squares from 2 inches to 4 inches on a side. The plain strips should also be doubled then from 12″ to 24″ wide.

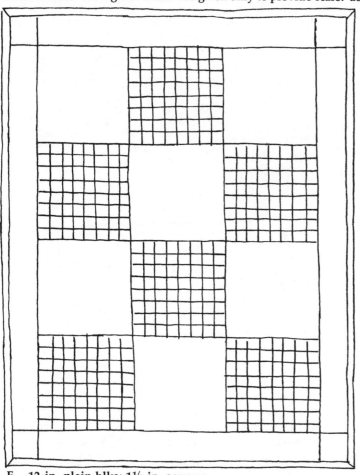

F. 12-in. plain blks; 1½ in. squares

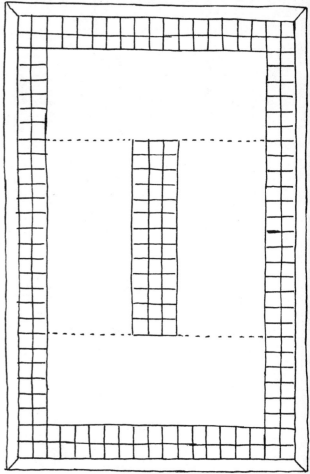

G. 12-in. strips; 2-in. squares

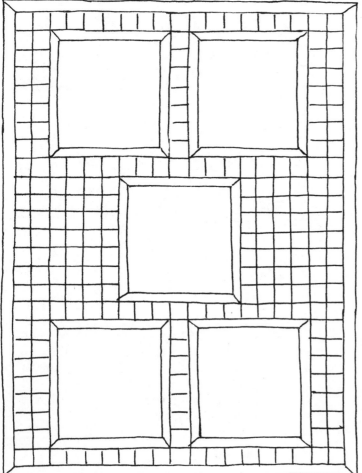

H. 12-in. blks.; 1½ in. strips; 3-in. squares

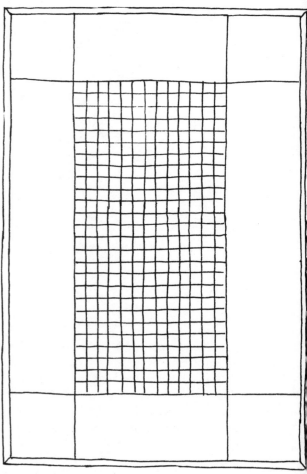

I. 8-in. borders; 1½-in. squares

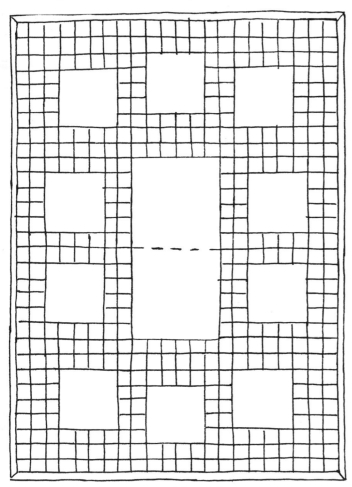

J. 212-in. lg. blks; 8-in. sm. blks.; 2-in. squares

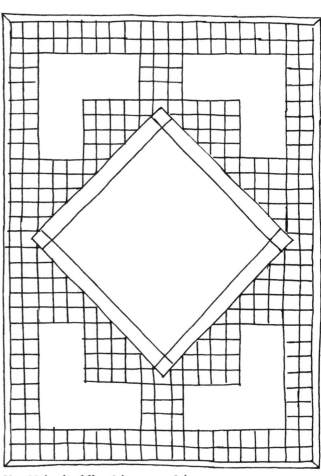

K. 22-in. lg. blk.; 6-in. areas; 2-in. squares

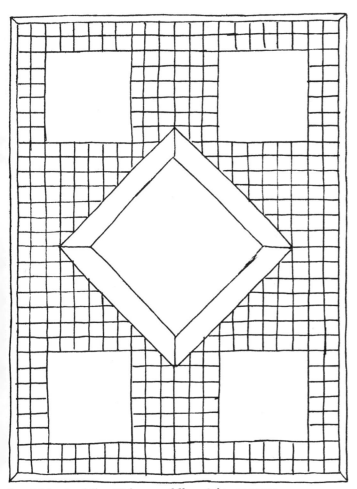

L. 16-in. lg. blk.; 12-in. sm. blks.; 2-in. squares

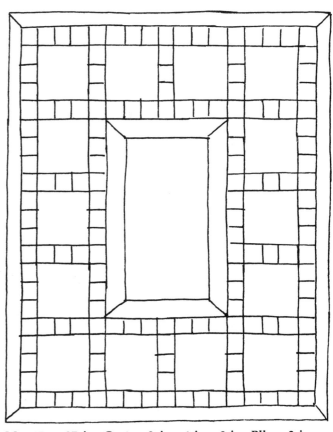

M. 15 × 27 in. Center; 3 in. strips; 9-in. Blks.; 3-in. squares

The sizes of the plain areas in these top designs are given in the captions beneath the diagrams. Most of these blanks are blocks in one or two sizes. The patterns in diagrams G and I, however, have plain strips rather than blocks. There are several fancy borders among the quilting patterns (which begin on page 292) that would suit these quilts beautifully. The strips could also be filled with a row of appliquéd, embroidered, fabric-painted, or crayoned motifs chosen from among the patterns given in the sizes that will fit the width of the strip. There could be one or two motifs repeated or several different motifs, as you wish. A new quilt top can be designed using bands of different border patterns selected from the border section. You could also design a border using one of the small motifs in this book repeated all the way around the quilt, like the elephant motif in the Elephant Parade border (page 143).

NOTE: There are several ways of using the motifs in this book as patterns for quilts. These methods include piecing, appliqué, and embroidery among the needlework techniques and using fabric paints and crayons from the field of textile decorating. The first two methods involve the making of *cutting patterns* described below. The last three methods use pattern outlines, which must be copied on the background cloth itself. This method of pattern transfer to cloth is explained later.

Cutting Patterns

The first step in making a pieced or appliqué quilt is to make a cutting pattern. **Do not cut the patterns from the pages of this—or any—pattern book.** If the pattern pieces are lost, they cannot be replaced.

1. Trace the pattern outlines onto tissue paper or onionskin paper with a No. 2 soft pencil. Use a ruler to straighten the lines and a compass to even out the curved lines.

2. To help you distinguish which pattern pieces to use for which size when a pattern is given in more than one size, the sizes are numbered in this book from the smallest size for any particular pattern to the largest. The sizes are given with the directions for each specific pattern. In addition, each shape needed for the pattern is marked with a letter indicating the approximate order in which the shape will be used. Thus, 1c, 2c, and 3c will designate the same-shaped piece in three different sizes, and "c" indicates that the piece will probably be used third. It was sometimes not possible to put all the shapes for one pattern on one sheet or even on consecutive sheets. Some of the

larger or more awkward pieces had to be mixed in wherever they fit, even with pieces in other sizes. This mixing has been held to a minimum.

3. Cut out the tissue paper patterns and retrace their outlines carefully on one of the cutting pattern materials suggested in item 3 of "Materials for Making the Cutting Patterns," page 6. You can make these patterns from medium-weight cardboard from the back of a pad of paper, from medium-fine sandpaper that will grip the cloth and not move while is is being traced, or from lightweight flat plastic sheets, such as the tops of margarine bowls or the sides of flattened bleach or laundry detergent bottles. All pieces should be marked (before cutting or after) with the name of the pattern and the number of the piece (including its letter if it has one). Cut the pieces carefully on the outlines so that the pieces will be accurate in size.

NOTE: If using cardboard or sandpaper cutting patterns, cut four or five patterns for each shape. These materials will wear along the edges and lose their shapes somewhat after being used a number of times. When the corners or edges begin to look noticeably rounded or worn, change to a fresh cutting piece.

Some of the larger pattern pieces in this book show only one quarter or one half of the shape needed. One edge of the piece will therefore be dots or dashes instead of a solid line. When tracing, place the tissue paper so that only one corner or one half of the paper covers the pattern piece shown. Draw off the solid lines of the pattern onto the tissue paper and mark the ends of the solid lines firmly. Then fold the tissue paper in half (or in quarters, as needed) so that the solid lines of the pattern piece touch the fold. Cut the tissue paper on the solid line. In this way, you will have copied the shape of the pattern on the other half (or three quarters) of the tissue paper wihout error and without needing to retrace. Finally, iron the tissue paper to smooth out the folds completely, and use the tissue paper as you would the other pattern pieces to make cutting patterns.

4. *These cutting patterns are finished-size patterns.* This means that they are the size of the shape after it is sewn in place, when the seam allowances are hidden in the seam. *The seam allowances must be added to the finished-size pieces before the cloth can be cut.* This procedure is explained fully in the section "Tracing the Pattern on Cloth," page 11.

5. A drawing of the finished block accompanies the patterns for all pieced designs. In these drawings, the sections representing the cutting pattern shapes are cross-hatched in a manner that shows the light, dark, medium, and white color areas. If the design is a scrap design, this too is indicated by different crosshatchings. Examine diagrams A, B, C, and D on pages 6 and 7. These show one single pattern used in four top designs. They also show four *tonal* designs. Where definite indications of light, dark, and medium shades are shown (this is tonal design), repeat the *shades* of a color in exactly the same position in each block in a single quilt, whatever colors you decide to use from block to block. Diagram A, page 6, shows the Jacob's Ladder design from page 51. Diagram B shows the same tonal pattern, but reversed. Diagram C shows the same tonal pattern as Diagram B, but the plain blocks are the same color as the dark sections of the pieced blocks. The look of the quilt would again differ if the plain blocks matched the lighter sections instead. The last of the four diagrams, D, shows the same tonal pattern as in diagram B, but this time half of the pieced blocks are given a half-turn to reverse the direction of their patterns. Small alterations in tone, direction, or top design change the looks of the finished quilt. Be sure to use the same tonal pattern for the entire quilt. A quilt containing blocks with several different tonal patterns is often unattractive.

Figuring the Number of Pieces for a Top

To determine the number of cloth pieces in each shape needed for a complete quilt top, the size, pattern, border (if any), and colors must all be chosen. Using the chart given on page 5, decide on the overall size of the quilt top in feet; then convert the figures to inches. Place these figures on a note pad under the headings *Length* and *Width*. Decide on the width of the border and of any rows of one- or two-inch-wide strips that will be pieced to the border to enhance its importance and beauty. Subtract the width of the border and any strips (multiplied by two for the two sides of the quilt) from both the length and width of the quilt top. The remaining figures give the dimensions of the center design.

The size of the blocks or center background material is usually a multiple of either a 2- or 3-inch square, which allows the blocks to be calculated to the nearest square foot. Thus there will be four 6-inch-square blocks in a 1-foot-square area. Decide how many blocks there are in a 1-foot area for the pattern size you have selected for your quilt. Multiply this by the number of square feet in the center area. A 9-inch block, for example, will go 16 times in a 3-foot-square area. Adjust the size of the center area—either larger or smaller—as needed to contain an exact number of whole blocks. Thus, if the number of 9-inch blocks that fits in a row of a given quilt size is 6 whole blocks

and 7 inches of a seventh block, add two inches to the width or length of the quilt top. The center area size may be either increased or decreased as necessary by up to 6 inches without changing the quilt size from one category to another. Adding or subtracting strips from the borders or making them wider or narrower is another easy way to maintain the correct top dimensions for your quilt.

Now that you have the number of blocks needed for the top, count the number of times a single pattern shape is used in a single block. Multiply that number by the number of blocks in the quilt top. The result is the number of pieces needed from a certain piece of cloth in that shape. It is usually better to trace these pieces all at once and also to trace all of the pieces needed for the entire quilt top from each of the pattern shapes at one time.

Tracing the Pattern on Cloth

If you are making a pieced quilt, trace the patterns onto the back of the cloth, where your sewing stitches will be placed.

If the patterns are to be appliquéd, trace them onto the front of the cloth so that the traced lines make a guide for your stitches.

As already noted (see page 10), these patterns are finished size and must have seam allowances added to them. To do this, place the first pattern piece in one corner of the cloth. Place it so as to waste as little of the cloth as possible. The sides of the pattern should be ¼'' from each edge of the cloth, *excluding the selvage edge.* (You may find it convenient to trim off the selvage edge before laying out your pattern pieces to avoid including it in a seam allowance by mistake.) Trace around the pattern with a light stroke. On light-colored cloth, use a No. 2 soft pencil; on dark fabrics, use a white conté pencil, which may be purchased in any art-supply shop. Lift the pattern and position it again on the cloth, taking care to leave ½'' between the new pattern edge and any part of the previously traced pattern line, and trying to position the pattern piece so that as little of the cloth is wasted as possible. Again trace the pattern outline on the cloth. Continue in this manner until you have traced all of the pieces needed from this cloth. See diagram N, page 14. Follow the same procedure for all the patterns needed from each of the different pieces of cloth.

Cutting the Pieces from the Cloth

Use sharp scissors. Cut the pieces apart halfway between the pencil outlines, leaving ¼-inch of fabric for seam allowance all the way around each piece. (Refer

Refer back to diagram A, page 6. In 12-inch square blocks, there will be 28 dark triangles per horizontal row × 8 rows down, or 224 dark triangles for a 7 × 8-foot double-bed quilt (solid outline, A); 16 × 60 or 96 dark triangles in a 4 × 6-foot children's bed quilt (dotted line, B); and 20 × 4 or 80 dark triangles in a 4 × 5-foot baby quilt (dot-dash line, C).

Adjustment of quilt sizes for 9-inch blocks

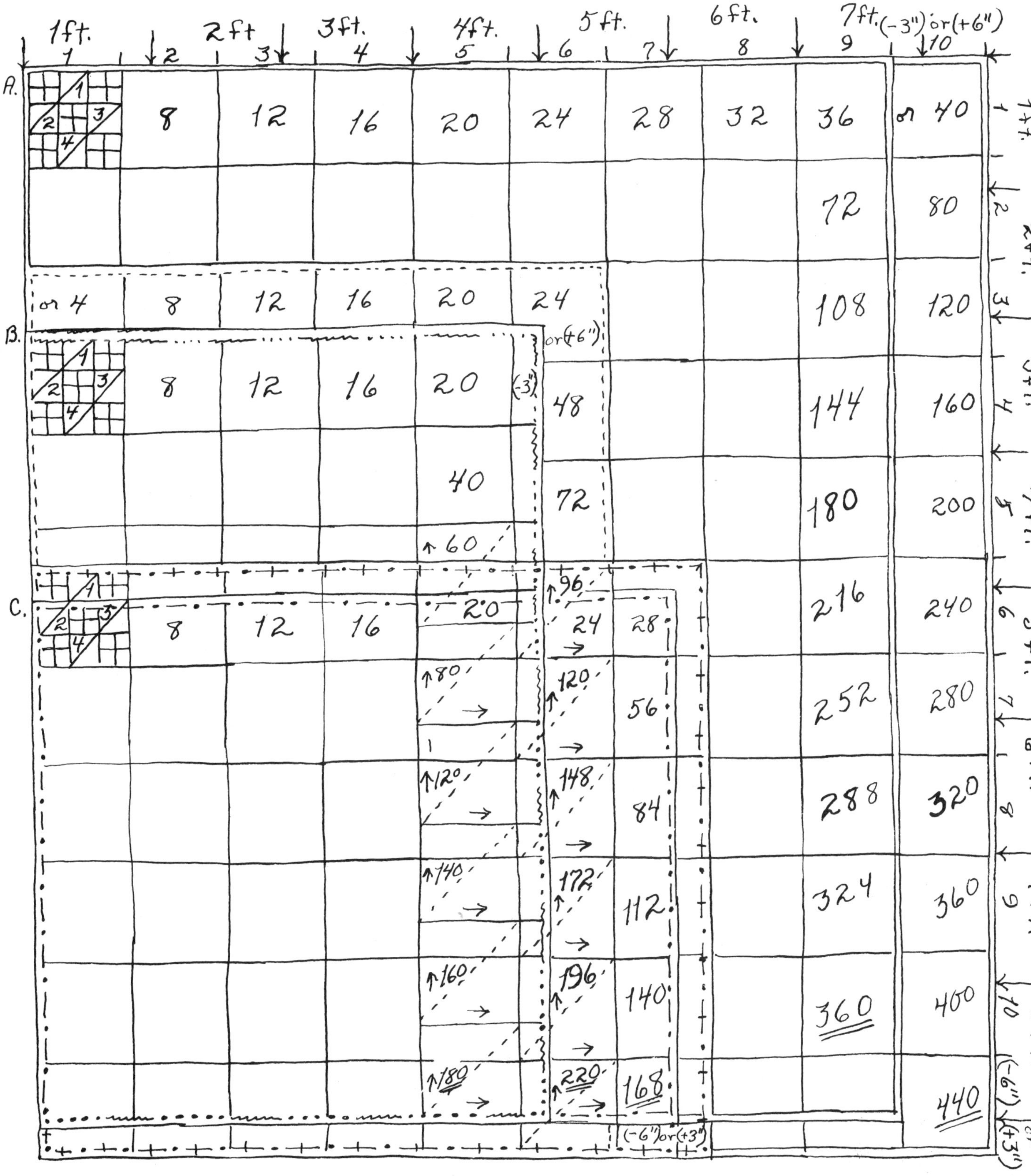

Top column headers: 1ft. (1) | (1) (2) | 2ft. (3) | (4) 3ft. | (5) 4ft. | (6) 5ft. | (7) | 6ft. (8) | 7ft.(−3") or (+6") (9) | (10)

Right side headers (top to bottom): 1ft. (1), 2ft. (2), 3ft. (3)/(4), 4ft. (5), 5ft. (6)/(7), 6ft. (8), 7ft. (9), 8ft. (−6") or (+3") (10)

A. (block diagram: 1, 2, 3, 4) | 8 | 12 | 16 | 20 | 24 | 28 | 32 | 36 | or 40

72 | 80

B. or 4 | 8 | 12 | 16 | 20 | 24 | | 108 | 120

(block diagram: 1, 2, 3, 4) | 8 | 12 | 16 | 20 | (−3") or(+6") | 48 | 144 | 160

40 | 72 | 180 | 200

↑ 60 | ↑ 96 | | 216 | 240

C. (block diagram: 1, 2, 3, 4) | 8 | 12 | 16 | ▲ 20 | 24 | 28

↑ 80 → | ↑ 120 → | 56 | 252 | 280

↑ 120 → | ↑ 148 → | 84 | 288 | 320

↑ 140 → | ↑ 172 → | 112 | 324 | 360

↑ 160 → | ↑ 196 → | 140 | 360 | 400

↑ 180 → | ↑ 220 → | 168 | | 440

(−6") or (+3")

To make a double-bed quilt (A) when using 9-inch blocks, 3 inches must be subtracted from the width or 6 inches must be added, and 3 inches added to the length or 6 inches subtracted. See diagram for adjustment of child's bed quilt (B) and crib quilt (C).

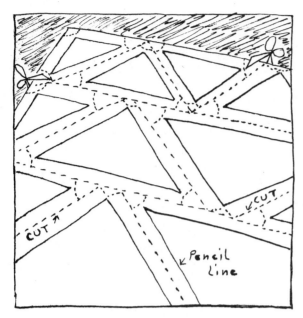

N. Cloth ready to be cut into added pieces, with seam allowance added.

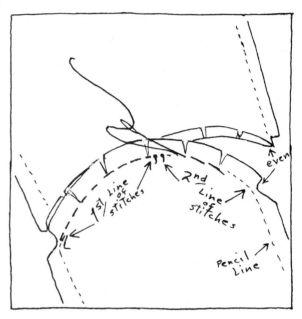

O. Sewing a curved seam: Start at the curve's center and stitch to one end of the seam. Then return to the center and complete the seam by stitching in the opposite direction.

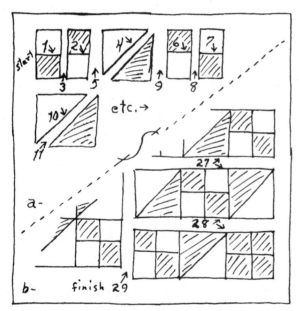

P. Piecing a block: Section a shows the steps to follow in assembling the smaller pieces of a block. After these smaller elements have been sewn together into larger units, the larger units can be joined to form the finished block (section b). Note that, in this step, only two long seams are used to combine the units into the finished block.

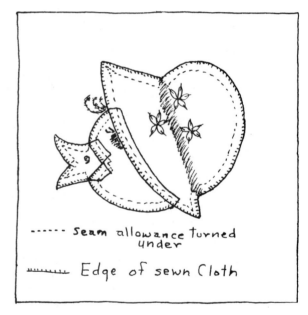

Q. Appliquéing a block.

to diagram N, on page 14.) Clip the seam allowance from all the corners to within ⅛-inch of the penciled line; this eliminates bulk when one piece is sewn to another. Straight-sided pieces do not need any more work. Curved pieces need to have the seam allowance clipped carefully at intervals along the edge to within ⅛-inch of the penciled line before sewing. See diagram O, page 14. On tight curves, clip the seam allowance every ½-inch, on long, shallow curves, clip the seam allowance about every 2 inches. This will allow the cloth to lie smooth after it is sewn. If the cloth pulls or bunches after the seam is finished, the seam allowance was not clipped often enough. On pieced seams more clipping can be done after the seam is sewn. In appliqué, however, the stitches will have to be taken out, the seam clipped, and the stitches resewn.

Organizing the Cut Pieces

Sort the loose pieces into groups, each of which will make one block after the pieces are sewn together. Within each pile, place the pieces in the order in which they will be sewn. (See the next two sections for instructions.) Each pile of pieces should form only one block. If the pieces needed for each block are assembled separately, any miscounting can be corrected before the cutting tools are stored away. To keep the groups of pieces in the correct order and keep them separated from one another, sew a single knotted thread once from bottom to top through all the pieces in a single pile. Leave about three inches of thread protruding from the top piece and clip the thread. You do not have to fasten this thread in any way. Sew all of the piles of pieces in this manner. When you are ready to begin sewing the first block, pull off the top two pieces and sew them together. Continue in this manner until all of the pieces have been sewn.

This trick of organizing the loose pieces needed for a single quilt is a traditional one used by quilters. I do not know when or where it originated, but it is at least 150 years old and very probably many centuries older than that. To me, cutting out the pieces is the least loved of all the quilting chores. Many times now I have cut out two or more quilts, assembled the pieces into blocks and placed the piles for each quilt in a small paper bag with the instructions and cutting patterns. Months later the pieces can be taken out and the quilt made without worry that any of the pieces may have gone astray or might have been miscounted. If you use this method, it is useful to store a diagram of the block and a diagram of the top design with the pieces. If the pieces are put away for any length of time, the directions and even the design of the pattern may be forgotten. If you just label the pieces with the pattern name

and then forget what the pattern looks like, it may take a lot of effort to pick out your pattern from several with the same name.

Piecing a Block

The directions for each block are given with the pattern. The sewing stitch is the running stitch with a back stitch taken every five or six stitches for reinforcement. In hand sewing the stitches should all be as small as possible. The smaller the needle used, the smaller the stitches can be made. A number 8 quilting needle is the best for making really small stitches. Before a beginner starts sewing her quilt blocks, she should take two strips of unbleached muslin or other scrap material and practice sewing the two pieces together. The stitch gauge is 5 to 6 stitches showing on one side of the cloth per inch. Some needlewomen count the stitches on both sides of the cloth, making their gauge 10 to 12 stitches per inch. Use either gauge. The important thing is to make each stitch and each interval exactly the same; this expertise comes with practice. Your stitching will take on its own characteristic look, which is as individual as your handwriting.

Many people think that hand sewing is much harder than machine sewing. On the contrary, in many ways it is easier. Most quilting patterns use small pieces of cloth that must be sewn together with many short seams. On the sewing machine this means constantly stopping to clip the threads and readjust the cloth. In hand sewing, these problems are absorbed in a smooth flow of turn, clip and sew that is relaxing to the spirit and absorbing to the mind.

The traced lines on the cloth should be on the *back of the material*. Place two pieces of the block together and adjust them so that the penciled lines on each surface are aligned. This is sewn as the first seam. Sew the seam from one corner to the next on the penciled line. Sew directly on the penciled lines. If you try to sew the pieces together by stitching inside the pencil lines, the pieces will not fit together properly, nor will they form a square. Open the two pieces of cloth and the seam allowance; press them open with your fingers. Then repeat this procedure for piecing the other elements of the block. Before sewing these smaller assembled pieces together, position them exactly as they will appear in the finished block; you can catch any errors early if you doublecheck yourself in this way. Calculate the fewest number of seams needed to sew all of the pieces together into the finished block, keeping the seams as long and straight as possible. See diagram P, page 14. Always stop sewing at a corner, no matter how shallow this corner may be. If the thread is not knotted, clipped, and restarted on the other side of the corner, the material will pull after it is sewn.

If sewing a seam with a sharp curve, start the seam at the center of the curve and sew to the left corner. Return to the center and sew a seam to the right corner. (See diagram O.) As the stitches are made, the concave top seam will have to be eased gently into position in alignment with the convex lower seam. Taking care with this adjustment will insure that the corners of the two pieces will be even at the end of the seam. *Do not try to make a pattern with pieced curves until you are an experienced hand sewer.* Piecing a curve is very difficult.

Appliquéing a Block

In piecing, the sections are sewn together to make a single layer of cloth. In appliqué, one piece of cloth (or more) is sewn over another, resulting in two or more layers of cloth.

Pin the appliqué sections to the background cloth, following the arrangement shown by the drawing of the finished block. Think about the placement as you pin the pieces. If one piece should look as though it is behind another piece (for example, a boy's shirt should be behind the waistband of his pants), then the seam allowance for that piece should be placed under the folded edge of the upper piece. See diagram Q.

The stitch used is called the hem stitch or the blind stitch. It is the same stitch used to sew a dress hem in place by hand, in such a way that the stitches do not show. See diagrams S and T. Practice this stitch on scrap material before beginning any work on the quilt. Try to make the stitches emerge exactly at the fold of the cloth on the traced pencil line. *The traced line must be on the front of the cloth for appliqué,* because the sewing is done with the cloth right side up. Clip the seam allowances on curves (see diagram N) in order to make the cloth lie smooth. The stitch gauge for appliqué should be at least 6 stitches per inch.

In machine appliqué, the pieces are cut on the finished-size lines *without* any seam allowance. The zigzag stitch is used, set for ¼-inch-long stitches that are as close together as possible. This makes the patch look as though it has been sewn to the cloth with satin-stitch embroidery. See diagram R. *These directions are applicable only to machine appliqué.* All hand-sewn appliqués must have seam allowances that are turned under. This fold of cloth keeps the edges of the pieces from raveling. If you wish to use outline embroidery, do your embroidering *after* the pieces have been firmly appliquéd in place. Embroidery thread

does not last as long as woven cloth. If you fasten pieces together with embroidery stitches, you risk having the stitches wear out after several years. Individual pieces may then be lost, ruining the looks of a quilt that probably can give many more years of wear.

Directions for Embroidery, Fabric Paints, and Crayons

Trace the patterns from this book onto tissue paper or onionskin paper with a No. 2 soft pencil. Place a piece of typing paper over the tissue paper pattern. If you do not have a clear piece of rigid plastic or an artist's lighted "transfer box," place the two sheets of paper against the window during the daytime. Trace the lines from the tissue paper to the typing paper. Then retrace the lines on the typing paper with a very black, permanent ink, felt-tip pen.

This pattern, when dry, can be used in the same manner as the onionskin or tracing paper pattern, with the pattern positioned behind the background cloth, to transfer the pattern as many times as is needed. In many cases, the black lines will show through the rather fine cloth without extra backlighting needed. Use a No. 2 soft pencil to trace the pattern on the cloth.

Any method of embroidery and any stitch or set of stitches can be used with these patterns. Use a good grade of embroidery floss, crewel yarn or metallic thread. The patterns given in this book do not show shading, but you may work the colored areas from dark to light if you wish to indicate shading in individual objects. The embroidery lines for the Dancing Elephant quilt (page 143) are 3-ply wool whipped to the surface of the cloth with hidden stitches of sewing thread.

Fabric paints create a stiff film of thin plastic on the cloth. This film cannot be penetrated by a quilting needle. If you use this method for decorating the quilt but wish to have lines of quilting stitches cross the designs, leave a thin line of uncovered cloth between the painted areas. A fabric-painted quilt can be very attractive. The designs are long-wearing, do not fade, and are completely washable.

The plastic film paints are a new media, but the art of decorating cloth with paint is ancient. Some of the finest dress fabrics in the 1840–1870 era had painted motifs; these can also be seen in fabrics used in the finest of the Victorian crazy quilts from that era.

Crayons were used on cloth household goods such as curtains, aprons, dish towels, and antimacassar sets in the 1920's and 1930's. This fashion became *passé* by the end of the 1940's and was subsequently forgotten by most hand workers. This is still an easy, economical

R. Machine appliqué, page 16.

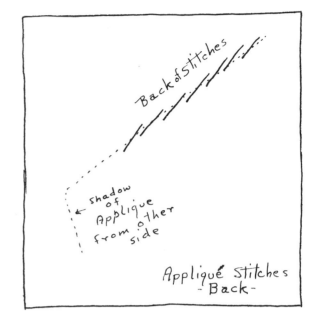

S. Hand appliqué, page 16.

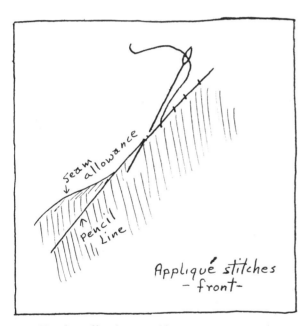

T. Hand appliqué, page 16.

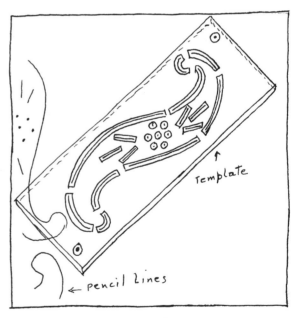

U. Placing a quilting stencil.

way of permanently decorating cloth for many purposes. The crayons actually dye the cloth. They are virtually non-fading and washable, and will last as long as the cloth. The color is rubbed into the pattern areas in the same manner used in a coloring book. To make the color a permanent part of the cloth, place the cloth between the two pieces of waxed paper; with a warm iron, smooth the design until all of the wax from the crayon and the paper has melted. Take care not to scorch the cloth. These colors will not stiffen the cloth, so the top made from crayoned blocks may be quilted as you choose. Outlining the pattern areas with embroidery stitches is another way of adding texture to the crayoned designs.

Quilting

Some quilting designs must be transferred to the cloth after the top is made. Others are only transferred to the top when it is in the frame. This means that the back-lighted transfer methods cannot be used. The transfer material or method must be erasable and not permanent. *Do not use carbon paper*. Warning: Many iron-on embroidery transfer patterns are indelible and cannot be used.

One solution is to make a transfer paper with a stick of carbon (available at art supply stores). Rub the paper all over with the stick, and then blend the carbon onto the paper with a cotton ball soaked lightly with lighter fluid. Take all precautions when using the lighter fluid. Do not inhale the fumes or use the fluid where there is danger of fire. When using this paper, take care not to smear the carbon onto the cloth. Next, pin the carbon over the cloth and then place the pattern sheet on the back of the carbon sheet. Draw over the lines of the pattern with a blunt tapestry needle. Do not touch the cloth and carbon paper more than is absolutely necessary. If you miss any of the lines in the pattern, you must draw them on the cloth with a pencil because the carbon and pattern cannot be replaced exactly once they are removed.

There are also iron-on pencils with a water-soluble lead. Check the needlework supply firms for these. The pencils are used on the paper pattern, which should be drawn in reverse. Turn your tracing paper pattern so that its right side faces down, and make your paper pattern by tracing the reversed pattern on your typing paper sheet. Redraw the outlines with the pencil; the resulting design is placed face-down on the cloth. Use a medium-hot iron to melt the wax of the pencil line onto the cloth. This method is useful when a complicated quilting pattern must be transferred to several places on the quilt top.

The last method is rather easier than the other two. Obtain a large sheet of acetate from a stationery store. This is a thick, clear, stiff but flexible plastic. It can be cut with scissors or an Exacto knife. Place the plastic over the pattern and mark it with a felt-tip pen. Cut the pattern into the plastic by making slits on the pattern lines. Do not make the slits more than 3 inches long. For longer lines, make two slits separated by a ¼-inch space of plastic. These are called *templates* when used in needlework. In painting they are called *stencils*. Using clear plastic will permit you to position the pattern exactly where it is needed (see diagram U). A No. 2 pencil or conté pencil can be used to trace the pattern onto the cloth.

For simple patterns of repeated lines or the heart outline on page 157, a yardstick or simple cardboard outline pattern may be used. Circles can be drawn around a dish or cup. Squares and oblongs can be drawn around boxes. There are many objects around the house that can be used to give quilting outlines. The best method for drawing a quilting pattern is to make a very light pencil line. On dark material use white or yellow chalk or conté pencil.(NOTE: Chalk comes off very easily.)

Quilting Frames

A lovely friend who started my real education in quilts and quilting, Retha Gambaro, had a one-liner she was fond of: "A quilt isn't a quilt until it is quilted." She dismissed all so-called tied quilts as beneath notice. In this she and I agree. A quilt with layers that are tied together at intervals may be quickly made, but it can never rival the true beauty of the low-relief sculpturing of even the simplest quilting pattern.

To be tight, smooth, and evenly quilted—or, in other words, to be professional looking—the quilt layers should be placed in a frame before being quilted. For the best results, even for beginners, the large room-sized quilting frame is easiest to use. The alternatives are, in order of effectiveness, a table frame, a lap frame, and finally the "quilt-as-you-go" techniques. A hooked rug frame is perfect for use on the smaller crib quilts that do not exceed the size of the frame. It is possible to quilt without a frame or by machine, but the results do not warrant the time, material, and effort spent.

The easiest frame to make and the least expensive (even today) is the room-sized frame, made from four 1″ × 2″'s from the lumber yard and four C clamps from the hardware store. The two boards that will be used as the frame's side bars should be cut at least 2 feet longer than the length of your quilt. The head and foot bars of the frame should measure 2 feet longer than the quilt's width.

To ready your frame for insertion of the quilt layers, take a piece of large waste cloth such as an old sheet. Cut this cloth in two across the width. Tack or staple one end of the cloth along the center section of the head bar; do the same with the other piece of cloth at the foot bar. Leave about 1½ feet of cloth free at each end of both boards. Now wrap the cloth loosely around the boards and fold the ends of the cloth under before basting it in place. Place the ends of the two short boards over the ends of the long boards and fasten the boards together at the crossings with the four C clamps. Diagram V shows the construction.

The frame's corners can be placed on the backs of four chairs or on four small sawhorses to raise the

V. 1. Cut cord approximately 2 feet long and attach a wooden dowel about 3 inches long at one end. Tie the other end to a nail driven into the side of the stand.
 2. Wind cord tightly around the crossed frame boards, as shown. Catch the toggle under the last winding to hold the cord in place.

frame to table height. If chairs are used to hold up the frame, they must have back supports that are higher than the top rail of the chair back. Each corner of the frame is inserted between these back supports, one chair to a corner, and the frame rests on the top rail of the chair back.

A fastening will have to be devised if sawhorses are used to hold the corners of the frame, but it must hold the frame firmly while in use and be easily released when the frame needs to be shortened. Some quilters use figure-8 lashings, as in diagram V above.

Probably the best solution I have seen was devised by quilters in West Virginia. The side boards of their frame (the ones without fabric attached) had holes just larger than the head of a 10-penny nail

drilled every 6 inches. A long nail was driven into the sawhorse or stand at each corner and the boards of the frame were fitted down over each. One hole was also drilled at each end of the head and foot boards, and these too were fitted down over the nails. Thus the nails held the frame boards together and fastened them to the sawhorse. See diagram W on page 20.

If you are obliged to use a smaller frame because there is just not room in your home for the large frame, choose a good quality table frame. There are several good frames on the market; some of the pattern services have plans for table frames that can be made in small home workshops. This frame should be made ready for use by tacking the waste material to the head and foot dowels and basting it in place in the same

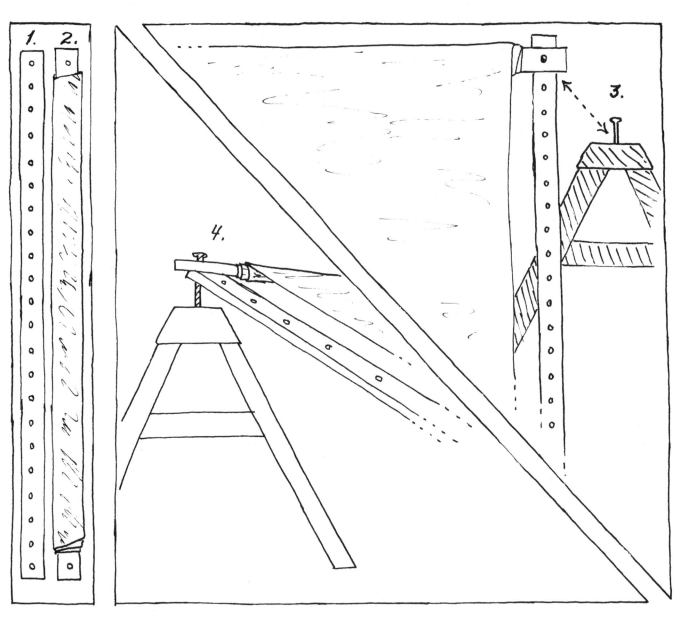

W. 1. One of the pair of sideboards. Holes are approximately 2½ inches apart.
    2. One of the pair of head and foot boards.
    3. All holes must be large enough to slide easily over the head of a 10-penny-size nail.
    4. Manner of fitting frame to stand.

manner as was used for the room-sized frame.

The following rules for placing the quilt in the frame may be used for both room-sized and table frames, the only difference being that in a pinch one person can put a quilt into the large frame (although the task is easier for two people). The table frame requires a minimum of two people for the task and it will take less time if there are three.

The backing for the quilt should be cloth either of the same weight as that used in the top or slightly lighter in weight. The backing should be about 16 inches longer and wider than the quilt top. Baste the backing to the loose cloth wrappings of the two shorter boards or dowels (the head and foot of the frame). Adjust the frame with the C clamps at the four corners (or roll the quilt on the dowels) until the backing is stretched tightly. A Dacron batt of the proper size (or one slightly larger, cut down to fit) should be used as the filler. Spread the filler smoothly over the backing. Then spread the top over the filler and pin the edges all

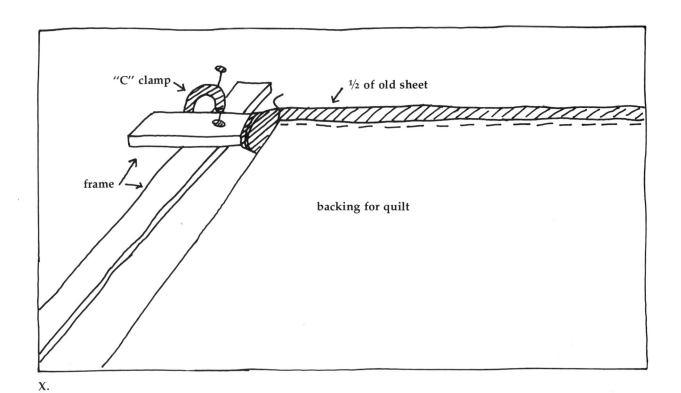

"C" clamp

½ of old sheet

frame

backing for quilt

X.

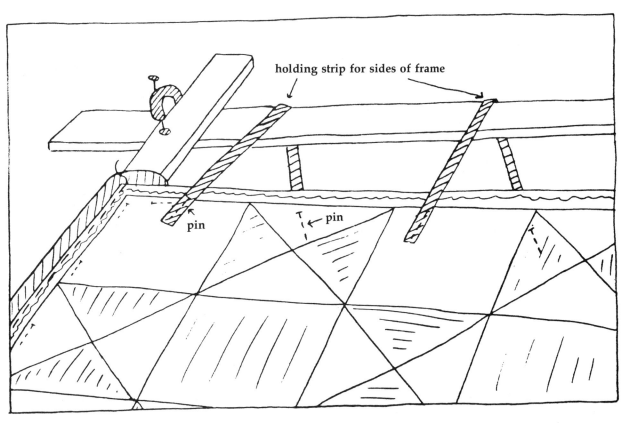

holding strip for sides of frame

pin

pin

Y.

21

around so the three layers cannot move.

There should be a space of about 4 inches between the side edges of the backing and the side bars of the frame. This space is needed to keep the quilt properly stretched along the sides. To keep the quilt edges taut, use holding strips made of waste cloth. (See diagram X on page 21.) The strips should be about 25 inches long. Pin one end of each holding strip to the underside of the quilt, spacing the strips about 14 to 18 inches apart. Pull the holding strips, one at a time, over the side bar, and pin them on the quilt top about 4 inches from where they are attached to the quilt's underside. The strip will form a "V" with its base at the side bar. If the quilt loosens as it is quilted, unpin one or more of the holding strips, pull the strip tight, and repin.

To ready a quilt for quilting in a lap frame, spread the three layers out one after the other with the backing on the bottom. After making sure that the layers are as smooth as possible, begin basting them together with 3-inch-long stitches, starting at the sides. Gradually work inward with the basting stitches. Do not allow the quilt layers to wrinkle or separate as you sew. When the quilt has been closely basted over its entire area, place the frame in the center of the quilt. Stretch the material over the bottom of the frame; then put the top of the frame in place and tighten it. When the center design has been quilted, move the frame and quilt the pattern in a different direction. Work outward, moving the frame in a spiral round the center until the entire quilt is finished.

The quilting stitch is simply a running stitch. Most quilters can comfortably reach about 12 inches in from the quilt's edge when sewing. Start your quilting at either the head or foot of the frame and stitch all the way across the width of that edge. When this edge strip is finished, unfasten the C clamps on that side and roll the finished section around the bars. The rolling will be done either on the head or on the foot—never on the sides. Restretch the quilt as you reattach the C clamps. Proceed with the quilting in sections in this manner until the quilt is finished. The holding strips can be discarded as the frame is shortened simply by pulling out the top pins and allowing the strips to hang until the quilt is taken from the frame.

Machine Quilting

Prepare a quilt for quilting on a sewing machine in the same manner as was described for quilting in a lap frame. Baste the layers firmly. *Only the smaller crib quilts can be sewn on a household sewing machine*—larger quilts are too bulky. You must roll part of the quilt in order to get some parts under the machine's sewing foot, and if the roll is too large, it won't fit under the arm of the sewing machine.

Only rather simple patterns and outline quilting can be done on a machine. Use a quilting foot and loose tension on both needle and bobbin. Start in the center and work outward toward the edges. Sew a line from the center toward each edge: center to north (the head), center to south (the foot), center to east, center to west. This will keep the tension between the stitches and the three layers of cloth equal in all four directions. Repeat in rotation until the quilting pattern is completed. If you are not careful to keep the tension equal in all four directions, the quilt will pull out of shape and one set of diagonal corners will be longer than the other.

Quilting by machine is much, much harder than quilting by hand, contrary to our machine-age thinking. Incidentally, machine-quilted quilts are not as valuable as those quilted by hand. Quilting is one of the few crafts for which hand work is easier, quicker, and produces better results than machine work. Surprisingly, hand quilting goes quite quickly.

Caring for Your Quilt

All quilts should be washable, but this is especially true for baby quilts. Use washable materials for the top and backing and soft Dacron batting for the filler.

When the quilt needs washing, use the gentle cycle on your washing machine; use the same laundry detergent you use for other baby clothing. Tumble-dry at medium heat, but remove the quilt from the dryer just before it is absolutely dry and finish by air-drying over the backs of two chairs. If you have a clothesline, hang the quilt in a U between two lines. Pin the two edges with clothespins about every 18 inches. Hang the quilt in the shade, if possible.

With proper care, a quilt will last many years. Dry-clean your quilt only very rarely and at long intervals, because the chemicals used in dry-cleaning are very harsh. Overdrying a quilt in a dryer or sunlight makes the cloth fibers brittle. *Never use an iron on a quilt.* The beauty of a quilt is in its puffiness, which ironing can completely destroy.

When a quilt is stored for a long time, unfold it at regular intervals (at least once a year) and refold it in another way so that the fold lines do not wear more than the rest of the quilt. For example, if the quilt is folded in fourths the first time, it should be folded in thirds the next time.

Many quilts have lasted 300 years, many more are still able to give use after 150 years. The quilt you make should be an heirloom for many future generations, but do use it. Wear is part of the charm of a family quilt.

Around the World

AUTHOR'S NOTE: In my drawings, I have tried to make the colors of the quilts clearer by using different shadings for each color. Some colors are the same value as gray, so the shading in the cross-hatching is the same. For those shades you will have to check the text, which will give the colors used in each quilt (where I have been able to obtain that information). The closer the cross-hatching is, the darker the color represented

3

Take a Square and Add a Square

This group of patterns is especially recommended for those beginning to learn hand sewing.

In the nineteenth century many boys and all girls learned to sew before they were five years old. They were given sewing scraps to cut into squares and then they pieced their squares either "hit or miss" or into four- or nine-patch doll or baby quilts. After practicing by sewing squares together, the beginner assimilated the basic skills and could progress to harder patterns with confidence. This is still an excellent way to learn to make quilts easily.

Quilters have available an infinite variety of colors and color patterns that can be arranged to modify the look of a pattern made with pieces of fabric cut in a single shape in a single size. All of the patterns in this chapter are made with squares. The first five illustrations show quilt tops made with simple color arrangements. Ideally, these quilts should be pieced row by row, but you may want to start from the middle and work outwards for some of these quilts; there is less chance of mixing up the color sequence. By varying the size of the squares from 1½ to 6 inches (patterns on page 29), you can make quilt tops in all the different sizes needed for modern beds—from crib to king size—using the same number of squares shown in the drawings.

Around the World/Around the World and Back

These are two traditional patterns. They have regained their popularity in the past two decades because they make beautiful quilts, especially if the plain and print succession is chosen carefully. These "patterns with squares" can be really eye-catching if the trick illustrated in these two tops is used for an effect. Choose a print or several prints that can be positioned as shown, with large motifs framed by the outline of the square. These can illustrate a theme of flowers, animals, or (as in the illustrated Around the World and Back) vehicles—or similar pleasantries. Study the way the fabric from one type of material forms rings or rows in the finished quilt top.

Aunt Emma's Baby Quilt

This quilt is mentioned in the history at the beginning of this book. It is a simple scrap quilt with every other square in white; the results can be quite effective. The colors used can be very bright or dark, and the white squares will lighten the pattern of the entire top.

Scattered Nine Patch

This pattern is based on the same principle of using white to lighten a darker pattern. Choose two contrasting colors or a bright color and a cheery print. The dark or plain-colored fabric should form the "petals" of the flowers and the second fabric is used in the flowers' centers. This is a more deliberate pattern than Aunt Emma's Baby Quilt. It should look quite nice in a tailored room.

Petticoat Lane

The last of this first group of five patterns is an original pattern—appearing for the first time in this book. Choose a group of eight color-related fabrics in plain and print materials. (The quilt illustrated on the cover, however, uses eight fabrics *plus* white.) If you can find a print material having three colors in several shades and then match the rest of the materials for the quilt to the shades in this print, the color scheme is sure to be a striking combination. There are two rows of white or light fabric in each section. The three rows dividing the sections are two shades of the same color with the darker (or the solid) in the center. This pattern is called Petticoat Lane, after a street in London, England. The name is not meant to limit the use of the quilt to little girls only—I just like the sound of it.

Around the World and Back

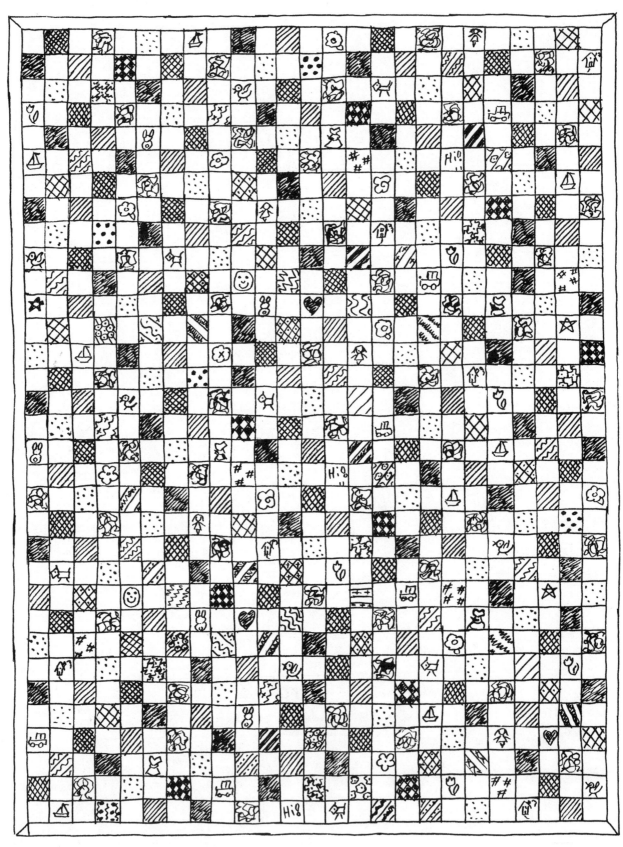

Aunt Emma's Baby Quilt

Scattered Nine Patch

Petticoat Lane

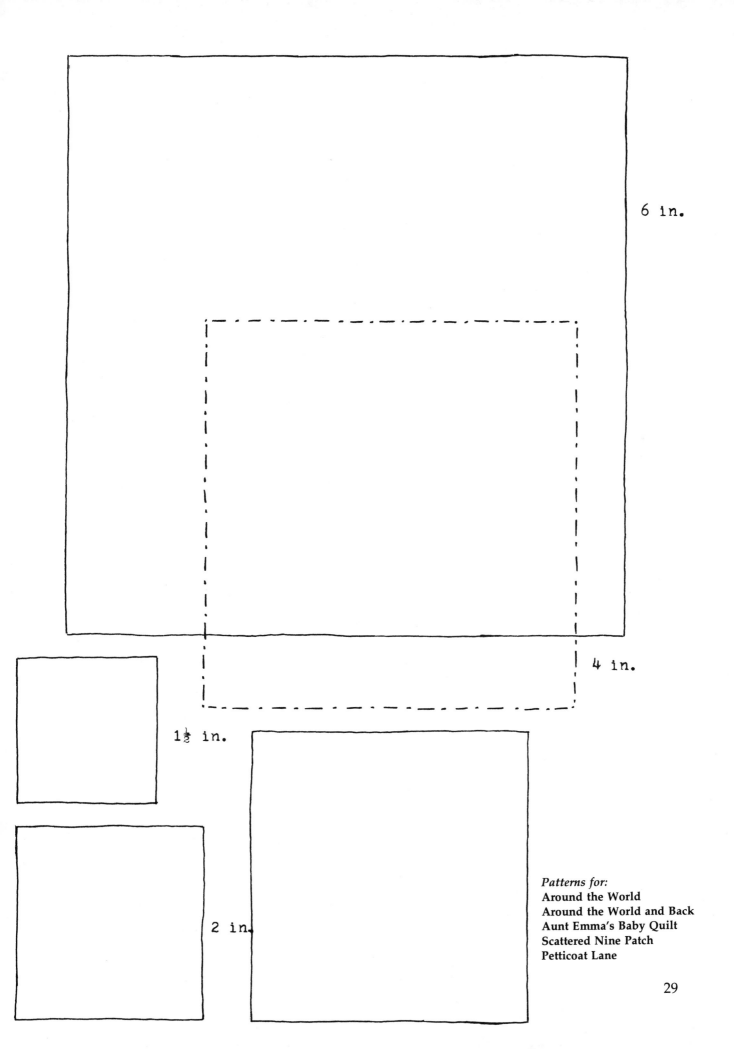

6 in.

4 in.

1½ in.

2 in.

Patterns for:
Around the World
Around the World and Back
Aunt Emma's Baby Quilt
Scattered Nine Patch
Petticoat Lane

Checkered Trail

This quilt is much more beautiful than the illustration shows. It should be pieced in either a red, blue, or green print material and unbleached muslin. The design shown is my own original design, but it is based on a rather uncertain and messy design from a nineteenth-century quilt. By arranging the colored pieces in four variations of an even nine patch (see page 32), I was able to straighten out the design to one that is easily pieced and that does not look at all like the earlier quilt. To see which of the four nine-patches goes where in the top, count the squares in the illustration in groups of three, across and down. A 2-inch pattern square will make the top shown in the crib quilt size. If 2-inch squares are used for a larger quilt, continue the pattern out to give the size needed for the top. The added work will be worth the effort when you see the finished quilt top. The smaller pattern pieces, 1a and 1b, are for 1½-inch squares. The larger pattern pieces, 2a and 2b, are for 2-inch squares. The *a* patterns are the individual squares shown in the nine-patch pattern blocks marked A, B, C, and D. Any of these variations can be used to make an entire quilt top. The larger *b* squares can be used to make the block

marked C, replacing the nine small squares. Since this block is all one color, the work can be much simplified in this way—for larger quilt sizes especially.

Nine-Patch Bouquet

This is a variation of the even nine patch. It should be made in rather subdued colors, but not pastels. This is a scrap quilt. Find as many large floral prints as are available. A few small floral prints can be used for variety. Cut the prints to frame a flower, using the pattern square. Choose a plain-colored material to match or contrast with each floral square. The lightly shaded squares in the drawing should be a soft, light green. There are four of these green squares in each block. The nine-patch blocks must be pieced together as shown in the drawing, with a very white lattice strip pattern (a) and green corner squares (b) between each two-pieced blocks, plus all around the outside of the Top. This pattern makes a neat quilt that will suit either a boy or a girl, and it can be used for larger quilts as well. The flowers are not pronounced enough to give an overwhelmingly feminine look to the pattern; besides, boys like flowers, too.

Before beginning any work on these quilts, please read the General Directions (which begin on page 4), including Piecing a Block, page 15. All pattern pieces are finished size; add 1/4-inch seam allowance on all sides.

Checkered Trail

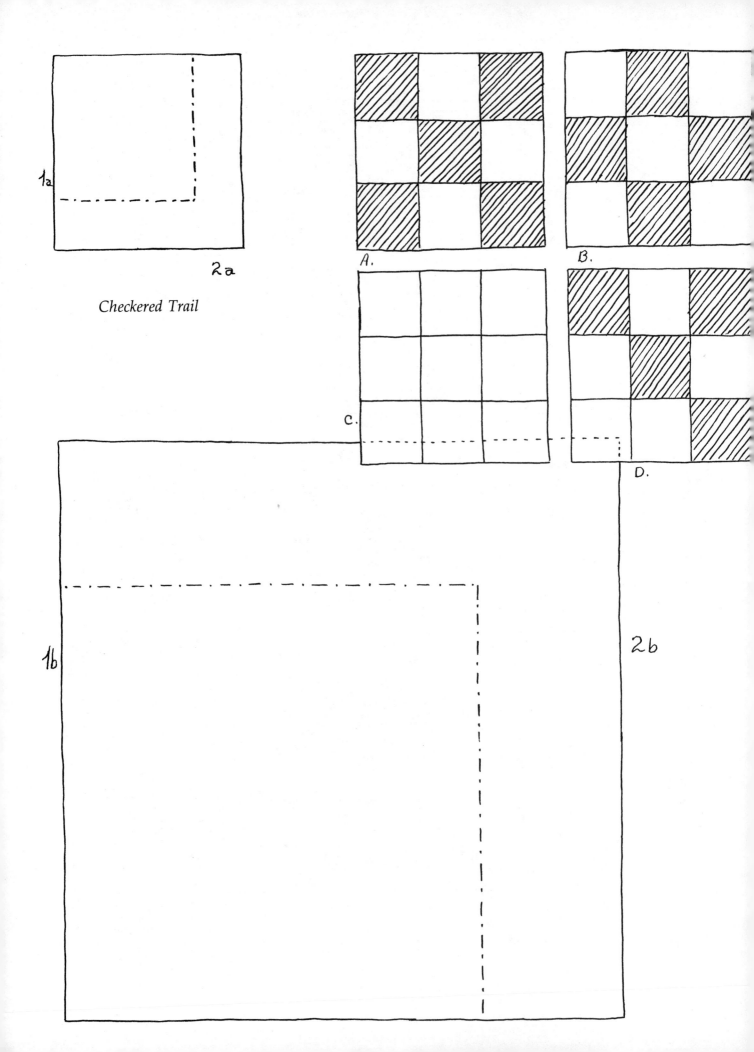

1a

2a

Checkered Trail

A.

B.

C.

D.

1b

2b

Nine-Patch Bouquet

a.

b.

4

Take an Old Pattern

Lone Star Baby Quilt—1850's

A friend sent me a photograph of this baby quilt after a quilt show. There was no information available to help with identification. I would guess from the unusual thistle decorations and the rosebud sprays in the corners that the baby this quilt was originally made for could have been of Scottish and English extraction.

The areas that show black on the drawing are deep red in the quilt. The second row from the center is a bluish grey. The third row from the center and the three diamonds in each point that correspond in cross-hatching to this row are deep gray. The fourth row is pink. The lighter colors are rather hard to make out, but one is goldish in tint, and another seems bluish. The thistles are bluish-gray, their leaves and stems blue-green. The rosebuds are deep red and most of the leaves are yellow-green, but a scattering of leaves on each spray is blue-green. These are not babyish colors, but they create a charming and original design.

To piece the center, cut out the required number of diamonds. Sort them into eight sections, each of which will reach from the center of the star to one of its points. Carefully watching color placement, sew five diamonds together to form the five diamonds along the outside of one point. When you sew the diamonds together, sew along the *inside* of your penciled line, in order to keep as close as possible to the actual outline of the pattern piece. Sew each of the remaining four rows, each of which will again consist of five diamonds. Sew the five rows together. (See the diagram below.) Make eight of these star points exactly alike. Be very careful to maintain the points of each diamond as you sew them together.

The four corner squares, made of white background material, should be cut 17¼'' square. Four triangles,

9⅜'' on the two short sides and 13½'' on the long side, will fill in the remaining spaces between the star's points. Sew four strips measuring 7⅞'' by 13¼'' to the long sides of the triangles to form the remaining background area. Appliqué the rosebud sprays and the thistles onto the background material after the quilt top has been sewn together.

This quilt will measure 4 feet by 4 feet when finished. It is not easy enough for a beginning quilter, but someone who has hand sewn three or four quilts should be able to make this design if extra care is taken with the sewing.

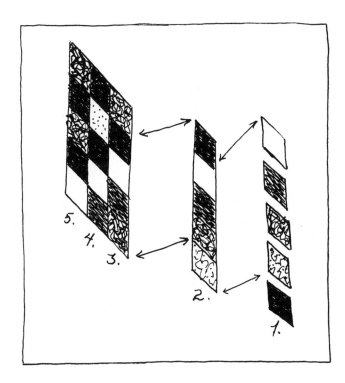

Before beginning any work on this quilt, please read the General Directions (which begin on page 4), including Piecing a Block (page 15) and Appliquéing a Block (page 16). All pattern pieces are finished size; add 1/4-inch seam allowance on all sides.

Lone Star Baby Quilt

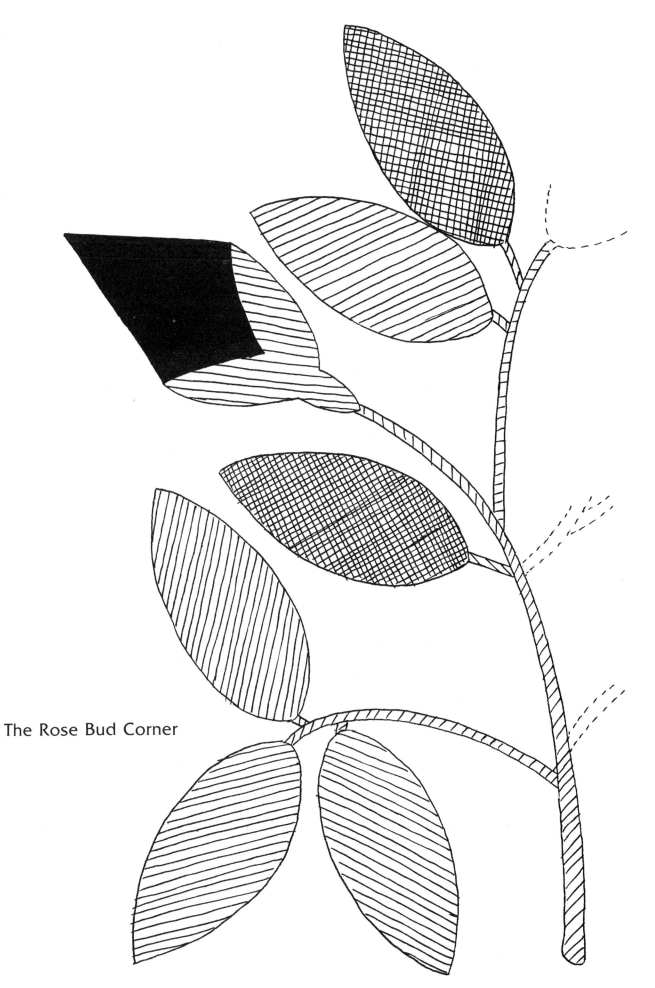

The Rose Bud Corner

37

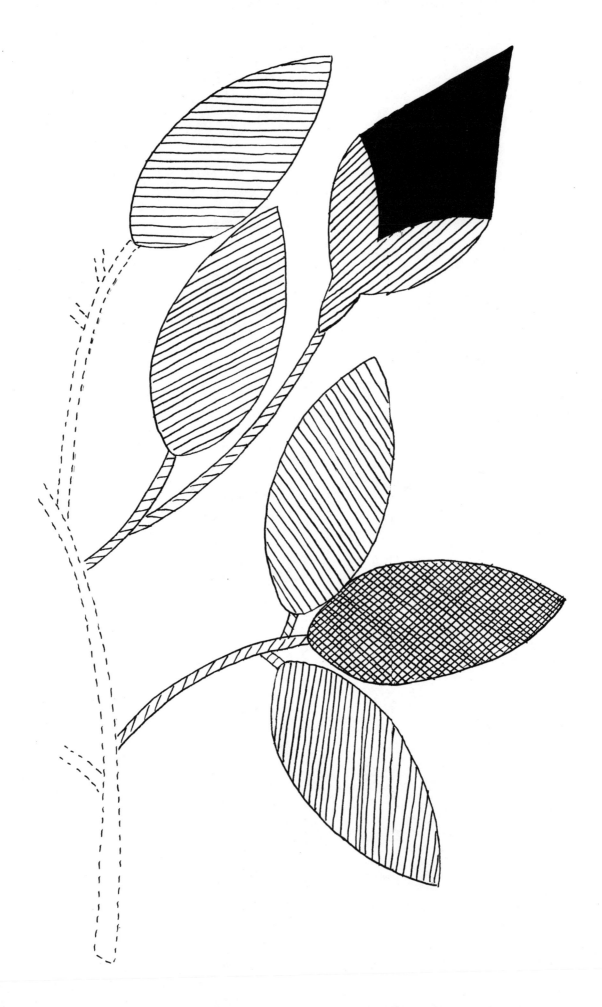

38

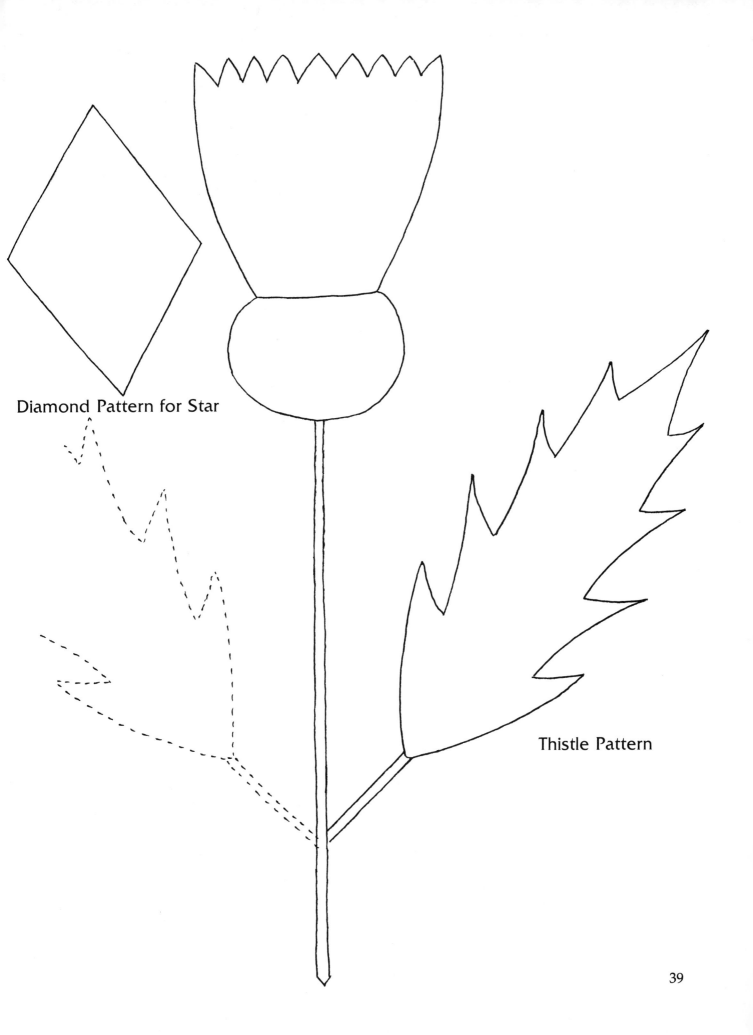

Diamond Pattern for Star

Thistle Pattern

39

A Pennsylvania Dutch Design for a Needlework Fractur-Schriften Birth Register

The originals of these handwritten, hand-illustrated documents are priceless museum pieces now. Your little one can have his or her own birth register using the patterns of bird, cradle, and tulip vine. Using the larger block sizes (12- and 18-inch blocks), a family register or friendship quilt can be made up as either the baby or larger-sized quilt.

On page 44 one of the shaded drawings shows a design for a birth register. Instead of using a motto, you may wish to place the names of the parents and the home town and state above the bird. The larger square illustrates a friendship block, which might also be part of a family register quilt. The motifs in this square are the correct size to be used as patterns for 6-inch-square blocks in embroidery, crayon, or fabric paints. Patterns are provided on the pages following for 10-inch-square blocks, 12-inch-square blocks, and 18-inch-square blocks. None of these patterns has to be made on squares. They may all be worked on oblong pieces of material of any length necessary for the size inscription you wish to record. Lengthen the stem of the tulip vine to fit the new length. The width of the design should remain unchanged.

The patterns for the three larger blocks should be appliquéd. The inscriptions or signatures should be embroidered or fabric-painted. The smaller tulip vine stems should also be embroidered or painted; the larger stems may be appliquéd if you wish. By using embroidery or fabric paints for the smaller patterns, even a beginner can use these designs.

Before beginning any work on this quilt, please read the General Directions (which begin on page 4) including Appliquéing a Block (page 16), and Directions for Embroidery, Fabric Paint, and Crayons, (page 16). All pattern pieces are finished size; add 1/4-inch seam allowance on all sides.

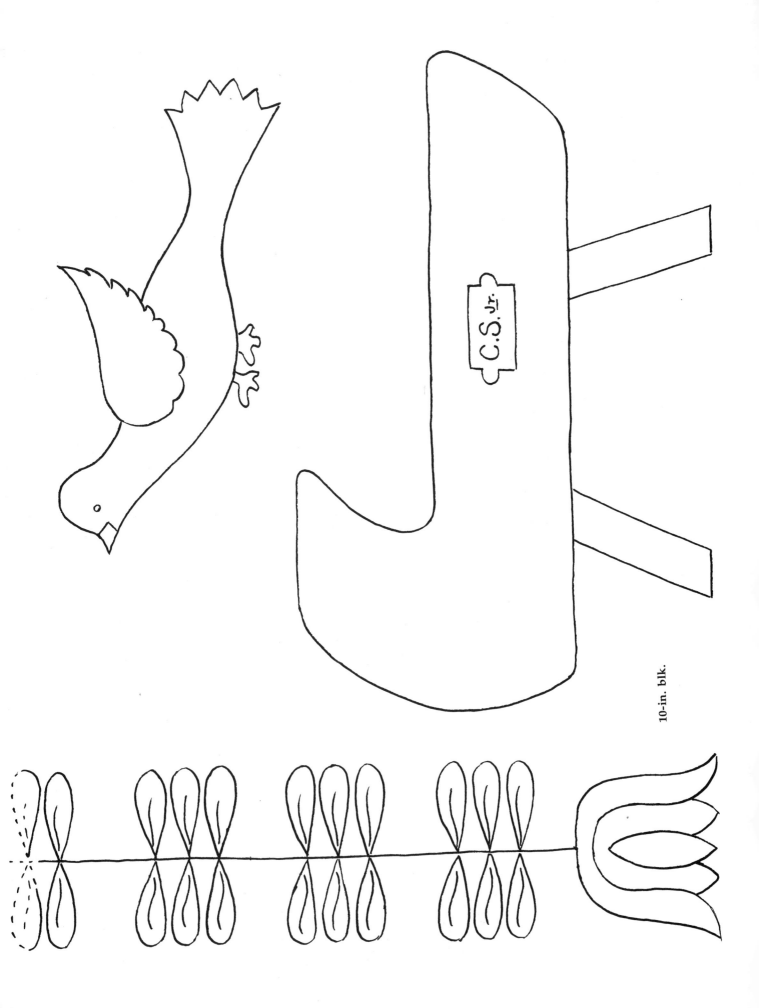

10-in. blk.

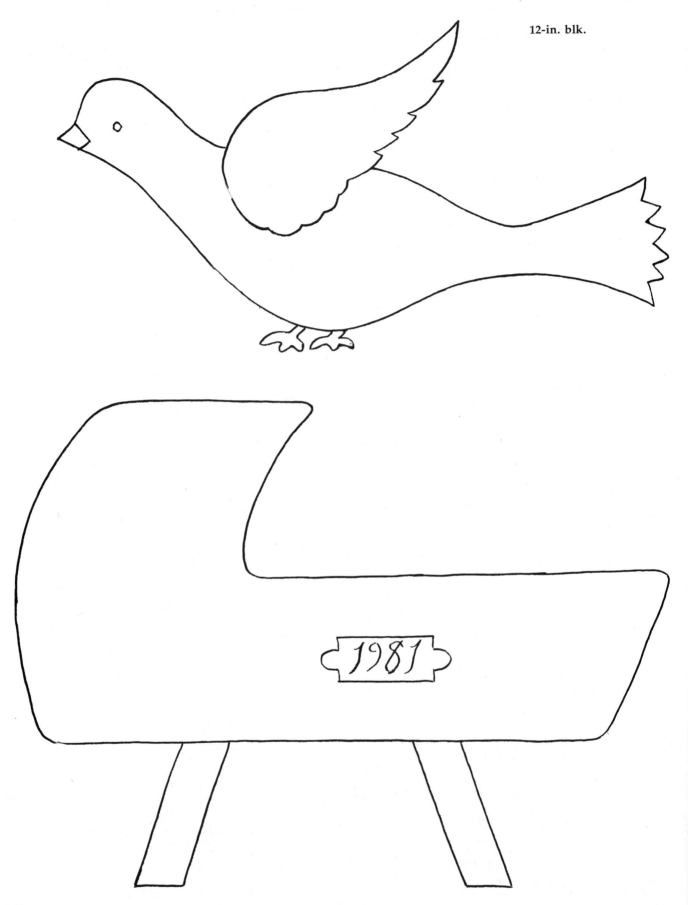

1981

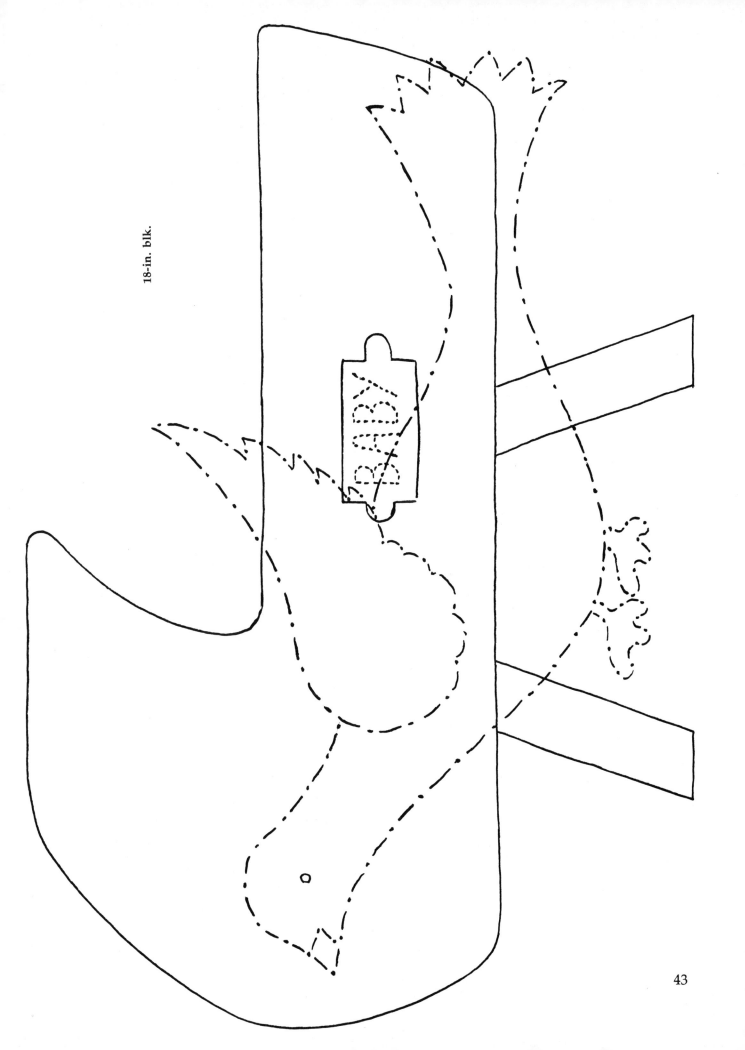

18-in. blk.

43

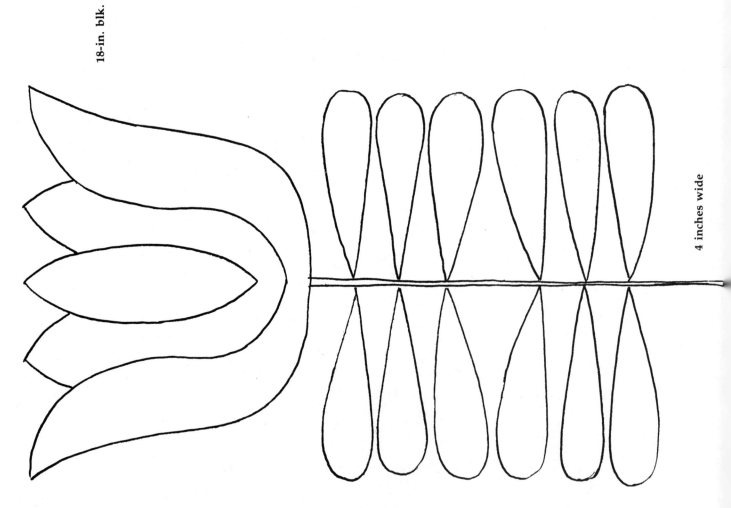

12-in. block

2½ inches wide

18-in. blk.

4 inches wide

44

6-in. blk.

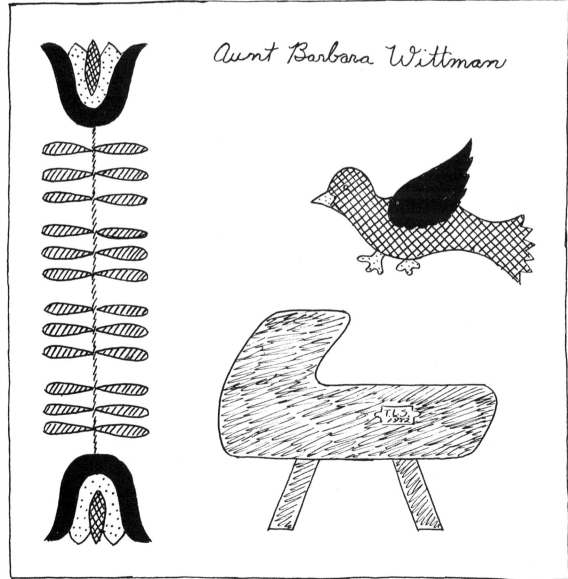

Peony Wreath—1840

(pictured in Frontispiece)

The cut-paper design is typical in many ways of the 1840's. The rage for cut-paper silhouettes, which began in the late 1700's, had progressed to become a fad called "Papeorama": sharp scissors and card-paper were used to cut flowers, animals, and people in scenes which could then be matted and framed. It was one of the arts taught to school children and was popular as a party pastime. Peonies were a favorite garden flower and they show up in many different forms in both silhouettes and quilt patterns of this era. Red and green on white were the most fashionable combination of colors for quilts of the period. The only way the blocks of the quilt from which this design was taken differ from the usual is that the color used for the appliqué is not a true red but a red-maroon print fabric.

To make a copy of the original baby quilt, see drawing D of the Frontispiece. The background block should be 12 inches square and made of unbleached muslin. Remember to add the seam allowance. The border is the Grapevine and Peony border in Chapter 6, page 282. Since the original pattern and border were made for a full-sized quilt, they may be used for any quilt from crib size to king size without any adaptation of the basic block necessary. With care, even a beginner can make this quilt.

Before beginning any work on this quilt, please read the General Directions (which begin on page 4), including Appliquéing a Block (page 16). All pattern pieces are finished size; add 1/4-inch seam allowance on all sides.

Peony Wreath — 1840

12-inch block

¼ of pattern

President Wilson's Sunburst Baby Quilt—1850

It is said that any child born in the United States can grow up to be President. The baby this quilt was made for grew up to be the twenty-eighth President of the United States. Baby Woodrow's father was the Presbyterian minister in Staunton, Virginia, and his cradle with its red print and white quilt is still in place in the nursery of the Manse, which is now a House Museum.

This baby quilt was made in the correct size for the cradle, but the pattern used was for an adult-sized quilt block, 12 inches square. It is one of the hardest patterns in this book and should not be attempted by a beginning quilter.

The complete quilt is shown in its cradle in drawing B of the Frontispiece. There are two pieced blocks placed on the diagonal in the center of the quilt. The original quilt is so worn and fragile that it is not touched any more than can be helped; thus the treatment of the borders is open to conjecture. Here I have shown a 3-inch-wide Sawtooth border similar to that used around the block itself. This border can be found in Chapter 6, page 287.

To make this block, follow diagram C. Piece four *b* and four *c* triangular shapes into an arc, forming one fourth of the circle. Piece this arc and shape *d* together. (See the directions for piecing a curve on page 16.) Make four of these sections. Piece two sections into a half-block. Repeat with the other two sections. Sew the two half-sections to center circle *a* and finish the last seams. If the curved seams begin to go out of alignment, take out the misaligned stitches back to the place where the seam began to mismatch and begin again. If this is not done, the block cannot lie flat. *This is a difficult pattern.*

The Sawtooth edge used around the blocks and for the border was very popular from about 1840 through the 1860's; it did not actually fade out of fashion until the 1890's. To make this design around the blocks, take one light and one dark *f* triangle; piece them into a square along the diagonal edges. Make thirty-four of these squares: see diagram A. Use pattern *e* as the square for two of the corners. See pages 287 and 290 for the border patterns, which are pieced according to the same method. Four variations of corner treatments for a Sawtooth border are given in Chapter 6, page 287.

The quilt top illustrated here is for an antique cradle. It is 23'' by 40''— a non-standard size that will not fit most modern cribs. A quilt of four pieced blocks, together with the border treatment, would make a better crib size. The border may be enlarged with either white or color-matching bands on the inner or outer edges, or both. Since the pattern is scaled to adult size, it is appropriate for any quilt in any size.

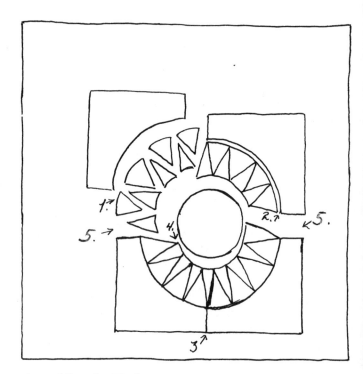

Assembling the Blocks

Before beginning any work on this quilt, please read the General Directions (which begin on page 4), including Piecing a Block (page 15). All pattern pieces are finished size; add 1/4-inch seam allowance on all sides.

48

President Wilson's Sunburst Baby Quilt
12-inch block

e

f

a

c

b

d

A.

B. 23 in. by 40 in. Top

49

Jacob's Ladder—Eighteenth, Nineteenth, and Twentieth Centuries

This pattern is one of the very old traditional American patterns that has never been either at the height of fashion or entirely out of fashion. To most quilters, this has always seemed to be a good pattern to make for a boy's bed. The evidence for this is in the many names the two versions (reverse color schemes) have been given over the years. The original is, of course, a name from a favorite children's story from the Old Testament. In addition, the design has been called The Tail of Benjamin's (Franklin) Kite, The Trail of the Covered Wagons, Wagon Tracks, Road to California, Rocky Road to California, Underground Railroad, and Stepping Stones. Most of these are names to set a small child dreaming. The traditional colors were dark blue and white. I have seen quilts made from this pattern in every color scheme as well as in scrap quilts; they are almost always pleasing because the pattern can be made with such neat seams. It is not too hard for a beginning quilter (it was the first pattern I attempted).

There are two sizes in the patterns. Nos. 1a and 1b are for a 9-inch-square block, Nos. 2a and 2b are for a 12-inch-square block. The 9-inch blocks are a little more dainty than the larger blocks. Before choosing the pattern size, read the General Directions at the front of this book and determine the size of your quilt. The directions for continuing the mathematics needed are on page 11.

There are two color schemes given for this block. The older, more traditional of the two uses two colors—light and dark—and is shown in the drawing labeled B. The color pattern marked A—in dark, medium, and light colors—was only made in the last two or three decades of the nineteenth century. It is not too popular for modern quilts, although it can be a very good-looking pattern if the colors are carefully chosen.

This is an even nine-patch pattern. There are nine large squares in each block. Four of these squares are made from one dark and one light *a* triangle in either size. Place two triangles face to face and then sew on the diagonal seam to make a square. The other five large squares in the block are each made up of two light and two dark *b* squares. Sew a light and a dark square together into an oblong. Sew another oblong, then match the dark to the light sides of each oblong and sew the center seam. The nine pieced squares should be put together in three rows, and then the three rows should be joined to make the block. Row 1 contains two large squares pieced from the *b* squares and one large square made from the *a* triangles. The large square made from the triangles is placed between the other two large squares. Row 2 contains two large squares made from the *a* triangles and one large square made from the *b* squares. The large square made from the *b* squares is placed between the other two large squares. Row 3 is identical to row 1. Study the drawings of the assembled block carefully to make sure that you arrange all the elements properly and position the colors correctly.

Before beginning any work on this quilt, please read the General Directions (which begin on page 4), including Piecing a Block (page 15). All pattern pieces are finished size; add 1/4-inch seam allowance on all sides.

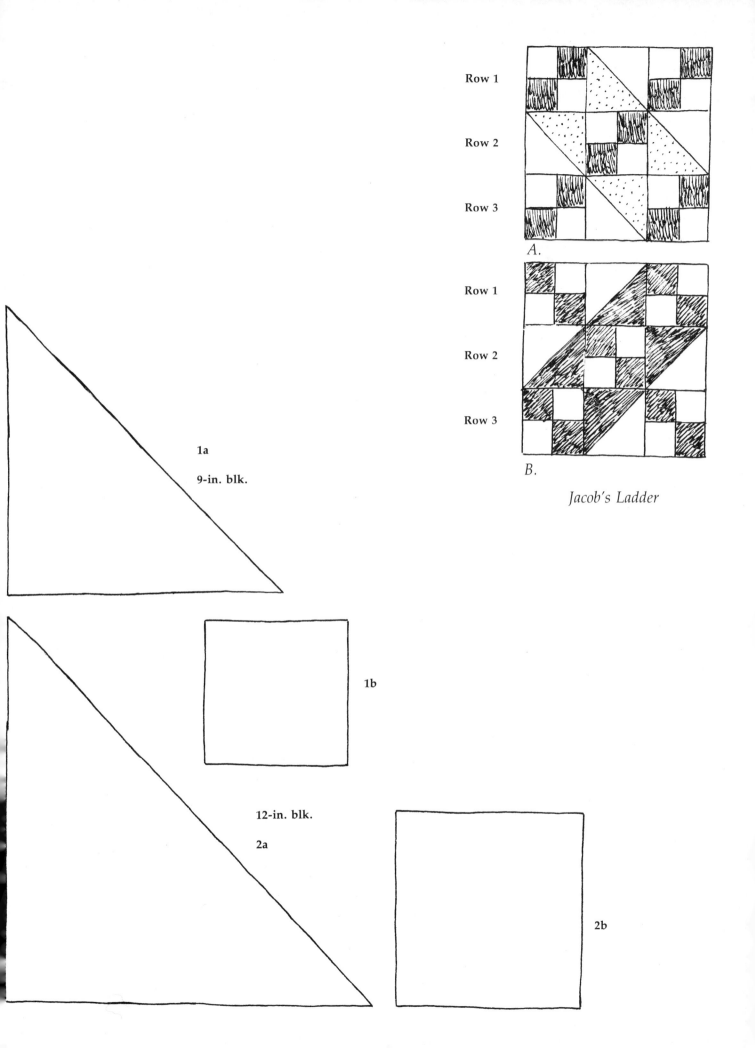

Row 1

Row 2

Row 3

A.

Row 1

Row 2

Row 3

B.

Jacob's Ladder

1a

9-in. blk.

1b

12-in. blk.

2a

2b

Jack-in-the-Box—Late Nineteenth Century

There isn't much information available about this pattern. It was one of those published in 1930's newspaper quilt columns, but it originated much earlier than that. If I were naming this pattern, I would call it something like Bow Knot because it looks like the fancy bow on top of a birthday gift. If the "ribbons" were cut from pretty print fabrics, with a different print used in each block, this would make a lovely child's quilt. The patterns are given in 10-inch and 12-inch square sizes.

The block is an uneven nine-patch—that is, not all of the nine patches are the same size. To piece the four corner squares, make an oblong from a *c* triangle and two white *d* triangles. Sew a second oblong from a print *e* shape and two white *d* triangles, which are placed on either side of the *e* shape. (See the block diagram.) Sew these two oblongs together, following the placement in the diagram, to make a corner square. Then sew one corner square on each side of an *a* oblong. Make two of these strips. The center strip is simply a white *b* square placed between two *a* oblongs. This pattern is a good one for a beginning quilter.

Before beginning any work on this quilt, please read the General Directions (which begin on page 4), including Piecing a Block (page 15). All patterns are finished size; add 1/4-inch seam allowance on all sides.

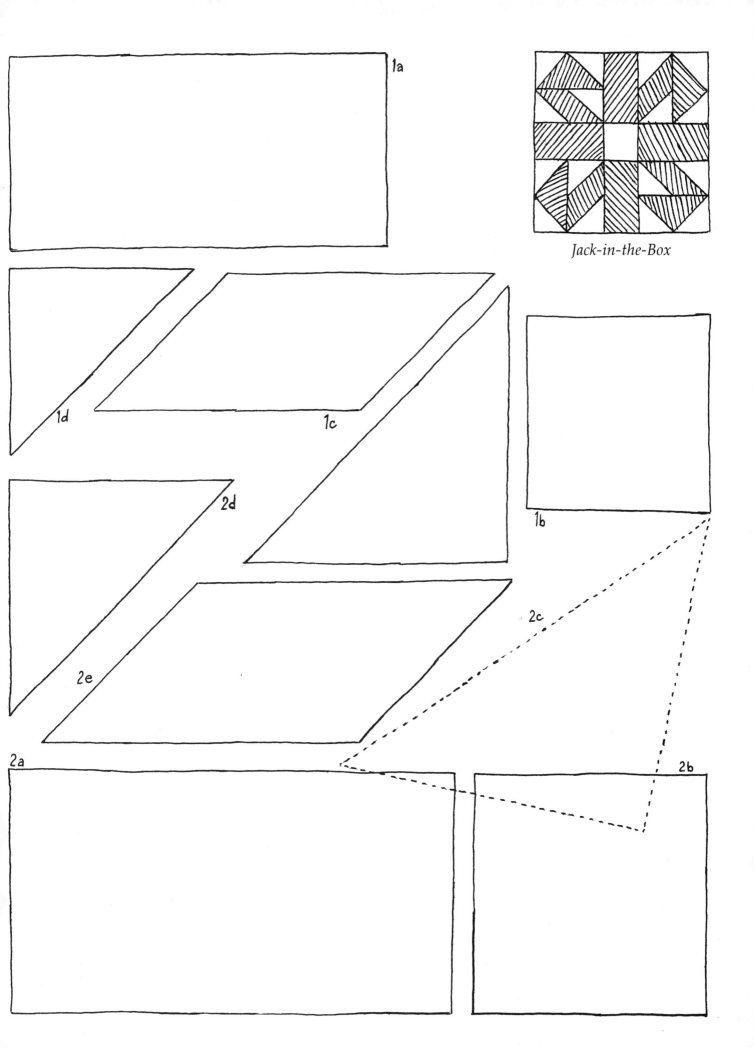

1a

Jack-in-the-Box

1d

1c

1b

2d

2c

2e

2a

2b

Puss-in-the-Corner—Mid-Nineteenth Century

This is one of a group of designs called Tile Puzzles, which were very popular in the nineteenth century; they have never gone out of fashion because of their neatness. The name is a part of childhood lore of the Victorian era. There are several possible color schemes for this design: All of the blocks can be pieced of one print or color and white; each block can be pieced of a different color or print and white; or the blocks' square patterns can be a dark color and their triangles a matching print with a white background. Any of these three color schemes would make a lovely quilt, and this design is easy enough for a beginning quilter.

The pattern is given in three sizes. The two larger sizes of patterns, which make 12-inch and 15-inch-square blocks, use only two shapes (a square and a triangle) to make the entire block (diagram A). To make the 9-inch-square block easier to piece, I have combined some of the color areas and shown this second way to make the pattern in diagram B.

Pattern A: To piece the 15-inch- or 12-inch-square block sizes, think of each block as divided into nine smaller, equal blocks with four squares in each block. The design is then, an even nine-patch pattern. Piece the center from four print squares; set this aside. Next piece four corner blocks of one print and three white squares. Each of the remaining four blocks contains four squares; each square is made from one print and one white triangle sewn together on the diagonal. When sewn into a block, these four squares form an arrowhead of print fabric. Sew these nine smaller blocks into three strips. Make two strips of one arrowhead and two corner squares each and the center strip of two arrowheads and the center square. Sew the center strip between the other two to make the large block. Consult diagram A continuously for the proper arrangement of colors and pieces.

The 9-inch-square blocks are made from five shapes. Two of these shapes, labeled 3a and 3b, are exactly the same (except in scale) as the patterns for the 12-inch- and 15-inch-square blocks. If you wish, you may use patterns 3a and 3b and follow the directions given for diagram A. If, however, you want to save a little sewing with very small pieces of cloth, follow these directions for diagram B: Cut the center square from pattern 3e. Set this aside after cutting it out of the print fabric. To make corner squares, sew one print and one white 3a shape into an oblong and sew one white 3d shape to the oblong to make a square. Make four of these corner squares. The arrowhead squares are each made of two pieced oblongs. Piece one oblong from a print 3c triangle and two white 3b triangles, one sewn on each side of the 3c triangle. Make the other oblong in the same way, but reverse the colors of the triangles. Sew the two oblongs together as shown in diagram B to form a square with a print arrowhead. Make four of these squares. Follow the color placement shown in diagram B carefully. Combine the nine squares into three strips; make two strips each containing an arrowhead square placed between two corner squares. The center strip contains two arrowhead squares placed on either side of the center square. Piece these strips to make the finished block.

Before beginning any work on this quilt, please read the General Directions (which begin on page 4), including Piecing a Block (page 15). All pattern pieces are finished size; add 1/4-inch seam allowance on all sides.

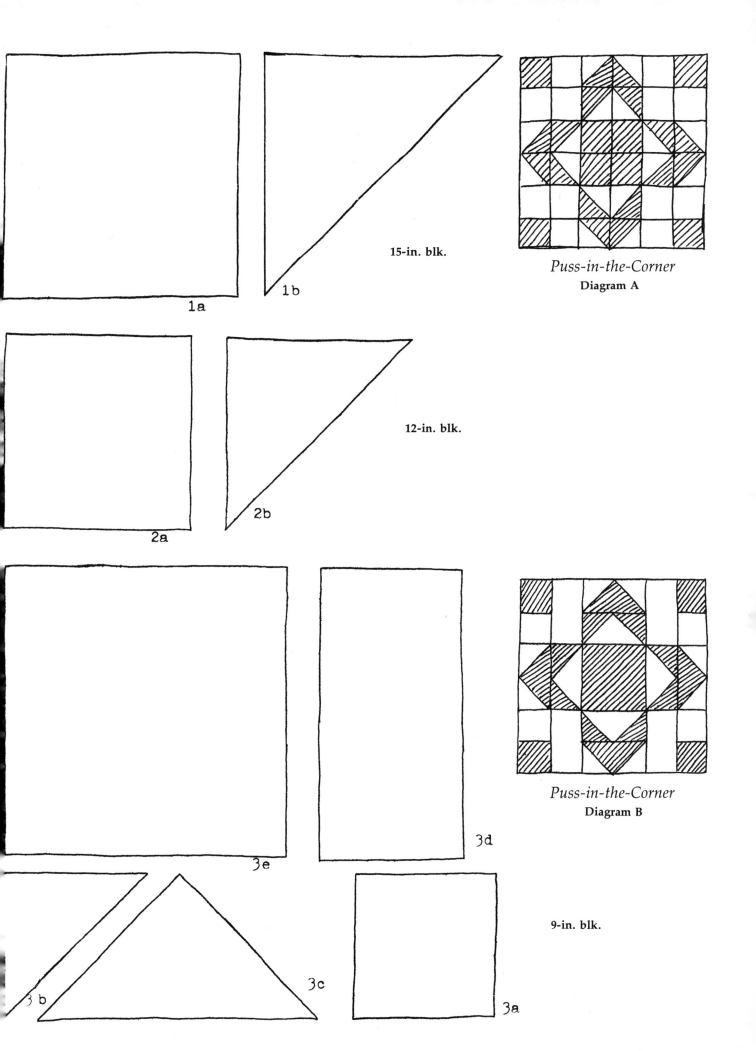

15-in. blk.

1a

1b

Puss-in-the-Corner
Diagram A

12-in. blk.

2a

2b

3e

3d

Puss-in-the-Corner
Diagram B

9-in. blk.

3b

3c

3a

Cat's Cradle—Nineteenth Century

This is another traditional nine-patch pattern with a name taken from a children's game. Six of the nine sections are made of pieced triangles and the other three are plain squares. This pattern should be made with bright contrasting colors, as indicated by the drawing. Any of the appliqué borders would look good with this pattern. For some reason, I would like to see it made with the King's Horses and King's Men border in matching colors. (See page 78.)

The patterns are given in two sizes, for 10-inch- and 12-inch-square blocks. For each block, you will need three *a* squares in a bright color and six *b* triangles in the same color material, as well as six triangles from pattern *c* in a contrasting color or print material and 18 *c* triangles in white or light-colored material. Piece together three white (or light) and one colored triangle into a large triangle of the same size and shape as triangle *b*. Make six of these pieced triangles; then sew them to the *b* triangles along the diagonal edges to make six pieced squares. Study the drawing for proper color placement. Piece the first row from one plain square and two pieced squares, in that order. The second row contains a pieced square, a plain square, and a pieced square. The last row is made from two pieced squares and a plain square. Sew Rows 1 and 2 together and add Row 3 at the botton to make a finished block.

This is an easy pattern and would be a good choice for a first quilt.

Before beginning any work on this quilt, please read the General Directions (which begin on page 4), including Piecing a Block (page 15). All pattern pieces are finished size; add 1/4-inch seam allowance on all sides.

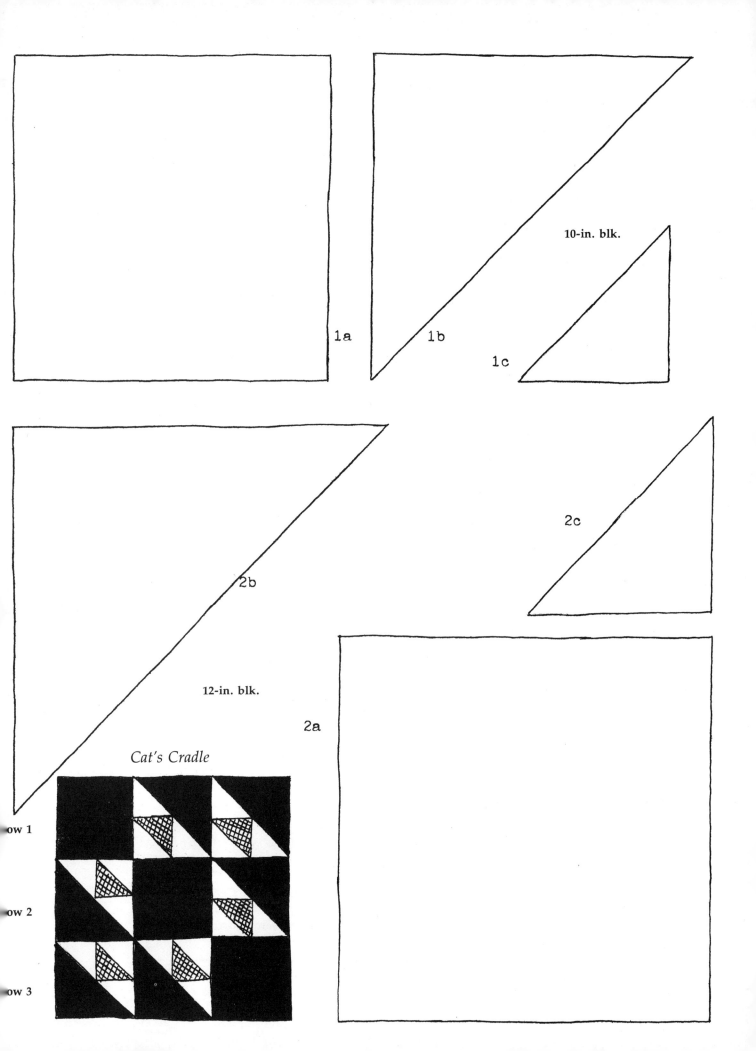

1a

1b

10-in. blk.

1c

2c

2b

12-in. blk.

2a

Cat's Cradle

ow 1

ow 2

ow 3

Broken Dishes—Nineteenth and Twentieth Centuries

This pattern is so easy that it was used as a utility pattern, to be made up quickly when a family needed more covers. There are only two triangles in this pattern. The larger is used to make plain blocks that are placed between pieced blocks. The four corner triangles, labeled *b*, can be white in all of the blocks to give the look described by the pattern name. However, more usual in the late nineteenth century was to cut these *b* triangles from dark blue-and-white print material which was economical and easy to obtain. This fabric was used throughout most of the country to make work dresses, aprons, sunbonnets, and so forth for women and children and work shirts for men and boys. The section pieced from the *a* triangles was usually made from two contrasting materials, light and medium in tone. The square might be made as shown in the drawing, but since this design was not usually made as a show quilt, the scrap material available was used mix-or-match, whether it looked good or not.

When made with care and well-matched material, this is as pretty a pattern as anyone could wish for, and it is so easy that any beginning quilter will be able to relax and enjoy making a first quilt.

The patterns are given in two sizes, for 9-inch- or 12-inch-square blocks. To piece one block, use eight light and eight dark *a* triangles and the four *b* triangles in the color of your choice. Consult the drawing for the proper arrangement of colors. Piece two *a* triangles of contrasting colors along their short edges to form a larger triangle. Make eight of these larger triangles. Piece two of these larger triangles together along their long edges, with colors in reverse positions, to form a square. Make four of these squares and piece them together to form a large square. Then piece the four *b* triangles to this large square along the triangles' long sides. The pieced sections may be the same two colors in all the blocks, or each block may be a different combination of three colors to make a scrap quilt. More than three colors should be avoided; too many colors in the block confuse the pattern.

Before beginning any work on this quilt, please read the General Directions (which begin on page 4), including Piecing a Block (page 15). All pattern pieces are finished size; add 1/4-inch seam allowance on all sides.

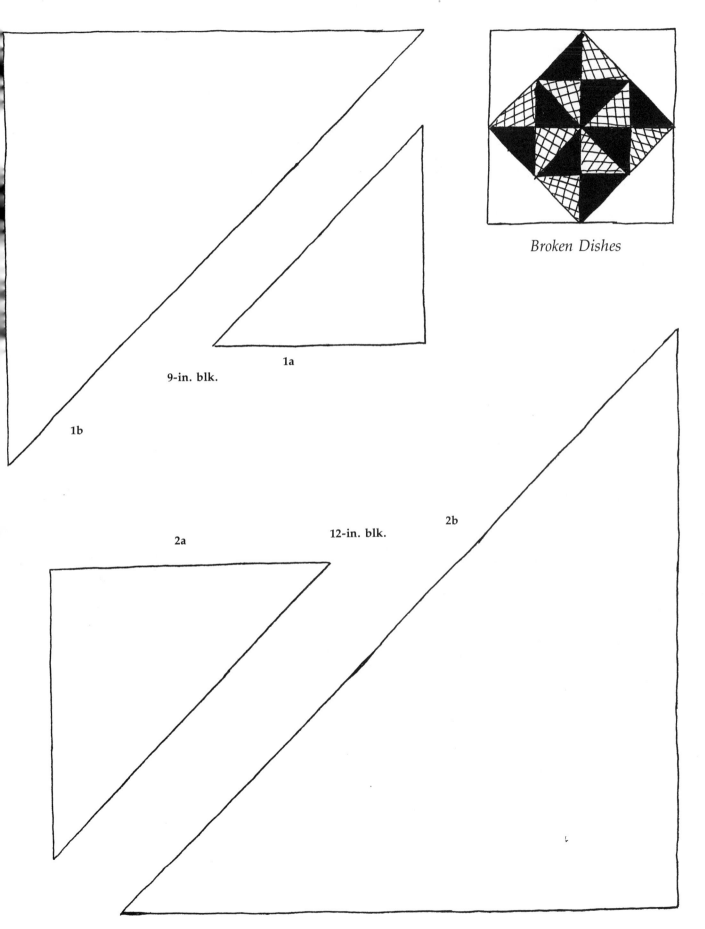

Broken Dishes

1a

9-in. blk.

1b

2a

12-in. blk.

2b

59

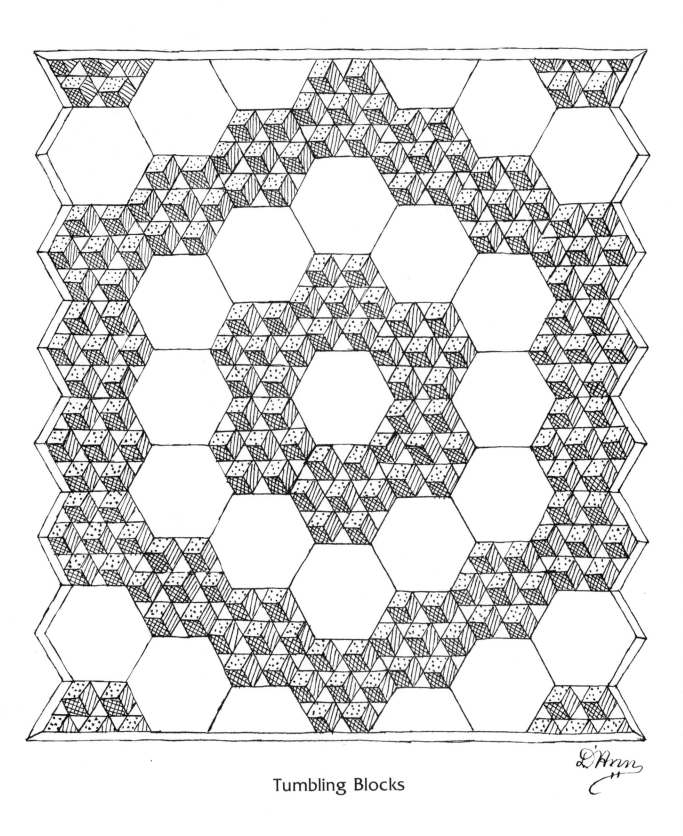

Tumbling Blocks

60

Tumbling Blocks/Babies' Blocks/Baby Blocks—Mid-Nineteenth Century

Quilts of all kinds made with diamond-shaped patterns were at the height of fashion in the early Victorian years, from about 1840 through the 1880's. Lone Star, Star of LeMoine, Double Tulips, Peony, and many other familiar diamond patterns competed for the quilter's attention, but variations of shaded, three-diamond patterns forming boxes in perspective were the most popular of all. Even Mary Todd Lincoln, in the midst of her duties as mother, wife, mistress of the White House, and hostess for the President, found time to piece at least one section of a box quilt, which is now in the Political Collection of the Smithsonian Institution in Washington, D.C. The three patterns provided here are representative of those pieced in cottons, wools, silks, satins, and velvets, according to the resources of the quilter. This style was popular not only in the United States and Canada but also in England and many other English-speaking countries.

Once you've chosen a pattern, there are two ways of piecing these diamond patterns—the English method and the American method. Neither is "preferred"; each has advantages and disadvantages, and so the choice of method is a matter of personal preference.

American method: Cut out the cutting patterns and the fabric pieces as instructed in the General Directions for piecing on page 15. Sew the pieces together to form a hexagon, consisting of units of three diamonds (light, dark, and medium) placed in the same relation to one another in each hexagon. One of the shadings (light, dark, or medium) may be a print material, but these shadings should be harmonious rather than contrasting colors. When there are as many units (hexagons) as are needed for the size quilt being made, sew the units together, making sure that the shading is in the same position for each hexagon sewn in place.

English method: This technique has one more step and uses a sewing stitch different from that used for the American method. After making the cutting patterns, cut out stiff paper patterns to the same size and shape as the cutting patterns, one for each diamond needed for the entire quilt top. The shiny pages from national magazines are exactly the right weight for this. In the past, old book pages, letters, maps, and other scrap papers were used in "box quilts." I have a lovely satin box quilt dating from about 1863. The paper that lines the fabric pieces has recipes handwritten in a beautiful, old-fashioned script.

Using the cutting pattern according to the directions on page 11, cut out the fabric diamonds—with seam allowance—for the quilt. Take one paper diamond (without seam allowance) and place it on the back of the fabric diamond. Fold the seam allowance of the fabric diamond over the paper diamond and baste it down firmly on all four sides. Repeat with two more paper-and-fabric diamonds in the other two shadings needed for a hexagon. Position two diamonds and sew them together along one edge by overcast stitches. These stitches should use a gauge of 12 to 16 stitches per inch or finer if possible. The stitches should almost touch but should be only long enough to cover the two edges of the fabric. Sew the third diamond first to one diamond along one edge and then, after knotting the thread and starting again, to the second diamond. Lay aside the hexagons as they are finished. When they have all been completed, lay the units in rows to match the colors—or form patterns with them. Sew the rows of hexagons together by overcasting. Remove basting stitches.

The advantage of the English method (which makes it worth the extra work) is that the points are automatically in the correct place and all points come together perfectly. Also, the size and shape of the diamonds are exact over the entire quilt, making the edges and corners of the finished quilt perfect without any adjustment. The English method does not require as expert a sewer or as much practice as does the American method—it just takes longer and is a little more tedious to execute. Try them both and choose the method you prefer. Many of the better American Victorian quilts in this style of pattern were made in the English manner. Incidentally, it is the only way to piece cloth that ravels easily, such as silks or satins, or cloth that is too thick, such as flanneled wools or velvets.

Each of the following patterns is given in three sizes. Choose the size that best suits the top size, material, and method you wish to use.

Tumbling Blocks

This is a rare variation of the box patterns that is different from the usual box design in two ways. The small hexagons (pieced from pattern *a*) are pieced into a larger hexagon in which they are separated by triangles (made from pattern *b*—see the drawing); these large pieced blocks are then made into a top by arranging them into a pattern with plain hexagons made from pattern *c*. (Pattern *c* is given as one quarter of a full pattern because of its size.) Because hexagons are almost impossible to visualize as top patterns, I have included the top pattern for this design on page 60. This same design can be used for the other two box quilt designs. By eliminating the plain hexagons, you can make a completely pieced quilt top.

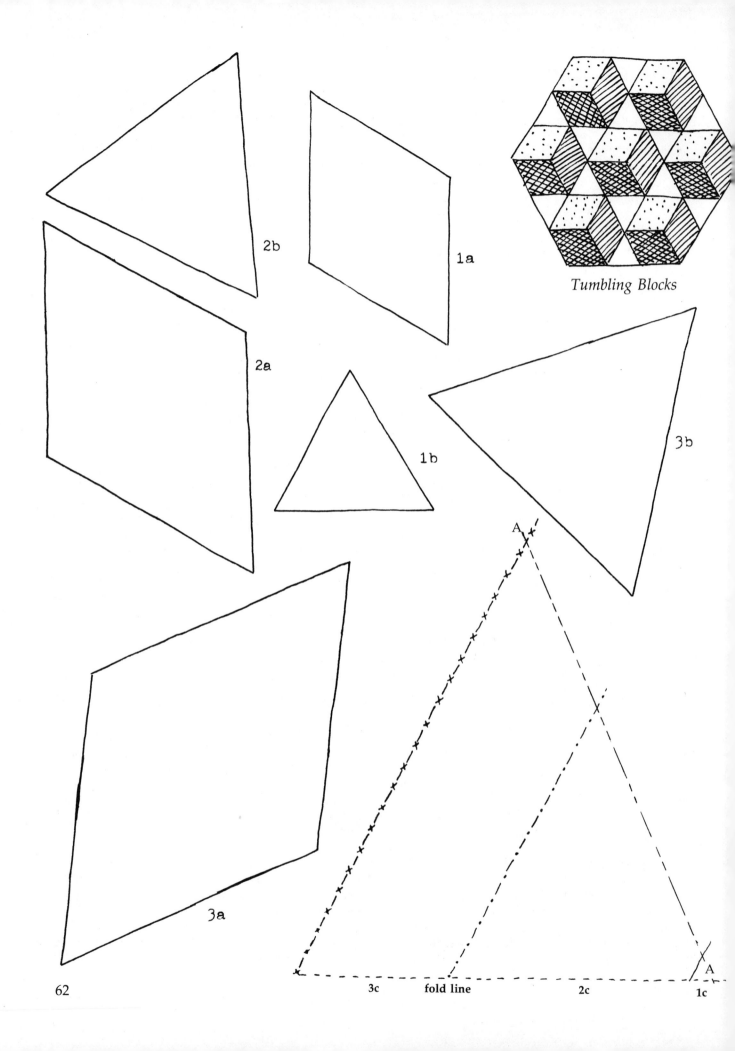

2b

1a

Tumbling Blocks

2a

3b

1b

3a

62

A

A

3c   fold line   2c   1c

¼ of pattern for plain hexagons. Attach pattern piece on page 62 below at line A (—— ·· ——).

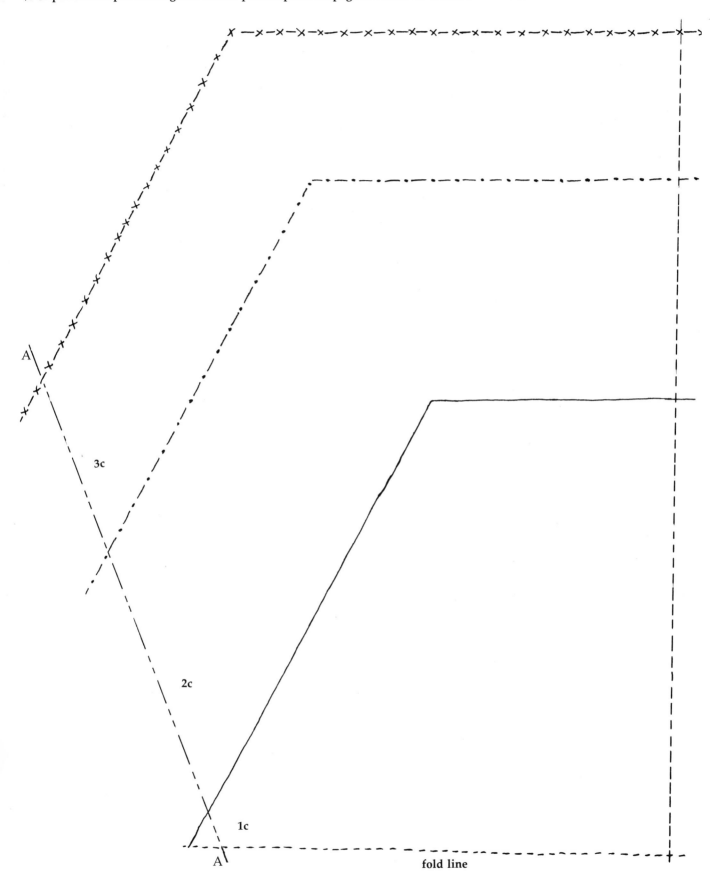

A

3c

2c

1c

A

fold line

Babies' Blocks

The most popular of the three patterns was—and still is—the one I have labeled Babies' Blocks. This has the same tonal pattern as Tumbling Blocks but without the triangles between the boxes; it is an overall pieced block pattern. Many quilt patterns have several names used interchangeably for similar patterns, as is the case with these three patterns.

Many interesting color designs can be achieved by varying the placement of the light, dark, and medium shapes. A quilt top might be made using only three fabrics, or using three shades of one color. A scrap quilt could be quite pretty, but the hexagons should be positioned carefully by laying them out in rows on a flat surface and arranging the colors in pleasing combinations before sewing them into the top.

The Tumbling Blocks top shows the preferred way to piece hexagon blocks into a quilt top, whether pieced or plain hexagons are used. It is probably easiest to move from the bottom of the quilt to the top, upwards along the sides. Piece strips and then join the strips together, following the design shown for Tumbling Blocks from left to right.

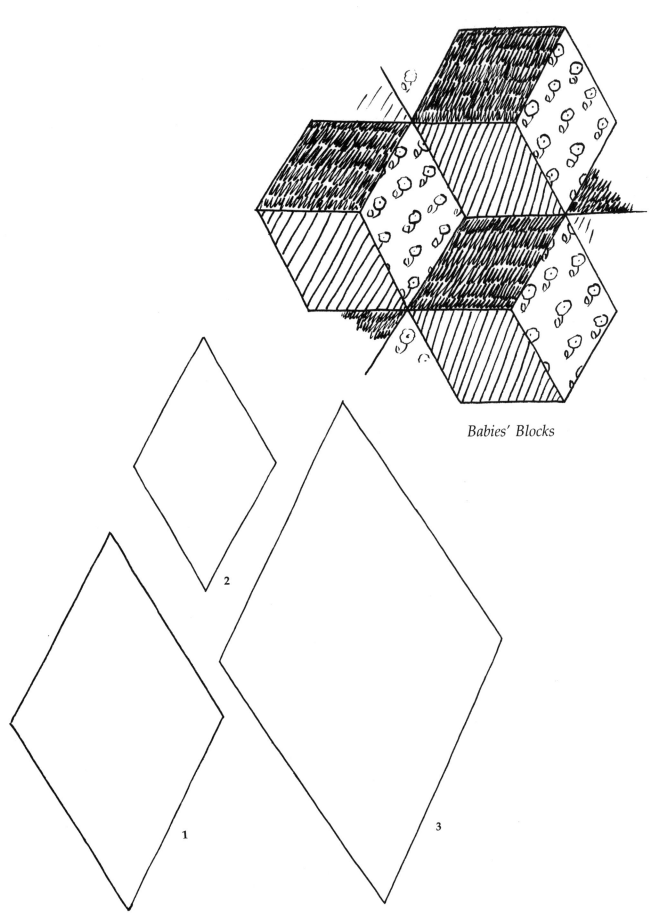

Babies' Blocks

1

2

3

65

Baby Blocks

Baby Blocks is a variation that looks very much like the Babies' Blocks pattern, but here the hexagon is pieced from two diamonds and a square rather than from three diamond shapes. The three pieces form a box with a slightly different perspective from the all-diamond boxes. Directions for piecing, color matching, and making a top are the same as those for the other two box quilts.

Baby Blocks

Before beginning any work on these quilts, please read the General Directions (which begin on page 4), including Piecing a Block (page 15), and item 3 of Cutting Patterns (for using 1/2 or 1/4 patterns). All pattern pieces are finished size; add 1/4-inch seam allowances on all sides.

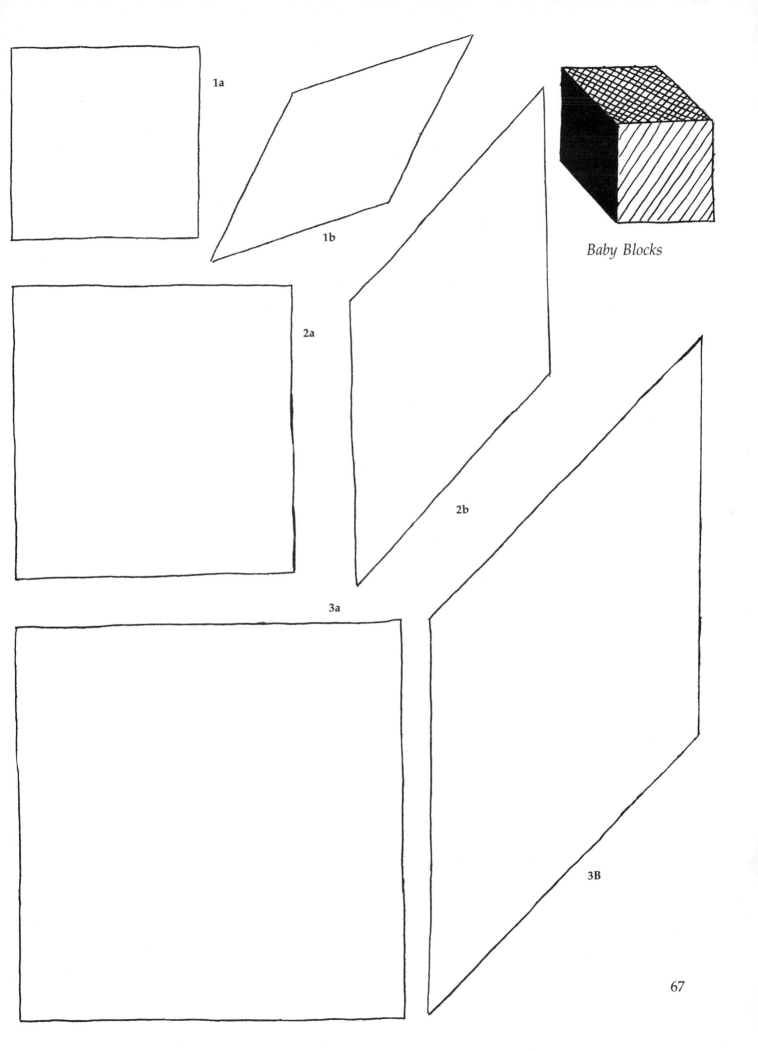

1a

1b

2a

2b

3a

3B

Baby Blocks

67

Melon Patch—1800

The Melon Patch (see Frontispiece, quilt A) is one of the earliest and most popular patterns designed with curved seams. The pattern here is given for 8-inch-square blocks. This size is small but will make a charming quilt for a bed of any size, from crib to king size. The colors used can be any color and white; however, this pattern is usually made using two tones of the same color or a matching plain color and print. For both smaller and larger quilts, reverse the dark and light areas of every other block, as shown in the diagram. You may use the same materials for the entire quilt or scrap fabrics. If you choose to make a scrap quilt, be sure to follow the tonal pattern shown.

The curved seams on four sides of the blocks are longer and shallower than those of most curved patterns. This means that greater care must be taken in sewing these seams to make the ends come out even. Read and follow the directions for piecing a curved seam on page 16 of the General Directions. When sewing curved seams, I have found that the concave edge takes less material than the convex edge. The pattern pieces take account of this difference.

This is a difficult pattern, as are all patterns with curved seams. It is also a lovely pattern when done carefully and will repay the effort of making it. The block drawing shows four blocks done in the suggested "Robbing Peter to Pay Paul" color scheme discussed above.

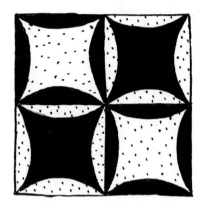

Melon Patch

Before beginning any work on this quilt, please read the General Directions (which begin on page 4), including Piecing a Block (page 15). All pattern pieces are finished size; add 1/4-inch seam allowance on all sides.

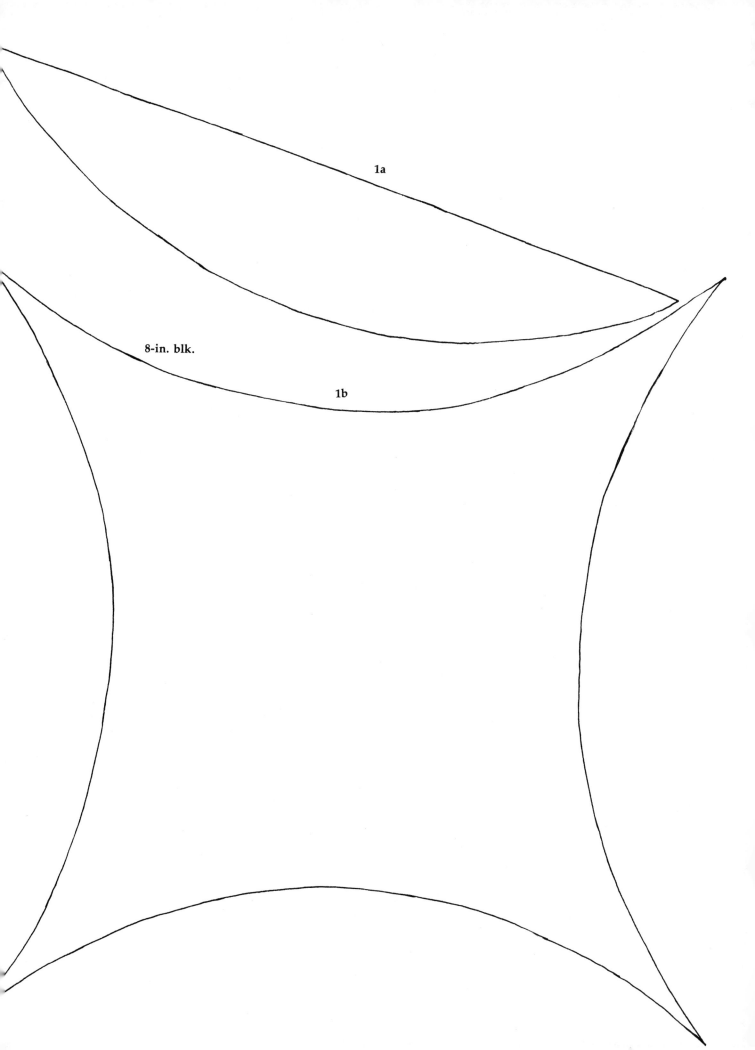

1a

8-in. blk.

1b

Retha's Baby Quilt—1959

This pattern is a variation of the Melon Patch pattern. Pattern *a* is a full oval instead of the half-oval of Melon Patch. It should be made either in one print or as a scrap quilt, with the oval pattern *a* white. The basic block is 6 inches from tip to tip of pattern *b*. Because of the oval *a* shape, the edges of any quilt made from this pattern will be scalloped. Pieces *a* and *b* should be used continuously over the entire top. Before choosing this pattern, read the Melon Patch directions and page 16 of the General Directions.

Pieces *a* and *b* will not mesh over the whole top unless they are fitted exactly in each block. The easiest way to piece the blocks is to sew two *a* ovals to each *b* pattern piece, placing the ovals on the bottom and on the left-hand side as shown in the block diagram. When the blocks are pieced to make the top, a row of ovals should be added to the top and right-hand edges of the quilt to complete the pattern.

This is a hard pattern and should not be attempted by a beginner.

Before beginning any work on this quilt, please read the General Directions (which begin on page 4), including Piecing a Block (page 15). All pattern pieces are finished size; add 1/4-inch seam allowance on all sides.

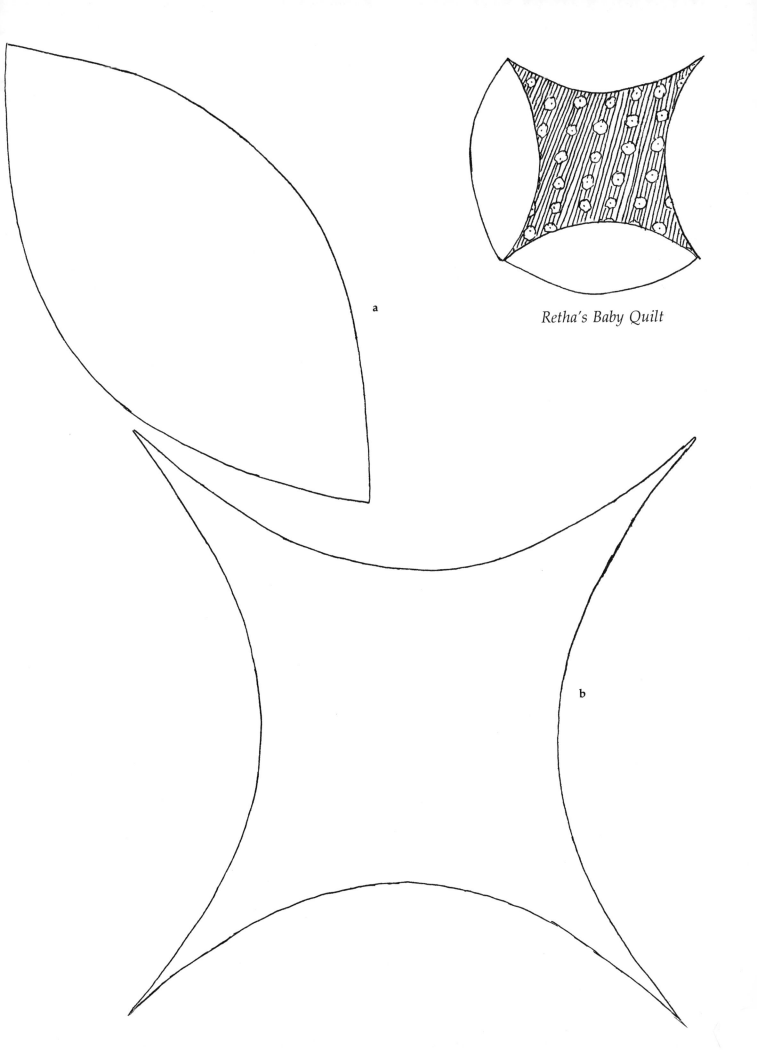

a

Retha's Baby Quilt

b

Humpty Dumpty Baby Quilt

72

5

Take Something that Interests Children

Children's Books

Alice's Humpty Dumpty—1981

"Don't you think you'd be safer down on the ground?" Alice went on, . . . in her good-natured anxiety for the queer creature. "That wall is so very narrow!"

"What tremendously easy riddles you ask!" Humpty Dumpty growled out. "Of course I don't think so! Why, if ever I did fall off — which there's no chance of — but if I did——" Here he pursed up his lips and looked so solemn and grand that Alice could hardly help laughing. "If I did fall," he went on, "the King has promised me — ah, you may turn pale, if you like! You didn't think I was going to say that, did you? The king has promised me — with his very own mouth — to — to —"

"To send all his horses and all his men," Alice interrupted, rather unwisely.

"Now I declare that's too bad!" Humpty Dumpty cried, breaking into a sudden passion. "You've been listening at doors — and behind trees — and down chimneys — or you couldn't have known it!"

"I haven't, indeed!" Alice said very gently. "It's in a book."

—from *Through the Looking Glass*
by Lewis Carroll

The Lewis Carroll books about Alice have always been favorites of mine and of many other people—there are whole societies given over to the pleasures of discussion and study of these enchanting social commentaries. To me Humpty Dumpty the egg becomes a real-life character, charming and irascible by turns. His comments on the use of words (making words his servants rather than the other way around) have always seemed like horse sense masquerading as nonsense. The scene above is the inspiration for the design of this quilt pattern. Humpty Dumpty sits serenely on his too-narrow wall while the horses and men, already rushing hither and yon, anticipate the fall.

The center is a 16-inch square including a 1-inch-wide band the color of either the wall or the border swags. If you choose to appliqué this pattern, cut the suit, tie, and collar separately from the egg-face. The eyes, nose, and mouth are large enough for appliqué, or you can embroider the entire face. To make the brick wall look more real, you might appliqué each brick in place; otherwise, embroider the lines between the bricks with white floss.

There are two borders: one appliquéd with the figures running clockwise to the right, and the other with the figures running "widdershins" (the old English word for counter-clockwise, or to the left). Because this pattern turned out so well, I have given it in two sizes: the 12-inch block size to be appliquéd, 2, and an 8-inch block size which may be embroidered, crayoned, or fabric-painted on other quilts. The 8'' border results in a quilt 4' by 4', the 12'' in a quilt 5¼' by 5¼'.

The Swag and Dot border in either size may also be detached as needed and used on other quilts. For larger quilts enlarge the center and the center band and/or add more borders. You might also add bands between the borders.

Before beginning any work on this quilt, please read the General Directions (which begin on page 4), including Appliquéing a Block (page 16) and Directions for Embroidery, Fabric Paints, and Crayons (page 16). All pattern pieces are finished size; add 1/4-inch seam allowance on all sides.

16-in. blk.

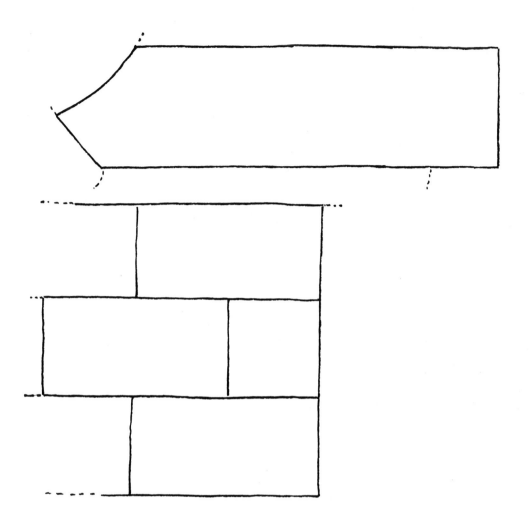

1. 8-in. blk.

King's Horses and Men Border

2. 12-in. blk.

2. 12-in. blk.

Mother Goose Characters—1981

Four sets of children in various period costumes appear in this quilt, illustrating famous nursery rhymes. Two children join to make a large center block, although you may separate them by giving each a pail and adding the section in dot-dash outline to Jill's patterns. Choose one of the quilt top designs given in the general directions on pages 6 and 7 and then pick the characters to fill the blank spaces. Some of the blank spaces may be filled with the embroidered words of the rhymes illustrated on the other blocks of the quilt. There are so many ways to use the blocks and make any size quilt needed.

These designs are given in only one size; however, the designs will fit on a 10-inch square if placed on the diagonal or on a 12-inch square if placed straight. The Jack and Jill figures will need a block at least 15 inches square when used together. The first pattern is a complete outline of the A figure. This can be used as a pattern for embroidery, fabric paint, or crayons, and it is also the diagram for use as a guide to placing the appliqué pieces. The appliqué patterns are marked B. There are small related designs in squares 1 through 9. These may be used on 3-inch-square corners for lattice strips between the blocks. See pages 6 and 7. The small designs are to be embroidered, fabric-painted, or crayoned. They could be useful as decorations on other needlework projects made for children.

Before beginning any work on this quilt, please read the General Directions (which begin on page 4), including Appliquéing a Block (page 16) and Directions for Embroidery, Fabric Paints, and Crayons (page 16). All pattern pieces are finished size; add 1/4-inch seam allowance on all sides.

1–2 Jack and Jill went up the hill
　　To fetch a pail of water,
Jack fell down and broke his crown
　　And Jill came tumbling after.

3 Little Nancy Etticote in a white petticoat
　　And a red nose.
The longer she stands
　　The shorter she grows.

4 Jack be nimble,
　　Jack be quick,
Jack jump over
　　The candlestick.

5 Little Bo-Peep has lost her sheep
　　And can't tell where to find them.
Leave them alone and they'll come home
　　Wagging their tails behind them.

6 Little Boy Blue come blow your horn.
　　The sheep's in the meadow,
　　The cow's in the corn.
Where is the little boy
　　Who looks after the sheep?
He's under the haystack, fast asleep.

7 There was a little girl
　　And she had a little curl
　　Right in the middle of her forehead.
When she was good
　　She was very, very good
　　And when she was bad, she was horrid.

8 Bobby Shaftoe's gone to sea,
　　Silver buckles on his knee.
He'll come back and marry me.
　　Pretty Bobby Shaftoe.

Mother Goose Quilt

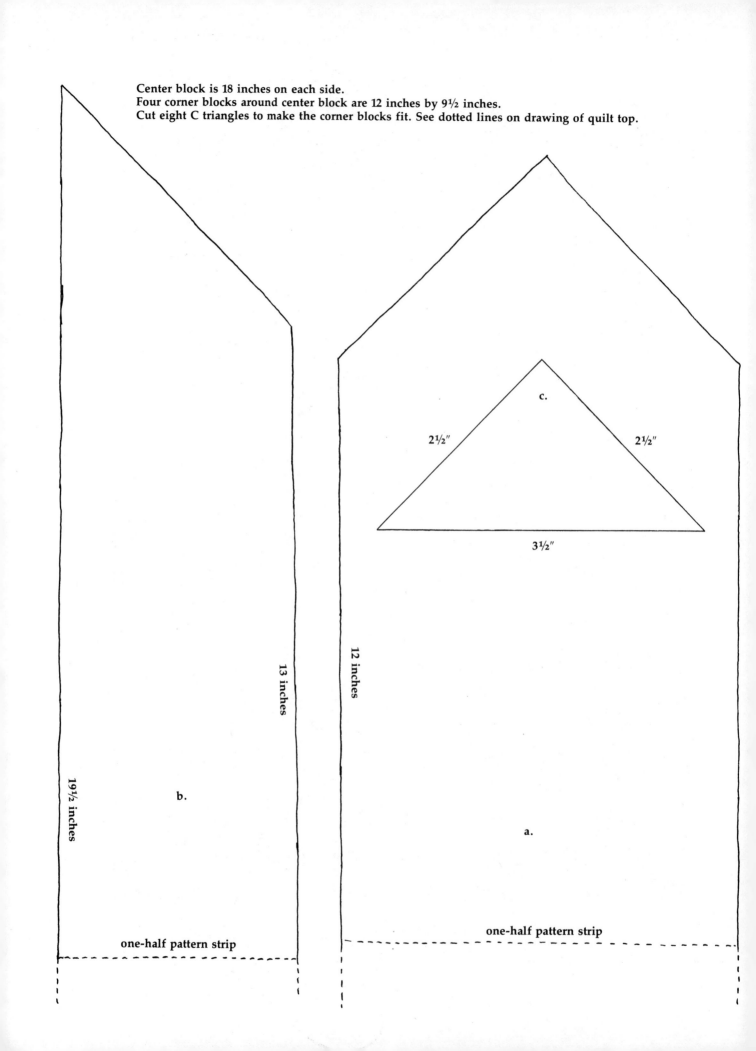

Center block is 18 inches on each side.
Four corner blocks around center block are 12 inches by 9½ inches.
Cut eight C triangles to make the corner blocks fit. See dotted lines on drawing of quilt top.

c.

2½"   2½"

3½"

13 inches

12 inches

19½ inches

b.

a.

one-half pattern strip

one-half pattern strip

Jack

A (12-in. blk.)

B (12-in. blk.) Appliqué

Jill

A (12-in. blk.)

B (12-in. blk.) Appliqué

Nancy

A (12-in. blk.)

B (12-in. blk.) Appliqué

90

Jack

A (12-in. blk.)

B (12-in. blk.) Appliqué

92

Bo-Peep

A (12-in. blk.)
93

a.

b.

c.

e.

f.

d.

e.

f.

i.

g.

h.

B (12-in. blk.) Appliqué

Boy Blue

A (12-in. blk.)

a.

e.

c.

d.

c.

d.

b.

f.

g.

h.

B (12-in. blk.) Appliqué

96

Little Girl

(12-in. blk.)

B (12-in. blk.) Appliqué

Bobby

A (12-in. blk.)

B (12-in. blk.) Appliqué

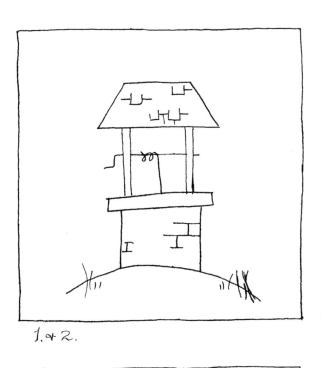

1. & 2.

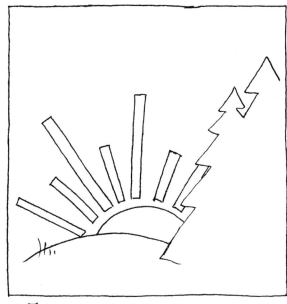

3.

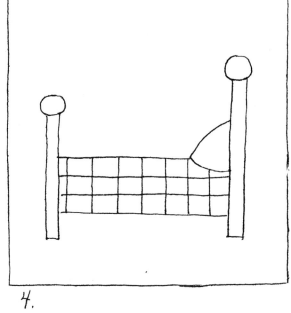

4.

7.

8

9.

American Patriotic Stories

Betsy Ross—1976

Everyone has heard the story of how Betsy Ross, who was a seamstress in Philadelphia, was asked by George Washington to make the first American flag. She persuaded Washington to have a flag with five-pointed instead of six-pointed stars. Whether this story is true or not, Elizabeth Griscom Ross really lived in Philadelphia and did make several well-documented flags for American forces fighting the Revolutionary War. Betsy Ross has passed into our country's folklore, and the story of the first American flag is taught to each new generation of children. It is one of those stories that, if it isn't true, ought to be—because it is true in spirit.

The patterns are given in two sizes. Pattern A can be used on a 10-inch square if placed on the diagonal or on a 12-inch square if placed straight. This is an outline pattern for use in embroidery, fabric-painting, or crayoning. It is also a diagram for use as a guide in placing the appliqué pieces. The appliqué patterns are marked B. They will fit on a 15″ by 20″ rectangle. This rectangle may be placed in the center of an 18″ by 30″ oblong. With the 9-inch-wide Stars and Stripes Border (page 289), it will form a 3′ by 4′ baby quilt.

Five Betsys in different-colored dresses could be used for the center of a twin bed quilt, suitably enlarged. You might also experiment with the figures of Paul Revere (page 109) and Betsy on a quilt center; Bobby Shaftoe of the nursery rhymes (page 99) could also impersonate John Paul Jones. The pattern for Betsy's dress is too large for these pages, so it was divided on the dot-dash line. This line should be eliminated when drawing the two sections as one pattern on a larger piece of paper.

> Before beginning any work on this quilt, please read the General Directions (which begin on page 4), including Appliquéing a Block (page 16) and Directions for Embroidery, Fabric Paints, and Crayons (page 16). All pattern pieces are finished size; add 1/4-inch seam allowance on all sides.

Betsy Ross

A (12-in. blk.)

104   *B* (15 x 20-in. blk.) Appliqué

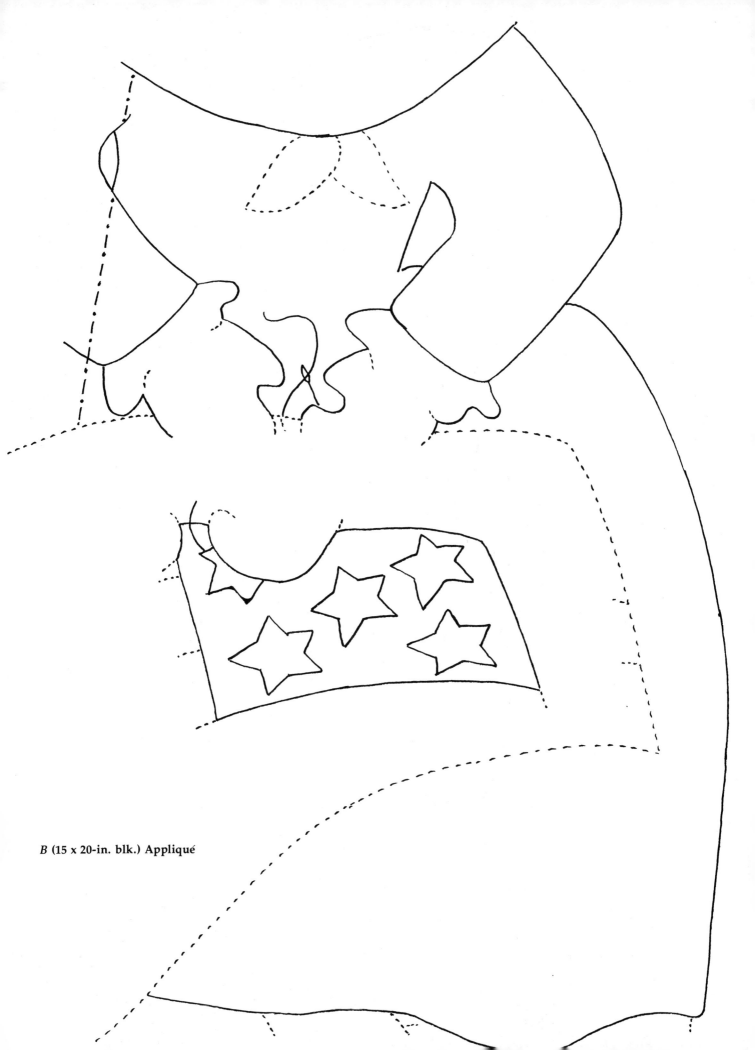

B (15 x 20-in. blk.) Appliqué

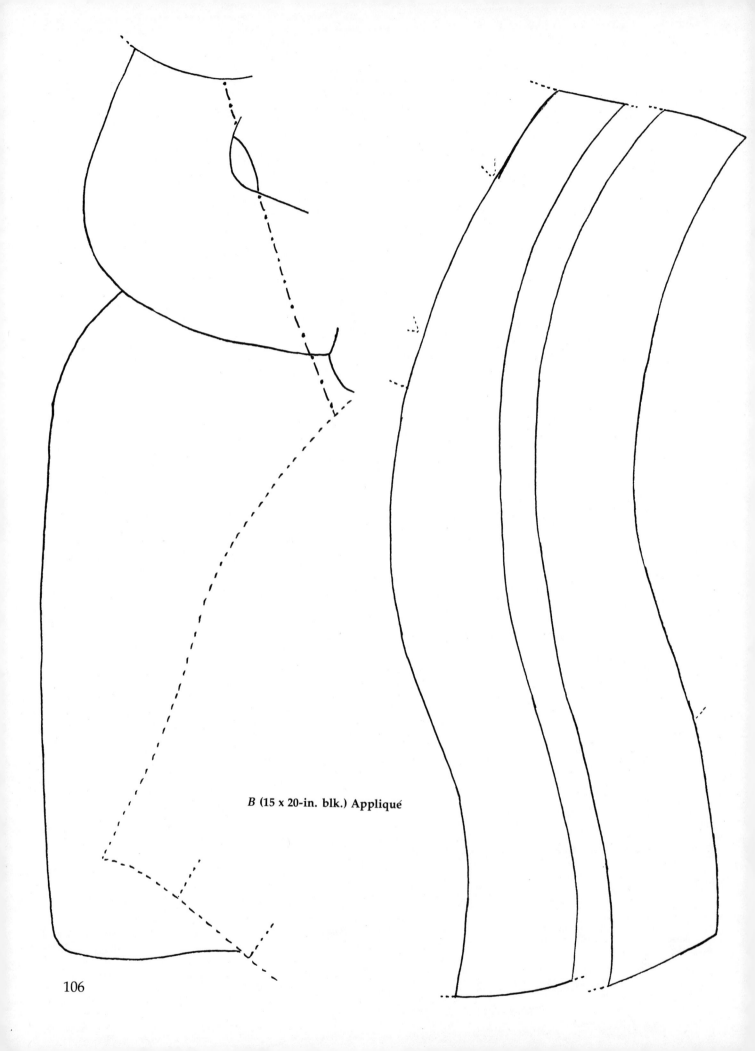

B (15 x 20-in. blk.) Appliqué

106

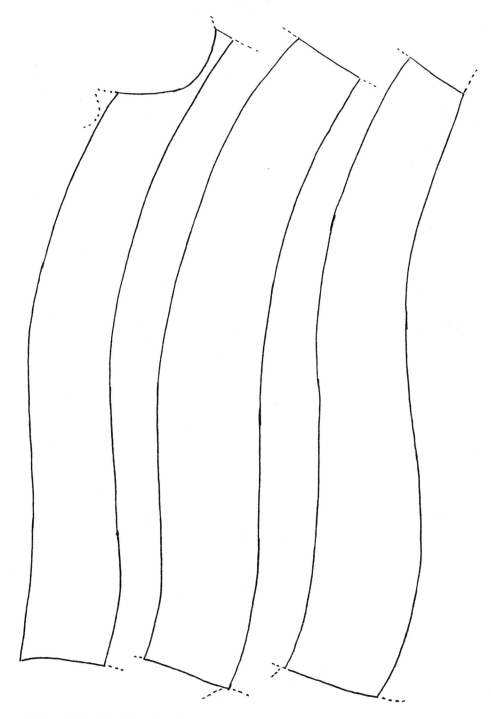

B (15 x 20-in. blk.) Appliqué

Paul Revere—1976

Listen my children and you shall hear
Of the midnight ride of Paul Revere
On the eighteenth of April, in seventy-five;
Hardly a man is now alive
Who remembers that famous day and year.

He said to his friend, "If the British march
By land or sea from the town tonight,
Hang a lantern aloft in the belfry arch
Of the North Church tower as a signal light, —
One, if by land, and two, if by sea;
And I on the opposite shore will be,

So through the night rode Paul Revere . . .

—Longfellow

The legend of Paul Revere overshadows the real-life story of a great man and patriot. This story, like that of Betsy Ross, is true in spirit and wrong only in details. It seems to me that the real story is even more in the American tradition than is the legend, because it tells how many men cooperated to defeat an enemy and how when one man was stopped another took up the task until it was completed successfully. Be that as it may, the figure of Paul Revere symbolizes for most American children an exciting part of American history.

The patterns are given in two sizes. The smaller *A* will fit a 10-inch square on the diagonal and a 12-inch square if placed straight. This pattern is to be used for embroidery, fabric-painting, or crayoning. Paul's uniform should be blue with light tan (buff) pants, waistcoat, and lapels. The shirt should be white and can be replaced with three tight ruffles of lace if you wish. The larger pattern *B* will fit on a 15″ by 20″ rectangle. See also the suggestions for various quilt top designs on pages 8 and 9. This design was made to be a pair with the Betsy Ross design and the Stars and Stripes Border, page 289.

Before beginning any work on this quilt, please read the General Directions (which begin on page 4), including Appliquéing a Block (page 16) and Directions for Embroidery, Fabric Paints, and Crayons (page 16). All pattern pieces are finished size; add 1/4-inch seam allowance on all sides.

Paul Revere

A (10-in. blk.)

B (12-in. blk.) Appliqué

110

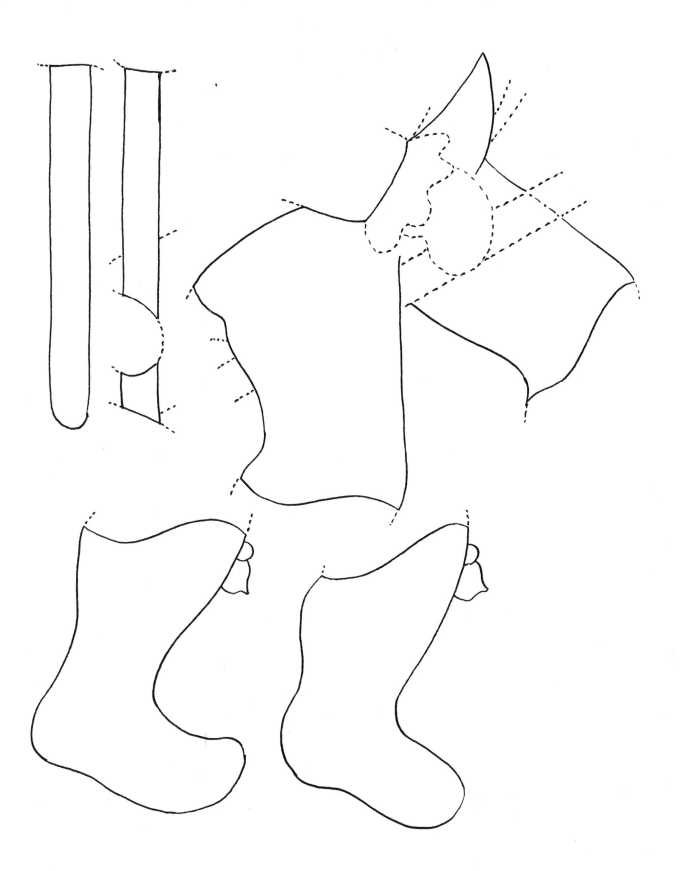

B (12-in. blk.) Appliqué

Fairy Tales

The Tinies—1977

There are fairies at the bottom of my garden,
They're not so very, very far away.
You go through the garden gate, and you just
keep straight ahead.
I do so hope they've really come to stay.

Rose Fyleman

Before I was two years old I could say this whole long poem. In fact, this was how I earned my first wages, standing on the counter of my grandfather's store and entertaining the customers. As far as I can tell, the "Little People" have been around me ever since, to see what I would be up to next. And they have always been welcome "at the bottom of my garden." So much of what we learn in our earliest years stays around to influence our thoughts and dreams in later years. In these two variations of the Little People of my imagination, The Tinies, I wish to share with you and your children a little of my own imaginative life.

The small patterns, *1A* and *2A*, are for 12-inch-square blocks if the design is placed on the diagonal and for 15-inch-square blocks when the design is placed straight. A top design can be chosen from those given on pages 8 and 9. These should be embroidered, fabric-painted, or done in crayons. A pretty effect can be obtained by coloring the designs and then outlining them in embroidery.

The appliqué designs, *1B* and *2B*, should be sewn onto an oblong 18″ by 24″ or larger. Use the embroidery pattern to see where the elements should be placed. The Hearts and Flowers quilting pattern (pages 294–297) was designed to go with this design.

Before beginning any work on this quilt, please read the General Directions (which begin on page 4) including Appliquéing a Block (page 16) and Directions for Embroidery, Fabric Paints, and Crayons (page 16). All pattern pieces are finished size; add 1/4-inch seam allowance on all sides.

1A (12-in. blk.)

1B (15-in. blk.) Appliqué

114

1B (15-in. blk.) Appliqué

1B (15-in. blk.) Appliqué

116

1B (15-in. blk.) Appliqué

2A (12-in. blk.)

2B (15-in. blk.) Appliqué

2B (15-in. blk.) Appliqué

2B (15-in. blk.) Appliqué

Bible Stories

Noah's Ark—1974

There are many beloved children's stories in the Bible—both Old and New Testament. Nevertheless, I believe that the story of Noah's Ark and the animals two by two has been made into quilt designs oftener than any other. The Smithsonian has a wonderful adult Noah's Ark quilt from the eighteenth century which has not only the Ark, Noah's family, and the animals, but also people, buildings, and vehicles of the eighteenth century cut from chintz fabrics, and all wending their way toward the Ark set in the center. Round and round they go, making three complete circuits. I've also seen a modern quilt design in which the needlewoman pieced the ark for the center block and arranged the animals in blocks set in two rows around this center.

My design is closer in feeling to the earlier quilt. It has the Ark built on one side of an appliquéd hill. Noah, with a shepherd's crook, is guiding the animals up the ramp. They go in a long **S** curve from the bottom of the quilt, threading through the flowers. Some animals are already aboard, and it is starting to rain. Clouds are beginning to cover a rather perturbed sun. To make this a larger quilt than the 4' by 5' crib size shown here, add two rows of 8-inch blocks all around with more "cookie cutter," simple animal shapes. By removing the beard and changing the color of the hair, Noah can become his three sons. Make the robe of flowered print and change the hairdo a little and Noah can become his wife and three daughters-in-law. Add a lattice strip between the blocks, as shown in the diagram. Some of the animals could be two each of: whales, lions, tigers, and zebras (from striped material), cows, horses, pandas, kangaroos, and monkeys. Don't put in a unicorn—they missed the boat, you know.

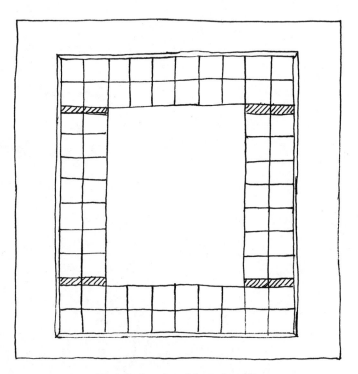

**Top design for enlarged quilt;
3-inch strips will fill out the new length.**

Before beginning any work on this quilt, please read the General Directions (which begin on page 4) including Appliquéing a Block (page 16). All pattern pieces are finished size; add 1/4-inch seam allowance on all sides.

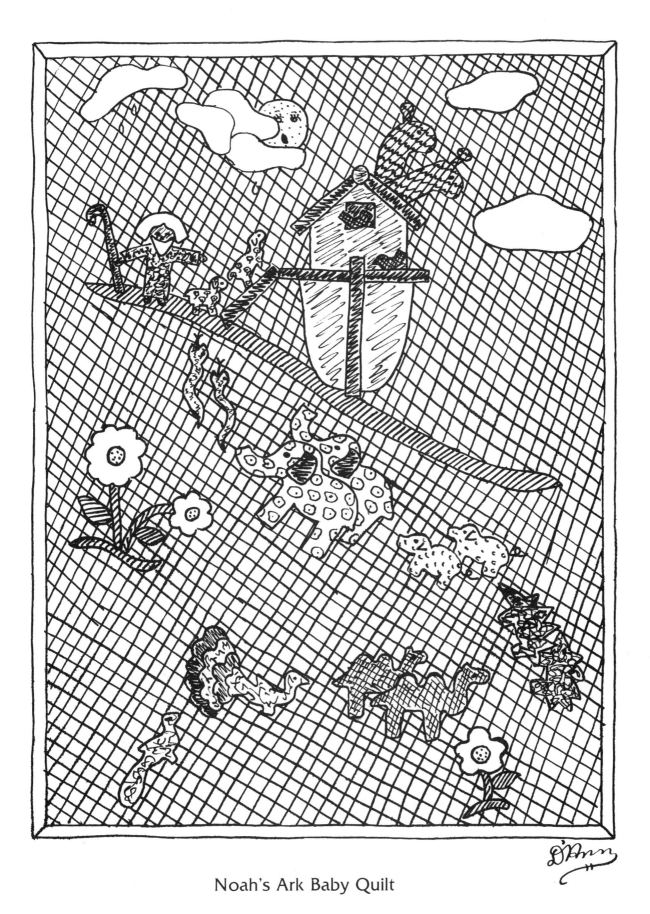

Noah's Ark Baby Quilt

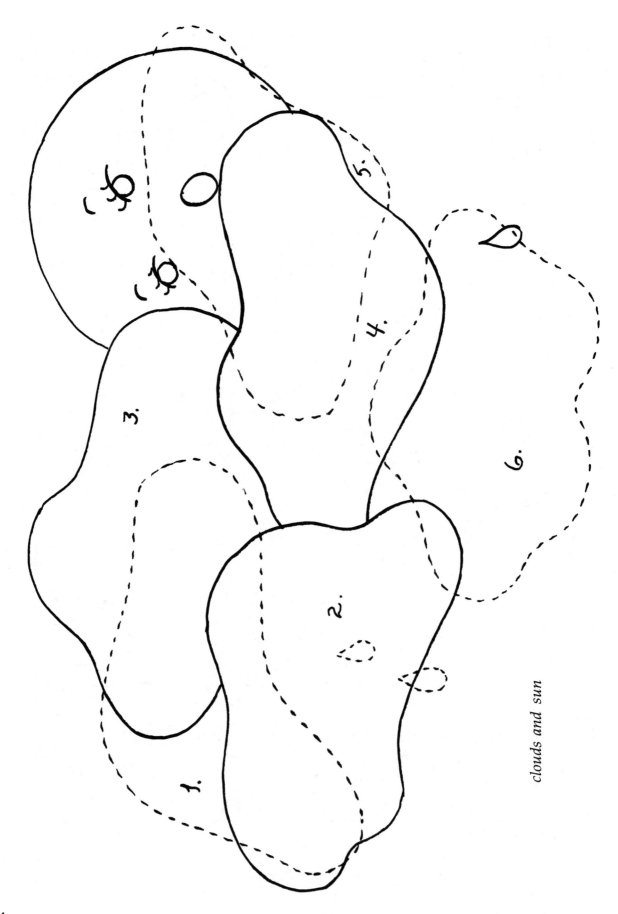

clouds and sun

124

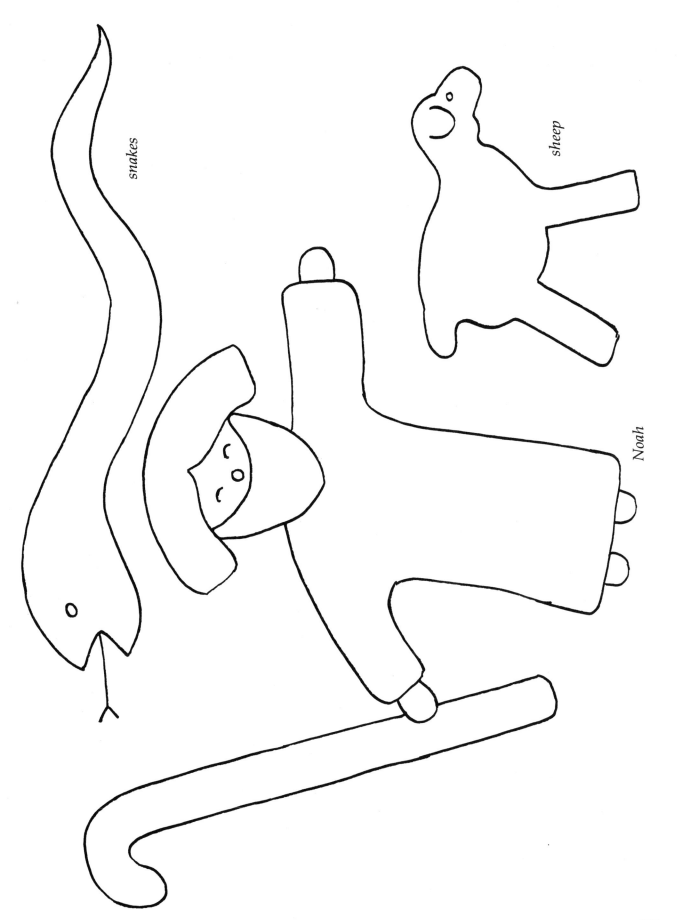

snakes

sheep

Noah

125

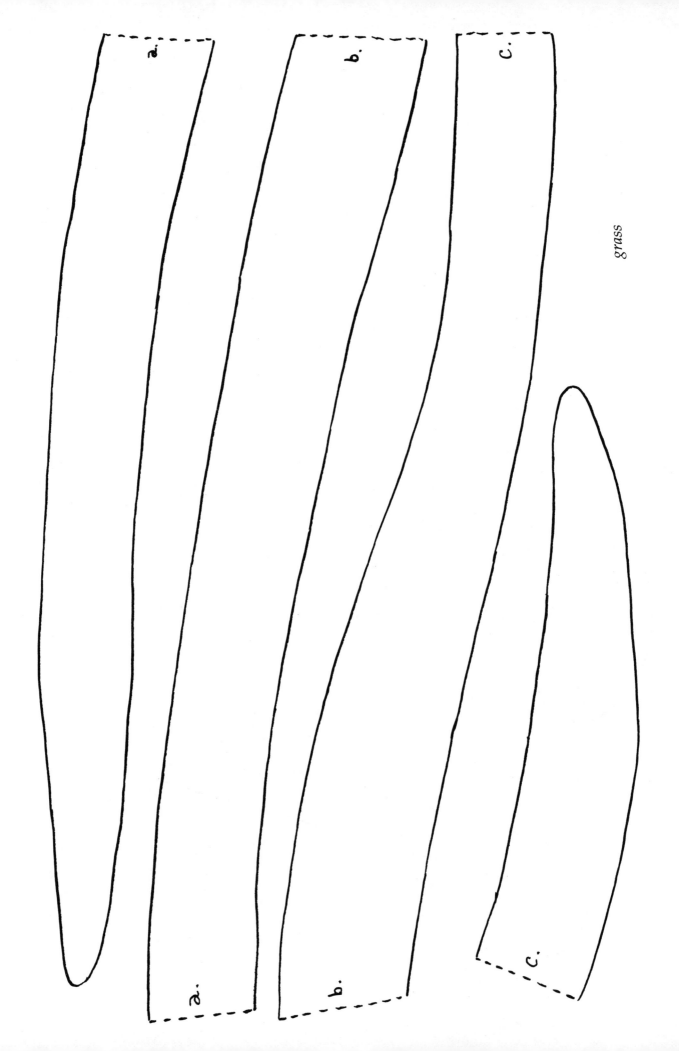

grass

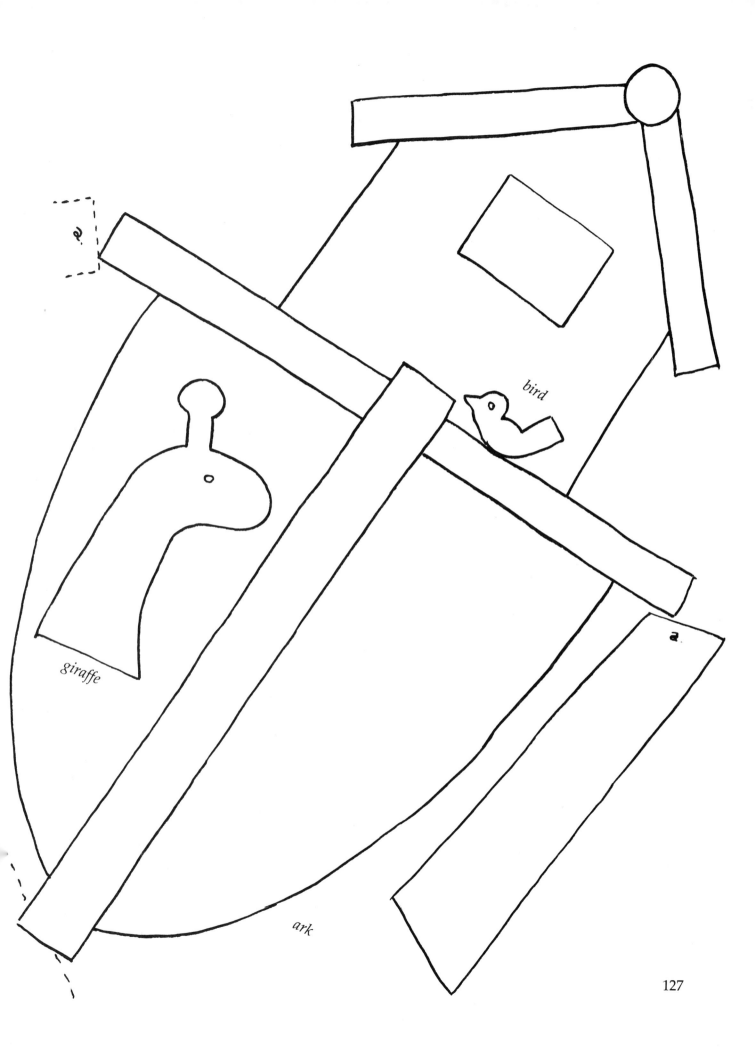

giraffe

bird

ark

127

porcupine

camel

elephant

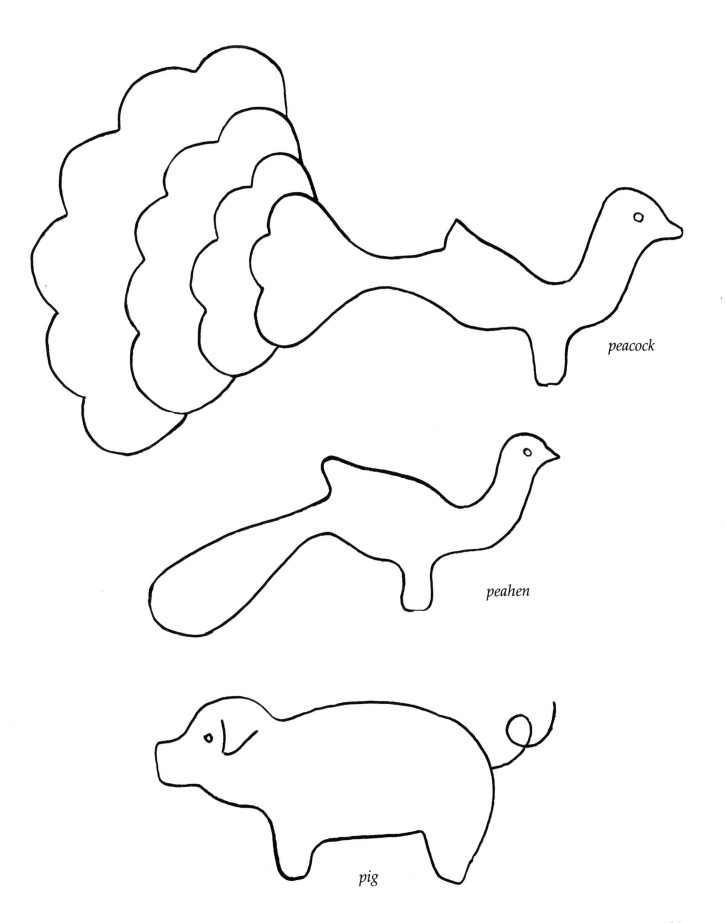

peacock

peahen

pig

flowers

130

The Owl and the Pussy Cat—1975

The Owl and the Pussy Cat went to sea
In a beautiful pea green boat;
They took some honey and plenty of money
Wrapped up in a five pound note.

They dined on mince and slices of quince,
Which they ate with a runcible spoon;
And hand in hand, on the edge of the sand,
They danced by the light of the moon.
— Edward Lear

Edward Lear wrote many nonsense verses, but this is the best-loved of all of them. The poem has always appealed to artists and has been illustrated in many engaging ways. The word-illustrations in the poem open the imagination, especially the "runcible spoon." I took the opening line and illustrated the words as a baby quilt design.

The pieces are in large, simple shapes for appliqué; they would serve very well as a first pattern for anyone who wished to learn appliqué techniques. The filler should be a Dacron batting so that the only quilting needed for this top would be outlining the motifs, on the outer edge of each piece, and ¼-inch inside each piece.

The background of the quilt is one sheet of cloth, 44" by 52". All of the motif pieces should be pinned in place to this background and then basted. To check that the pieces are in the correct position, look at the top design on page 134. To make the large curves on the edges of the background cloth, cut a large pattern from heavy paper. Grocery bags opened out are very useful for making large patterns; if they are not large enough, two can be taped together with masking tape. The paper needed for the curved-edge pattern must be 3' long by 4" wide. Draw a line ½-inch from the top and then the bottom edge the full 3-foot length of the paper. Place a noticeable mark at 1-foot intervals on the bottom line. You will have four marks in all, including marks at the beginning and end of the line. Mark the top line in the same way, but start the marks 6 inches from each side edge; you will have three marks

in all with the middle mark 1 foot from the two end marks. Fold the paper, accordion-pleating it on each of these marks. The pleats will be 6 inches wide. Now draw an S curve from the bottom mark on one side of the top pleat to the top mark on the other side of the pleat. When you are satisfied with the shape of the curve (it will look best when opened if the top and bottom curve are flattened about 1½ inches from the edges) cut the paper, without unfolding it, on the curved line. Place this pattern on the top and bottom edges (the short edges) of the background piece and trace it on the cloth. For the two sides, the pattern for the first 2 feet should be traced at the top and bottom of the side; then fill in the small center area with a smaller curve only 2 inches deep. See the drawing of the quilt top. The corners should be rounded off from the end of the top curve to the end of the side curve. For both the small center curve and the corner curves, you can make trial drawings (on paper) which are then cut out for patterns.

The appliqué patterns for sails and mast are drawn at one quarter of their actual size. Draw a graph with lines 1 inch apart on a piece of paper 32" by 26" wide. Copy the outlines from the small graph to those squares on the large graph that exactly correspond in placement with the squares crossed by the outlines on the small graph. This is not hard to do, taking very little time or artistic ability. It is such a useful tool for the quilter that I hope many readers will try to use graphs for making small patterns larger.

The colors used in the original top are as follows: the background material is a very pale olive green. The boat sections are all pea green (which borders on medium olive green). The cat is gold. The owl is medium brown and tan with white rings around brown and yellow eyes, and a yellow beak and feet. The water and sails are white; the mast is the same green as the rest of the boat. The island is tan, the trunk of the palm brown and its fronds pea green. The note of color that sparks the whole quilt is the pennant, which is flamingo red (slightly yellowish but not orange). The binding is made of background material carefully cut on the bias to fit around the curves without pulling.

Before beginning any work on this quilt, please read the General Directions (which begin on page 4), including Appliquéing a Block (page 16). All pattern pieces are finished size; add 1/4-inch seam allowance on all sides.

The Owl and the Pussy Cat
Baby Quilt

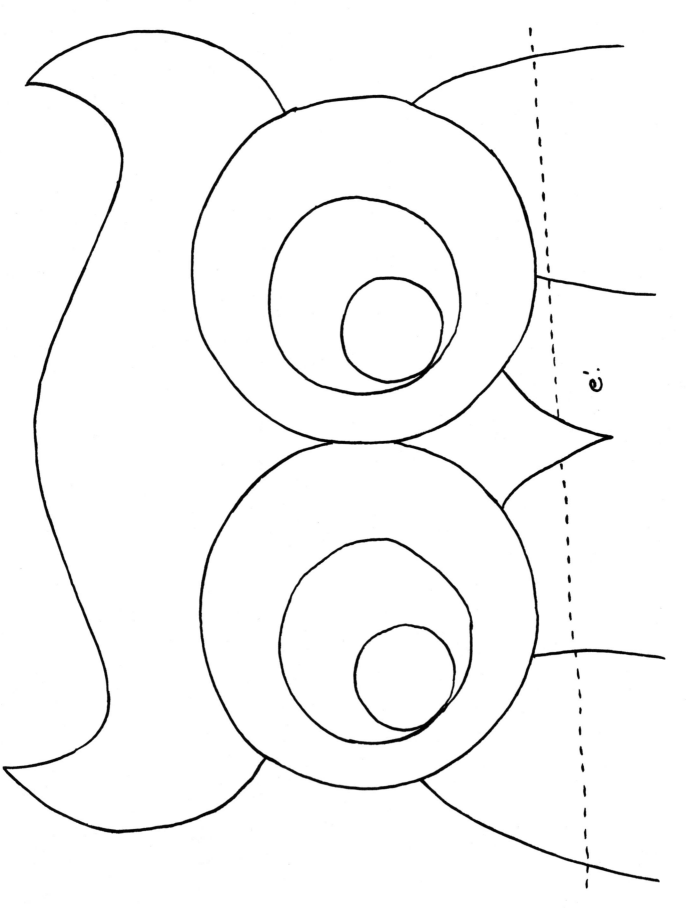

136

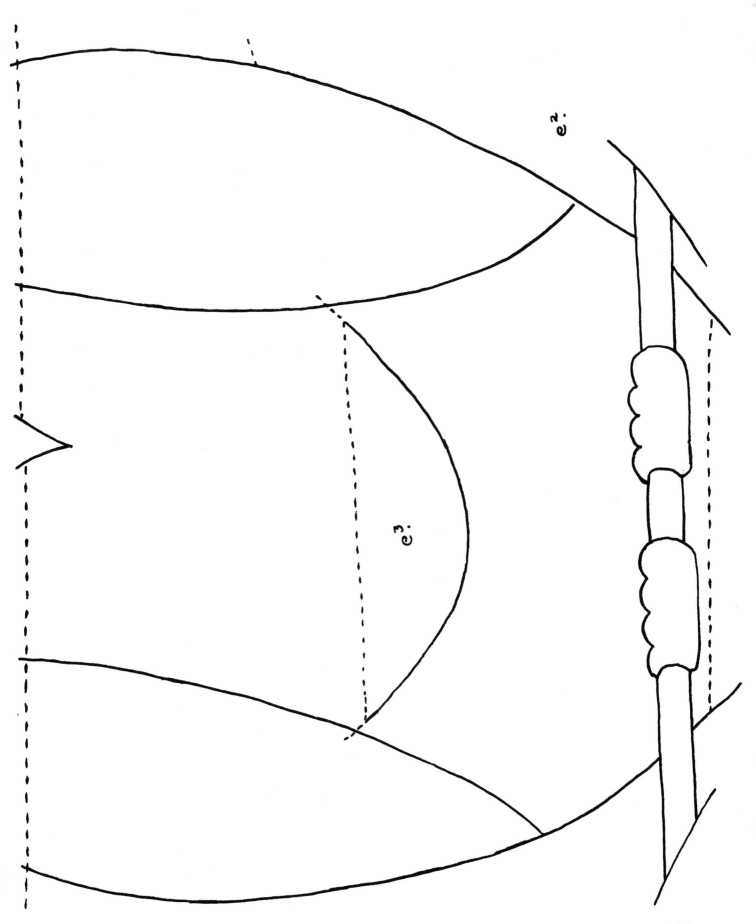

e².

e³.

137

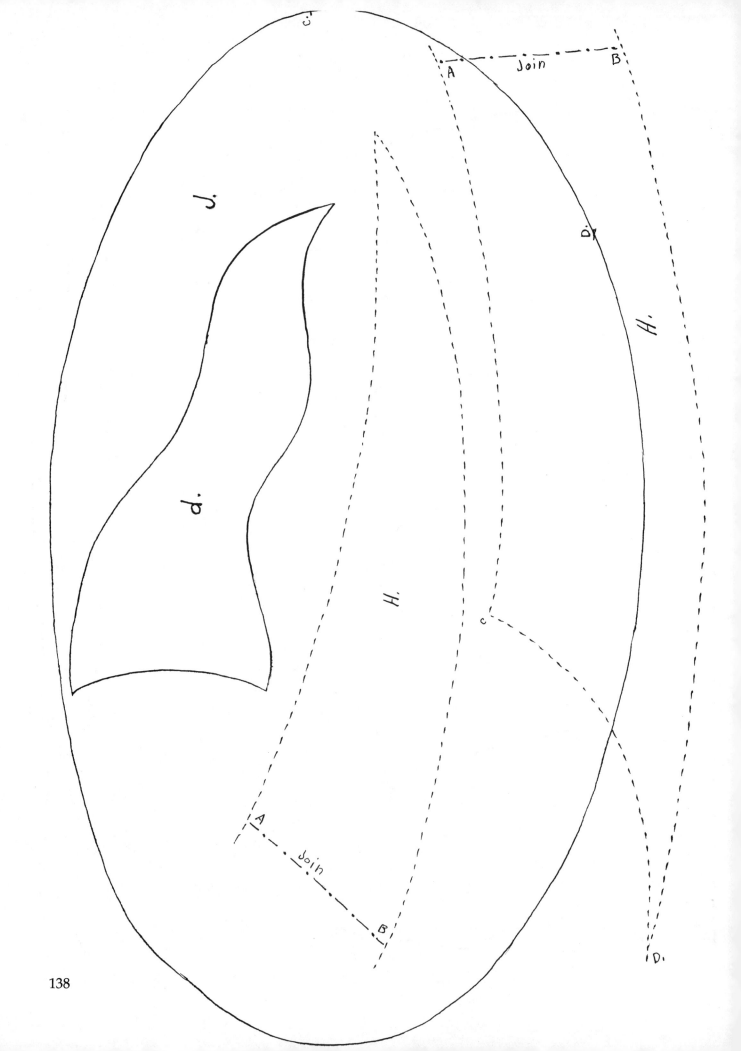

G'

K.

G²

139

K.

E.

Join

L.

F.

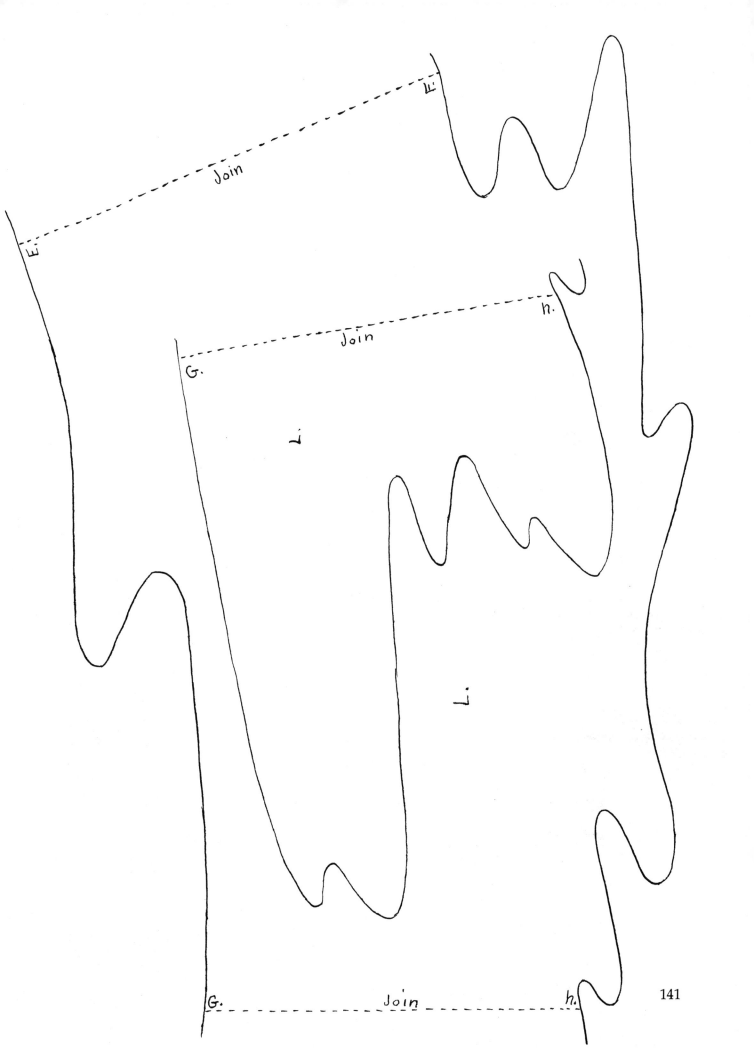

F.

Join

E.

Join

G.

h.

J.

L.

G. Join h.

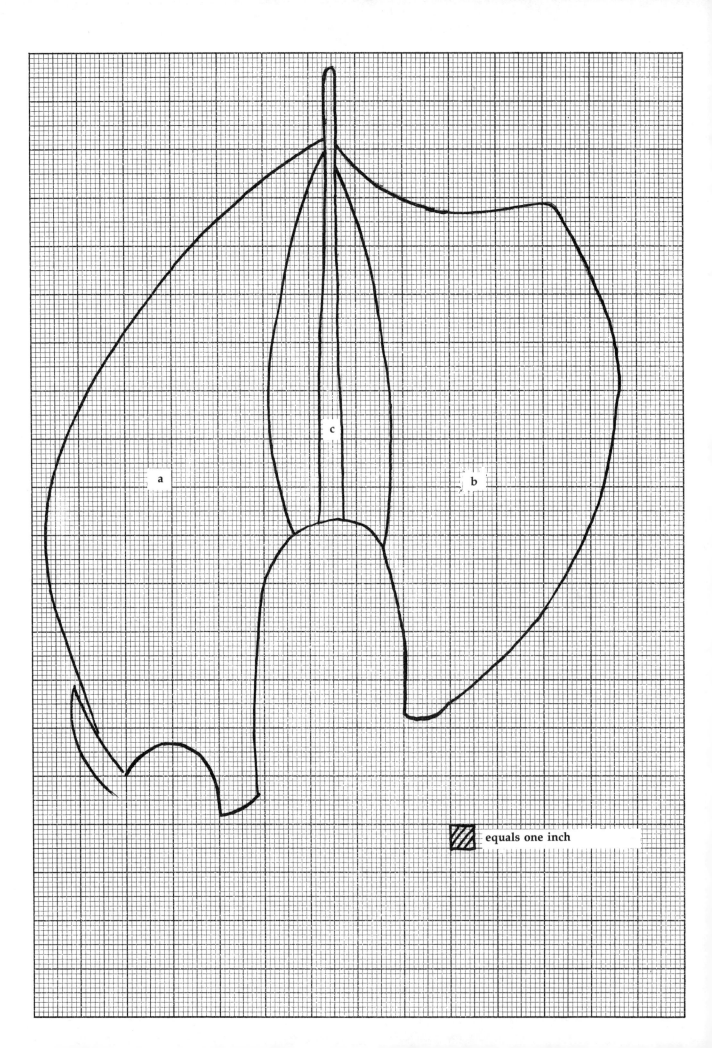

a

c

b

equals one inch

The Dancing Elephant Baby Quilt

Animals

The Dancing Elephant—1977

Spring is in the air—the flowers bloom and butterflies flutter. So, of course, an elephant would feel like lightly tippy-toeing in a ballet step or two. His friends join trunk to tail in a Circus Parade border. This is one of the happiest quilts I have ever designed and made.

The background of the center oblong and the border strip are white. The strips between the center and the border and around the outside of the quilt are yellow gingham. The large elephant is a soft blue-grey with yellow toes and white tusks. The circus elephants, the flowers, and the large butterfly, as well as the binding, are a bright red print with touches of white and yellow. The small butterflies are the same yellow as the elephant's toes.

To emphasize the embroidered details—flower stems, leaves, butterfly bodies, and the inner lines of the elephant's body—I used a three-ply synthetic yarn in the appropriate colors. This was laid along the pattern lines of the designs, penciled in on the cloth. I then used a couching stitch (tiny stitches evenly spaced directly over the yarn) in sewing thread, pulled to hide itself in the fibers of the yarn.

The center for this crib quilt is 12" by 24". The inside gingham band is 2 inches wide, the white border band is 7 inches wide, and the outer gingham band is 3 inches wide. These measurements could be doubled to make a twin-bed-sized quilt border. The center should be enlarged to 30" by 30" for a twin-bed-sized quilt. Place one elephant on the left and reverse the patterns to make a second elephant for the right side.

The elephant pieces for the border should be pinned nose to tail with the bottom of the feet about 1 inch from the lower edge of the white border band. The length of the nose and tail can be altered slightly when necessary. Place the same number of pieces on opposite sides of the border. If you make the larger border for twin size, pin the animals in place and adjust them up or down until they fit the length of the bands. All the animals should be at the same level on the band.

Before beginning any work on this quilt, please read the General Directions (which begin on page 4), including Appliquéing a Block (page 16) and Directions for Embroidery, Fabric Paints, and Crayons (page 16). All pattern pieces are finished size; add 1/4-inch seam allowance on all sides.

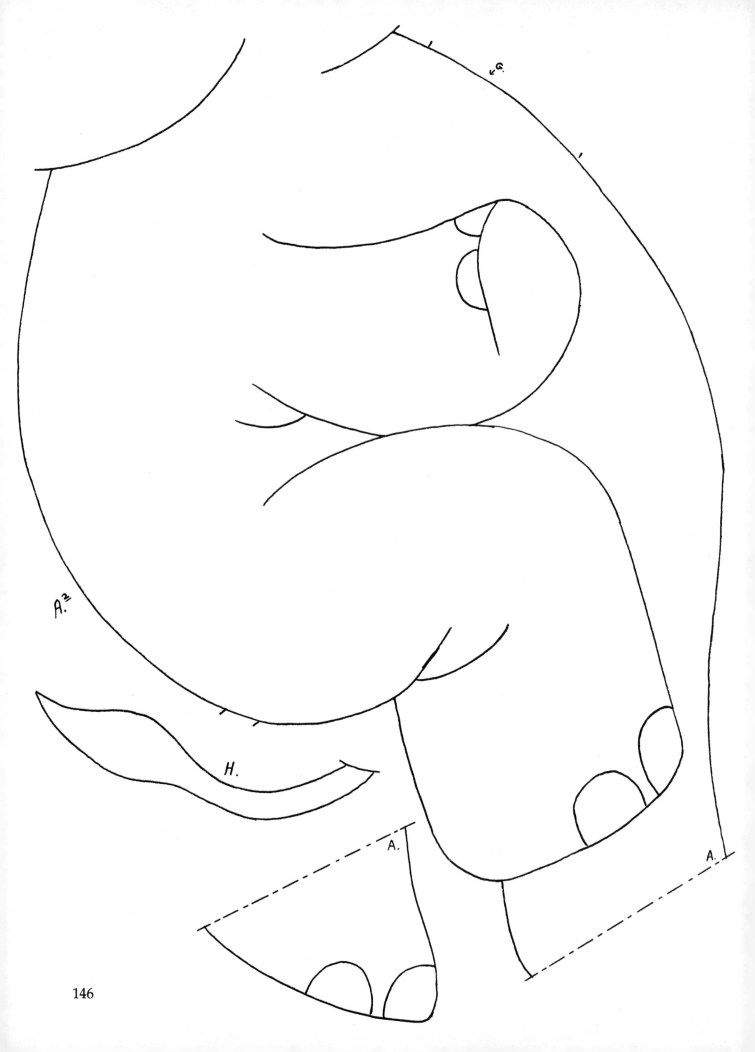

G.

A.²

H.

A.

A.

146

C.

D.

e. optional tusk

E.

F. mouth

1.

1.

D.

C.

B.

2.

2.

A.²

147

Baby Chick (1940) and Duckling (1980)

In the 1920's children's coloring books that could be used with the newly improved wax crayons became a thriving part of the publishing business. Almost as quickly as these books came on the market with their simplified and attractive outline designs, quiltmakers found them and began to trace off the designs for use in embroidered quilt blocks. Indeed, some of the designs are so simplified, with such nicely proportioned parts, that they have been used for appliqué (as was one of the designs further on in this book—Flying a Kite, page 263). The pattern used for the basic outline of the chick and duckling was given to me with a group of other patterns by Mrs. Jeanne Hindman of Ohio. There were no quilters among the younger members of her family, so I inherited a wonderful two-generation collection of quilt patterns and printed materials on quilts started by Mrs. Hindman's mother

and continued by her for over sixty years. This simple, unmarked cardboard cutting pattern was among the rest. It is hard to date something with so little information, but the design of the outline appears similar to those drawings for children designed in the decade of 1940-50. To make this pattern resemble the designs traced directly from coloring books, I have added a sailor hat for the duckling and a bonnet for the chick, and have also placed them in appropriate landscapes.

Consult pages 6 and 7 for top design suggestions. Use 12-inch square blocks for the backgrounds. The little birds and their clothing can be appliquéd with embroidered details; they can also be entirely embroidered, fabric-painted, or crayoned, or you can use a combination of these techniques. To make a quilt as the design would originally have been used, alternate the two designs on white blocks. Between each two pattern blocks place a plain block cut from a pleasing print material.

Before beginning any work on this quilt, please read the General Directions (which begin on page 4), including Appliquéing a Block (page 16) and Directions for Embroidery, Fabric Paints, and Crayons (page 16). All pattern pieces are finished size; add 1/4-inch seam allowance on all sides.

149

Kitten and/or Puppy in a Basket—1930's

Just as the Victorians liked their needlework flowers set neatly in vases, the needlewomen of 1920-30 liked flowers and animals in baskets. A quilt block of this pattern was given to me by a Tennessee quilter. It is an interesting change from the usual color scheme in that the kitten is white and the background is a blue-and-white print. The basket is yellow. I have added a pattern for a puppy, because although I do not have a copy of this substitute pattern, I have heard that they were available then.

The background should be a 12-inch square in a pretty print—dark for the kitten and light for the puppy. The kitten is white; the puppy is a light brown material. The basket should be a light tan or yellow or even light green. To fit the puppy in the basket, reverse the basket and handle patterns.

The motifs are placed on the background block on the diagonal. After the appliqué is finished, embroider the details of the animals in appropriate colors. This quilt should be put together according to diagram E on page 7. The lattice strips should be 3 inches wide. They can be cut from the same material as the baskets, or they can contrast in a plain color with the main color of the background print.

Before beginning work on this quilt, please read the General Directions (which begin on page 4), including Appliquéing a Block (page 16) and Directions for Embroidery, Fabric Paints, and Crayons (page 16). All pattern pieces are finished size; add 1/4-inch seam allowance on all sides.

10½-in. block

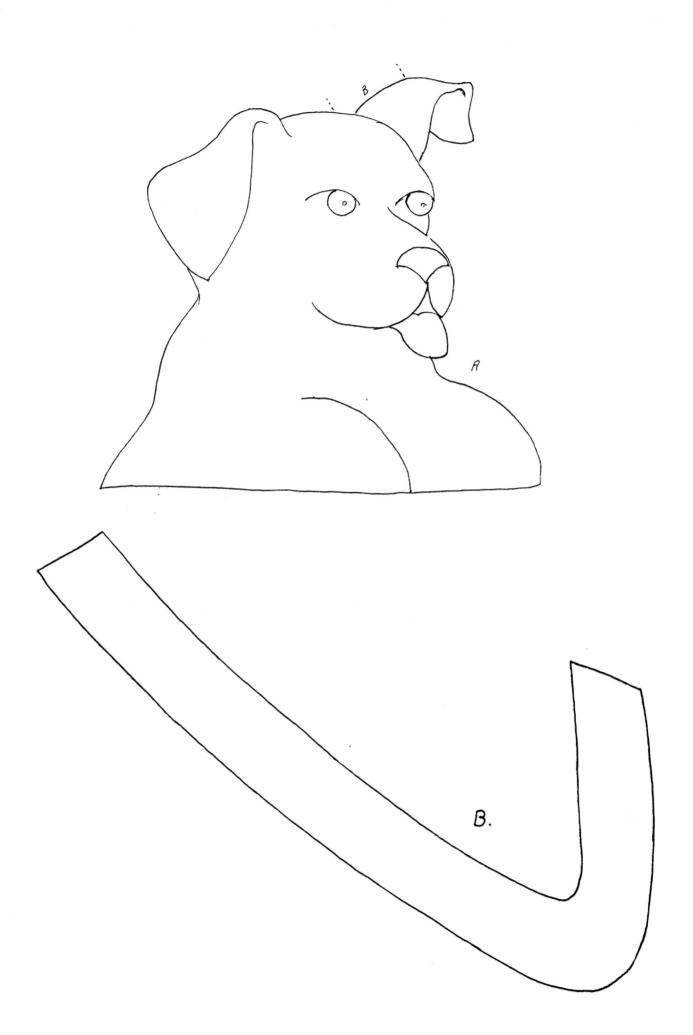

B

A

B.

Tweety-Pie—1965

Two little birds cuddling in front of their first house with a huge heart and lots of flowers as a romantic background were chosen for this crib quilt in traditional pastels. The birdhouse, birds, and flowery branch are all appliquéd. The large background area in white is quilted. The results give me one of the most beautiful baby quilts in my collection. The appliqué is not difficult, but the quilting requires a degree of skill and experience that only the making and quilting of several quilts gives one. This is definitely not a quilt for a beginner.

The white background should measure 40″ by 56″. The outlines for the birdhouse and its roof, pattern numbers 20 and 21, are too large to be given on these pages, so the patterns have been reduced in scale and shown on a graph that measures ¼-inch to 1¼ inches. This means, then, that the lines of the enlarging graph will need to be 1¼ inches apart. Draw the patterns for the roof, the house, and the heart for quilting separately. Directions for enlarging patterns from graphs are given with The Owl and the Pussy Cat, page 131.

In the original quilt the house is pale green, the leaves medium green, the branch and the roof light brown, and the flowers bright pink with yellow centers. The two birds are: light pink, with pink flowered print body, yellow feet, and yellow bill for the female (closed eyes); light blue, with blue flowered print body, yellow feet and bill, and white eye with darker blue iris for the male. Cut these out and arrange them on the center of the background material as shown in the diagram on page 156. All of the patterns are marked with a number followed by a period. The numbers in parentheses with arrows show which pieces surround the selected pattern piece. The arrows on these numbers show where these surrounding pattern pieces touch the selected pattern piece. There are twenty-three individual patterns; however, the roof has two pieces, and the flowers with their round centers are used five times. The dot-dash lines can be used as cutting pattern lines to go behind the smaller pieces and raise them for a more three-dimensional look (for example, the birds' bills). The patterns are all correct in size. The diagram has minor discrepancies; they are due to difficulties in drawing and should be disregarded.

Mark the quilting pattern last. Cut out a large heart, following the enlarging graph. Use this to outline a heart in pencil (make a double line) with top, widest side point, and bottom point each exactly 5 inches from the sides of the material. Use a yardstick to mark the diagonal lines crossed inside this heart outline. Do not cross these lines over the appliqué pieces, which will be outlined. Cut a good heavy cutting pattern for the dogwood-shaped flower (see page 164) with a hole cut out as the pattern for the flower center. Draw little freehand V's marking the petal edges inside the flower outline. Cut two more patterns for the leaf shapes or draw these freehand. There is no placement pattern for these shapes. Fill in the background of the quilt outside the heart outline with flowers and leaves in clusters that do not quite touch each other (see the quilt-top drawing). Quilt the birds' breasts with an upside-down shell (that is, scallop) pattern all over. The birds' heads should have the same pattern quilted in back of the features. The wings should be quilted in outline every ½-inch to the center. Quilt the tails in straight lines half an inch apart from the body outward. The remainder of the appliqué pieces are simply outlined on the edge of the piece and ¼-inch inside the edge. The binding should be cut from the same material as the background.

Before beginning any work on this quilt, please read the General Directions (which begin on page 4), including Appliquéing a Block (page 16) and Quilting (page 18). All pattern pieces are finished size; add 1/4-inch seam allowance on all sides.

Tweety-Pie Baby Quilt

155

156

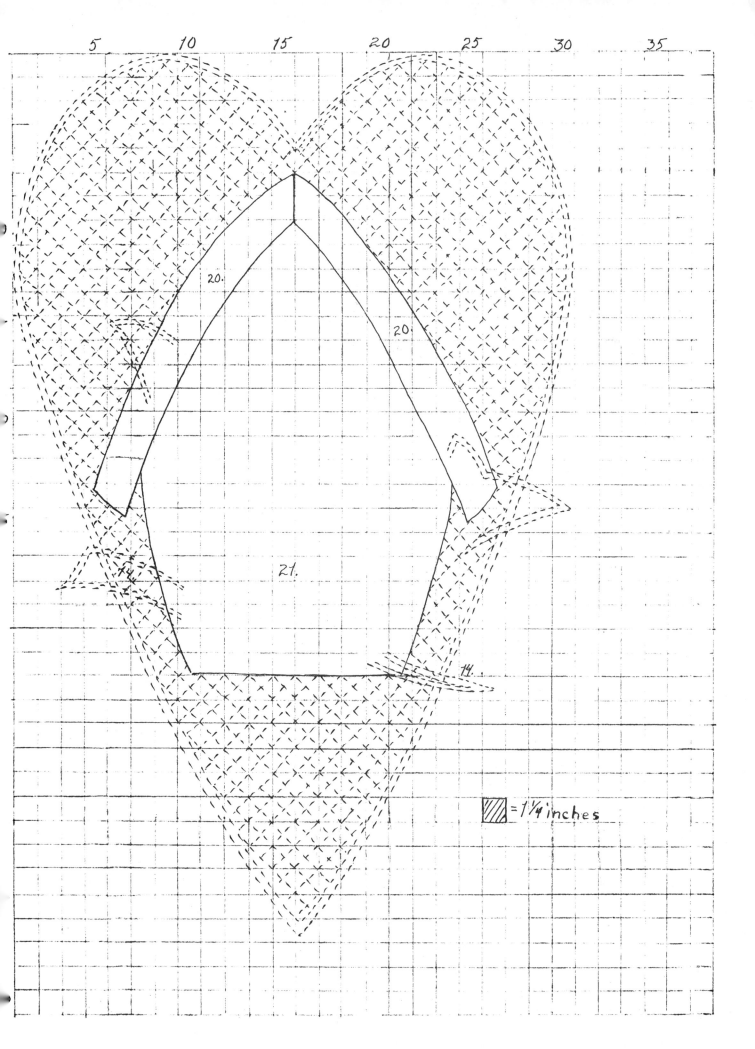

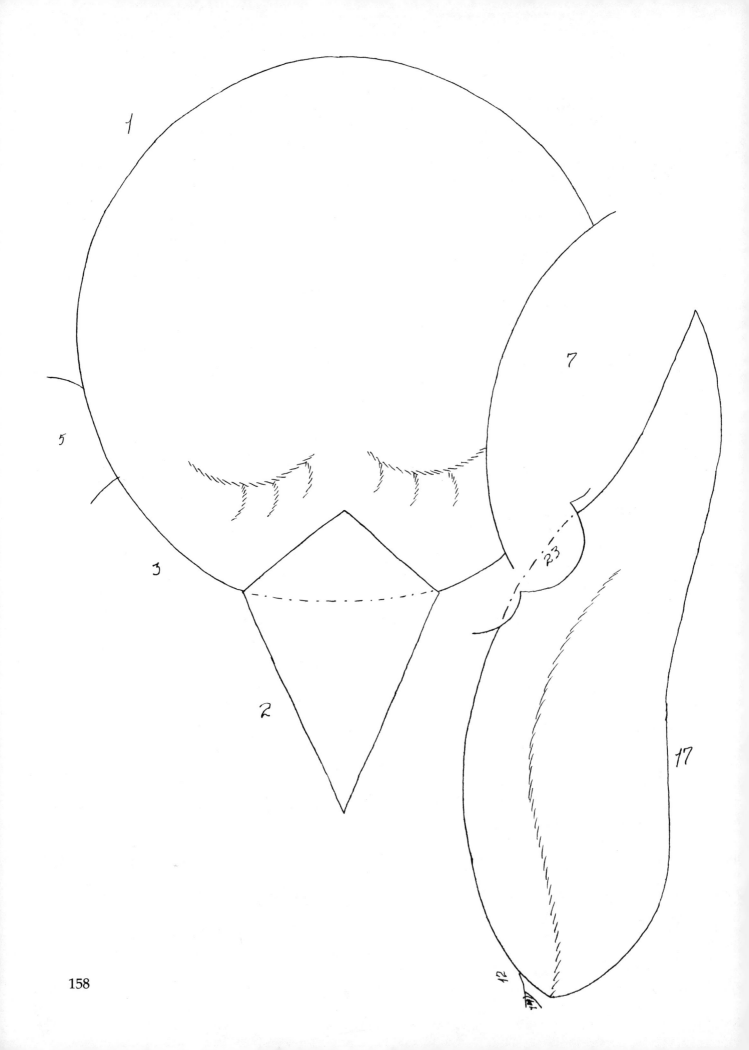

158

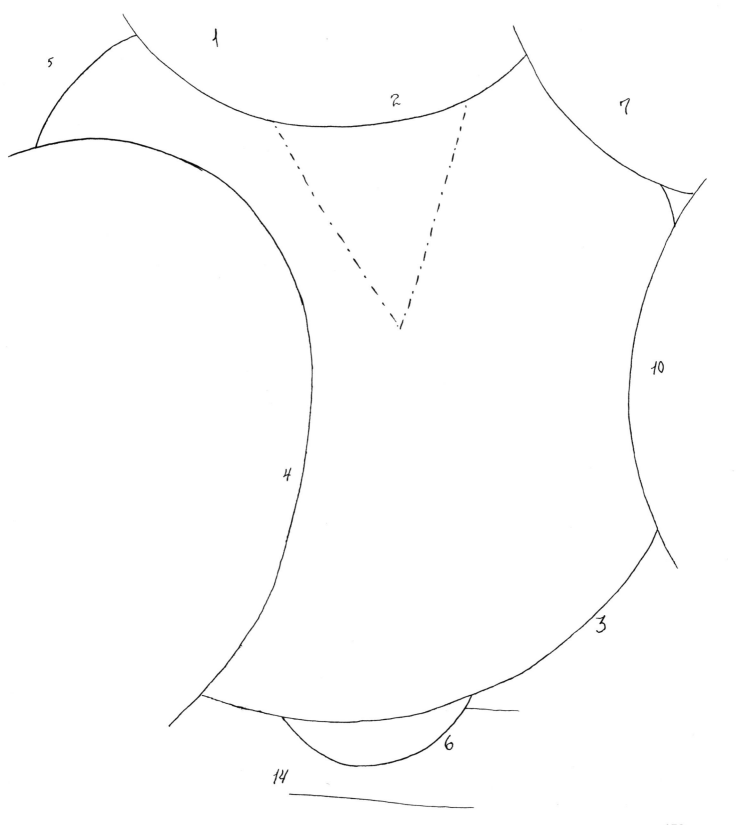

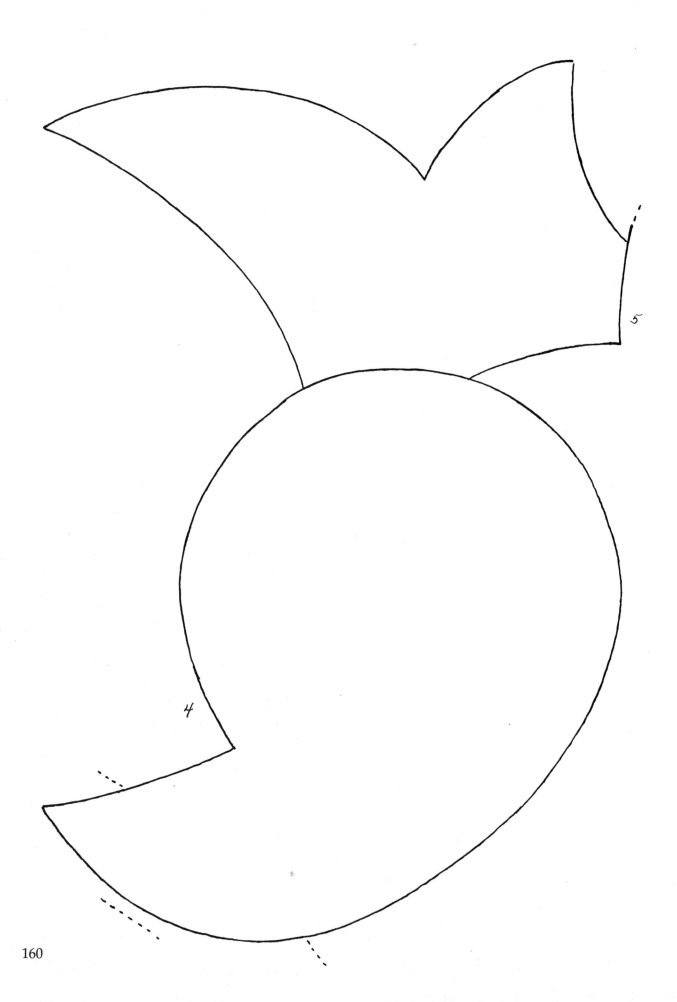

5

4

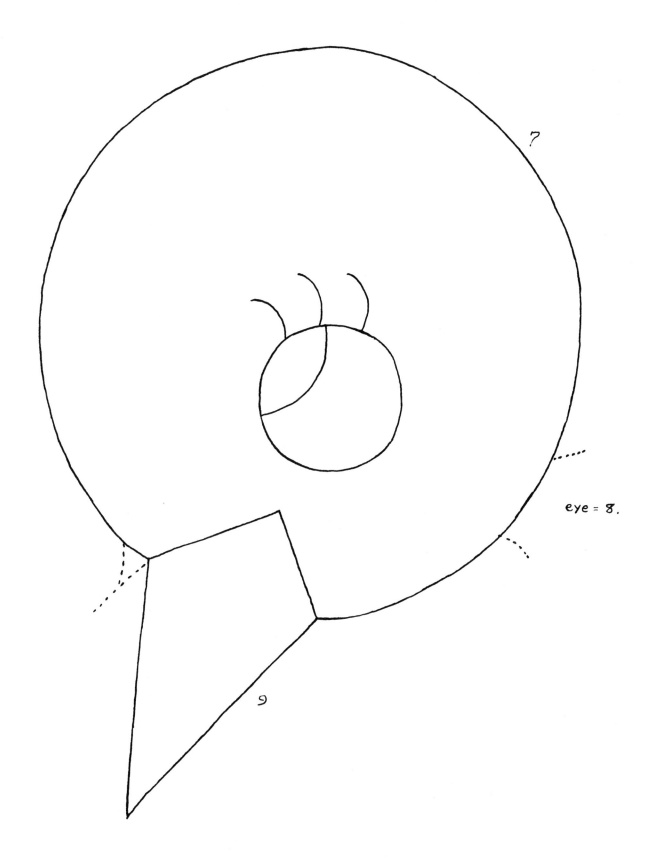

7

eye = 8.

9

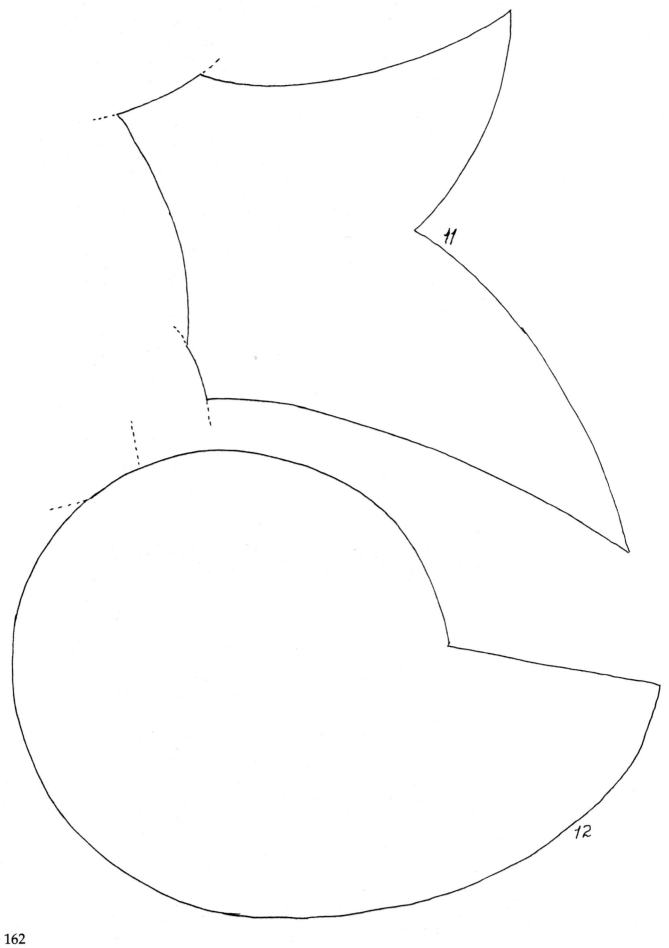

11

12

162

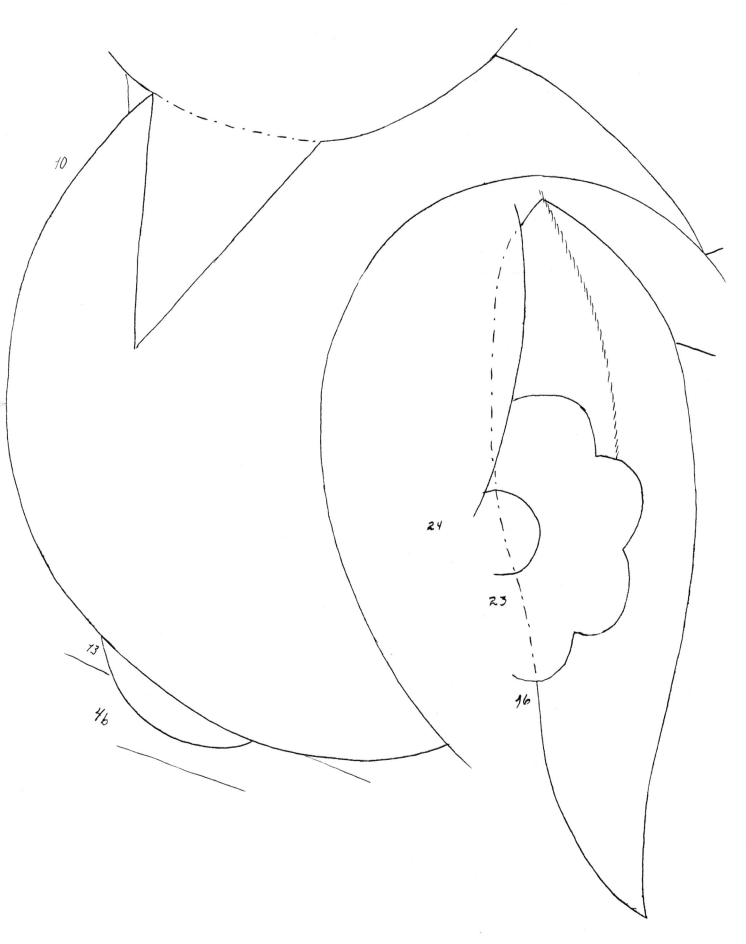

10

24

23

16

13

4b

16

15

23

164

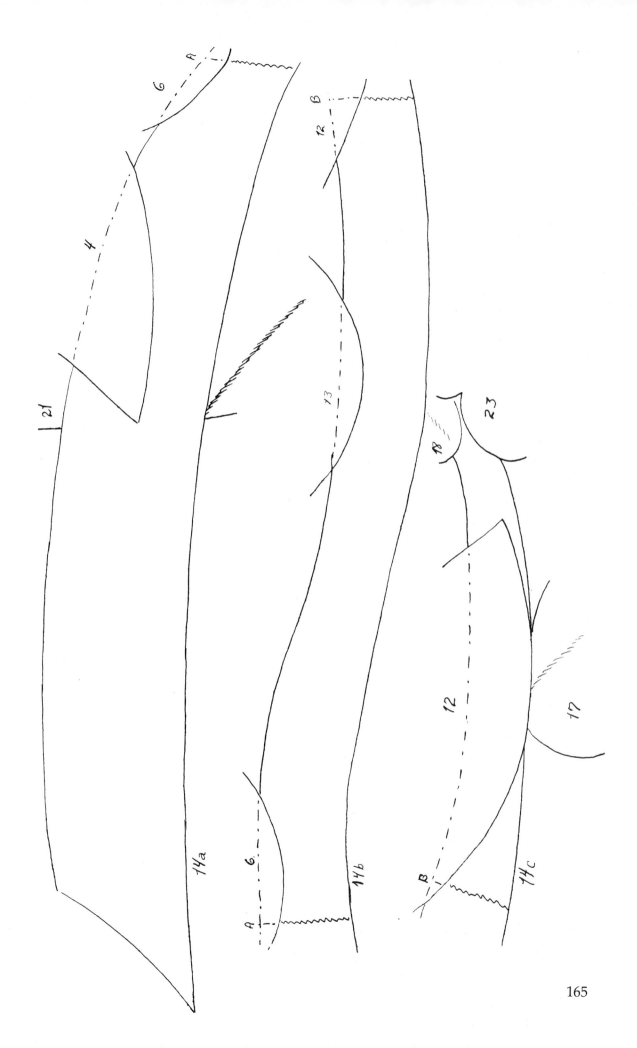

165

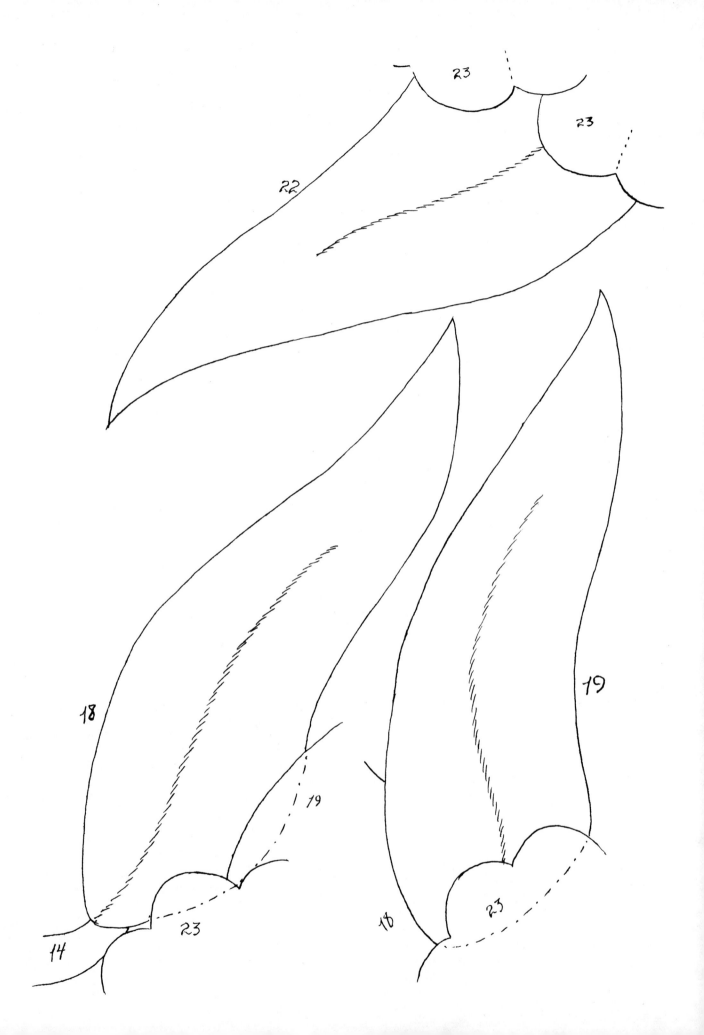

Children's Toys and Games

The Ethnic Dolls—1977

In my library there are several books with pictures of people in very attractive foreign folk costumes. With these colorful and interesting costumes in mind, I designed a quilt for little girls with their favorite toys—dolls—in foreign or (to use the current term) ethnic costumes. The twin-bed-sized quilt top design has spaces for five dolls. I have included patterns for only eight dolls, using great restraint; there were about thirty costumes I would have loved to include. In the end my choice was determined by the fact that the costumes chosen would fit a given silhouette fairly well and are not as well known as others that could have been shown. Also, these costumes represent a people from each of the most populated areas of the world. They are, in alphabetical order, Alsace-Lorraine (a border region between France and Germany), Anatolia (a region of Turkey), Bolivia (a South American country), Czechoslovakia (Eastern Europe), Hunza (a region of the Himalayas in northernmost India), Liberia (a West African country), Norway (a Scandinavian country), and Wales (part of Great Britain).

All of the dolls will fit a 12-inch-square block. The oblong doll blocks for the quilt shown are 11'' by 15'' (except the center doll block), with two triangles added to each of the four sides (see diagrams on page 179).

The patterns for these dolls are small and complicated, so they would be quite confusing if they were given for appliqué. These designs should be done in embroidery, fabric paint, crayons, or a combination of these media. Folk costumes are always very colorful—and these are no exception. They may be completed in the color combinations of your choice. The only part of these costumes that has a traditional color you may not want to vary is the huge ribbon headdress (hairbow) of the Alsace-Lorraine doll. Traditionally, the costume of a Roman Catholic must have a red hairbow. Protestants of this region wear black hairbows.

This quilt top has a very complicated design and should be attempted only by expert sewers, though 12-inch doll blocks can be used in any basic top design. After you have cut one white oblong for a doll background oblong as described below, you will find it convenient to lay out your fabric with right sides together. But do not attempt to cut out two pieces that join across a center axis of the quilt as though they were one piece. Remember to add ¼'' seam allowance on all edges.

Cut from white fabric:

1 a oblong for the center doll block, 10'' × 14''

4 a oblongs for the doll oblongs, 11'' × 15''
2 b oblongs for the top and bottom floral oblongs, 10'' × 11''
2 c oblongs for the right and left side floral oblongs, 7'' × 14''

Be sure to cut these pieces two at a time, right sides of fabric together, so that you have two sets of two each of the patterns, one set the reverse of the other.

	4 A^1 triangles for center oblong
	4 A^2 triangles for center oblong
	4 B^1 triangles for top and bottom oblongs
	4 B^2 triangles for top and bottom oblongs
	4 C^1 triangles for side floral oblongs
	4 C^2 triangles for side floral oblongs
	4 D^1 appliqué border rectangles, 27'' × 6''
	4 D^2 appliqué border rectangles, 33'' × 6''

Cut from blue fabric, again with right sides together:

for the doll oblongs	4 #5 lattice strips, 14'' × 2½''
	4 #6 lattice strips, 18'' × 2½''
	4 #7 lattice strips, 21'' × 2½''
	4 #8 lattice strips, 16'' × 2½''
for the center oblong	4 #1 lattice strips, 10½'' × 2½''
	4 #2 lattice strips, 12¾'' × 2½''
for the top and bottom oblongs	4 #3 lattice strips, 8'' × 2½''
for the side oblongs	4 #4 lattice strips, 11¼'' × 2½''

See dimensions in the exploded top diagram on page 180 for the ends of the lattice strips.

Directions for sewing:

Choose five of the ethnic dolls and embroider or

167

The Ethnic Dolls Child's Quilt

Quilting Manual, © 1970, 1980 Dolores A. Hinson, Dover
Publications, Inc.

color them to the five white doll oblongs labelled a in the exploded diagram of the quilt top on page 180. Decide which of the dolls you would like to use as the centerpiece of your quilt. Begin joining the background pieces from the center of the quilt. Piece two sets of A¹ and two sets of A² triangles together, joining the small triangles together so that the 90° corner angles (the angles opposite the diagonal sides) meet to form a larger triangle. Center these sets on the sides of the center oblong, A¹ sets at the top and bottom, A² sets at the sides, placing them so that about 1″ clearance remains on each side of the new triangles to each corner of the center oblong. See Diagram A on page 179. Arrange one #2 lattice strip and its reverse on the sides of each A² triangle. Finish the center section with one #1 lattice strip and its reverse on the sides of the A¹ triangles. Lay this center assembly aside.

Attach lattice strips to each of the other doll oblongs, following the top diagram on page 180. Use the lattice pieces as follows:
Upper right corner oblong: Top, #8; Left, #6; Right, #7; Bottom, #5
Upper left corner oblong: Top, #8; Left, #7; Right, #6; Bottom, #5
Lower right corner oblong: Top, #5; Left, #6; Right, #7; Bottom, #8
Lower left corner oblong: Top, #5; Left, #7; Right, #6; Bottom, #8
Set these four units aside.

Construct the two units containing the top and bottom floral oblongs. Each of these oblongs has four B triangles pieced to it: B² triangles toward the center block and a large triangle pieced from two B¹ triangles pointing toward the top and bottom edges of the quilt. See Diagram B on page 179 for the placement of the B triangles. Once you have joined the B triangles to the oblongs, appliqué flowers to each unit, following the top drawing on page 180 for placement or arranging them as you choose. Lattice strips #3 and their reverse should be sewn to the two B¹ triangle units. Then these flower oblong units too can be set aside.

Construct the two floral units to be placed to the right and left of the center oblong: Piece two sets of C¹ triangles together, again matching 90° angles, to make two larger triangles. Piece one of these triangle units to the left side of the floral oblong that will be to the left of the center oblong and the other to the right side of the floral oblong to the right of center. Position two C² triangles on the inner edges of the side floral oblongs, the long edge closest to the center oblong, following Diagram C on page 179 for placement. Piece. When all C triangles have been joined to the side oblongs, appliqué flowers to the unit according to the top drawing or to your own preference. Then finish each of the side oblong units by adding #4 lattice strips and their reverse to the sides of the C triangle units for each oblong.

You should now have nine finished units to be assembled for the body of the Ethnic Dolls Quilt:
1 center oblong unit
4 corner doll oblongs
2 floral oblongs for top and bottom
2 floral oblongs for left and right sides
Join them in this manner:
Sew the left side floral unit to the bottom seam of the upper left corner doll oblong. The seam should start at the outside, with lattice strips #7 and #4 placed exactly even. The doll unit will be longer at the inner corner than the floral unit. Continue by adding the top floral unit to the right side of the doll unit, again matching the edges of the outer lattice strips, #8 and #3.

Sew these three combined units to the center unit as follows: The lower corner of the two lattices #5 and #6 fit into the notch in the center of the two lattice strips #1 and #2 (see the diagram showing how the lattice strips meet on page 181). Start the seam at the center of the V and sew to the top corner, the point where the B² triangles meet. Return to the center and sew the second seam to the other corner, near the left edge where the C triangles meet. Now the two side seams, where lattice #2 and triangle C² meet and lattice #1 and triangle B² meet, may be sewn from this corner outwards. Be sure to break your thread and knot it before proceeding anew from the points where the C² and B² triangles meet.

Sew the upper right doll unit to the right side floral unit, beginning at the outer lattices and joining lattice #7 to lattice #4, and moving toward the center. Then sew these two units to the remaining side of the top floral unit, beginning at the outside #8 and #3 lattices and again moving toward the center. Fit the #6-#5 lattice corner to the notch where lattice strips #1 and #2 meet, then sew in place from the center of the notch to where the other seams begin, first on one side, then on the other. Then sew the center unit to the right floral oblong along the #2 lattices and the C² triangles, breaking and knotting thread as before.

Sew the right lower doll unit to the bottom floral unit: sew these combined units to the remaining side of the right-side floral unit; then sew this section to the center unit exactly as described for the upper units.

Add the lower left doll unit to the left floral unit and bottom floral unit and sew the remaining seams to the center doll unit as before.

Sew one D² border piece to a D¹ border piece for the upper left corner of the quilt. Repeat for the opposite corner (the upper right). Use reverse patterns and sew the other two border corners. Add the border floral appliqués as shown in the top drawing or any way you choose, but make them as close to mirror images as possible.

Sew each border to the completed body of the quilt in turn: Start the first seam in the corner between the D²-D¹ pieces. Sew the D² piece to the #8 lattice. Stop at the next corner, knot off and break your thread, and, with a new piece of thread, continue by sewing the D¹ border to the #3 lattice. Return to the first corner you began sewing from and sew D² to the #7 lattice and

then to the #4 lattice, stopping and knotting your thread as before. Each border corner should be sewn in turn in this manner.

The last task is to sew each of the 1-½" seams between the D border strips on each side of the quilt.

Then congratulate yourself on a job well done.

NOTE: It is possible to sew around a corner, but this almost inevitably results in the thread being either too tight or too loose. To achieve the best results, an expert seamstress will always knot off her thread at a corner and begin again at the other side of the corner.

Before beginning any work on this quilt, please read the General Directions (which begin on page 4). Read directions for all of the different techniques described, because they are all used in this quilt. All pattern pieces are finished size; add 1/4'' seam allowance on all sides.

Alsace-Lorraine

Anatolia

Bolivia

Czechoslovakia

174

Hunza

175

Liberia

176

Norway

Wales

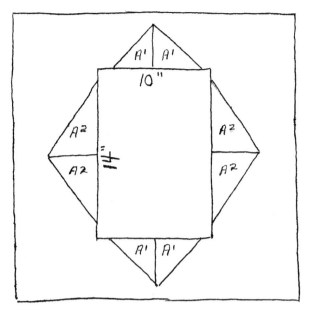

A. Center Doll Block

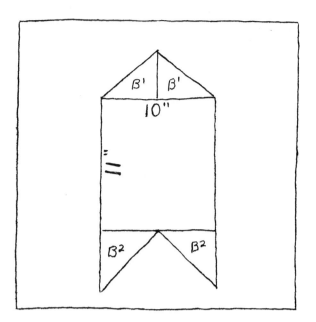

B. Top and Bottom Flower Blocks

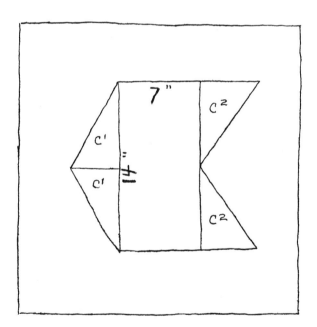

C. Right and Left Flower Blocks

179

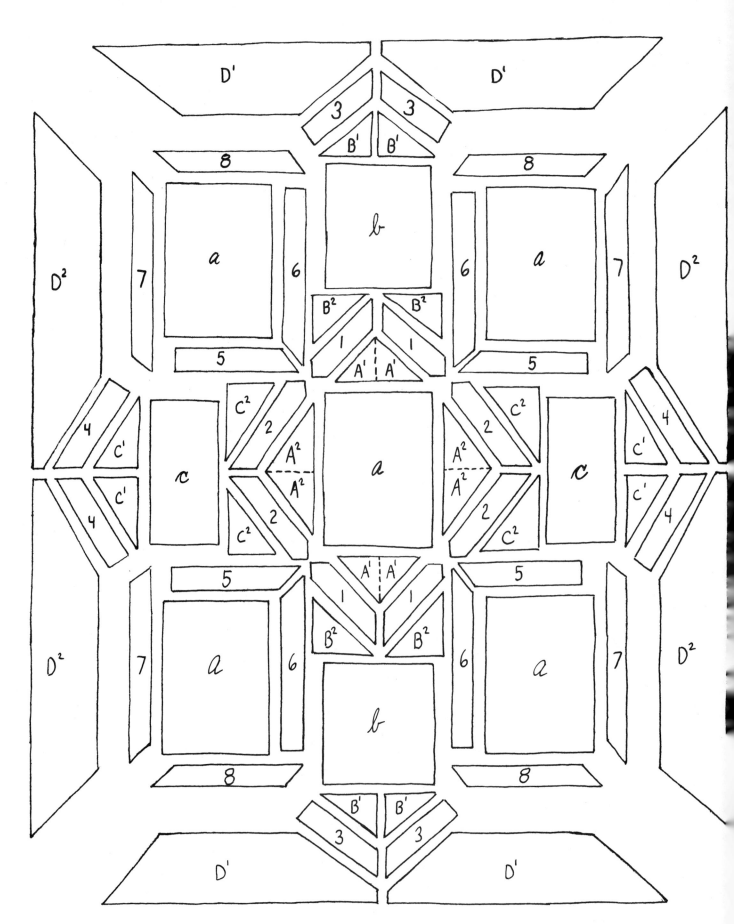

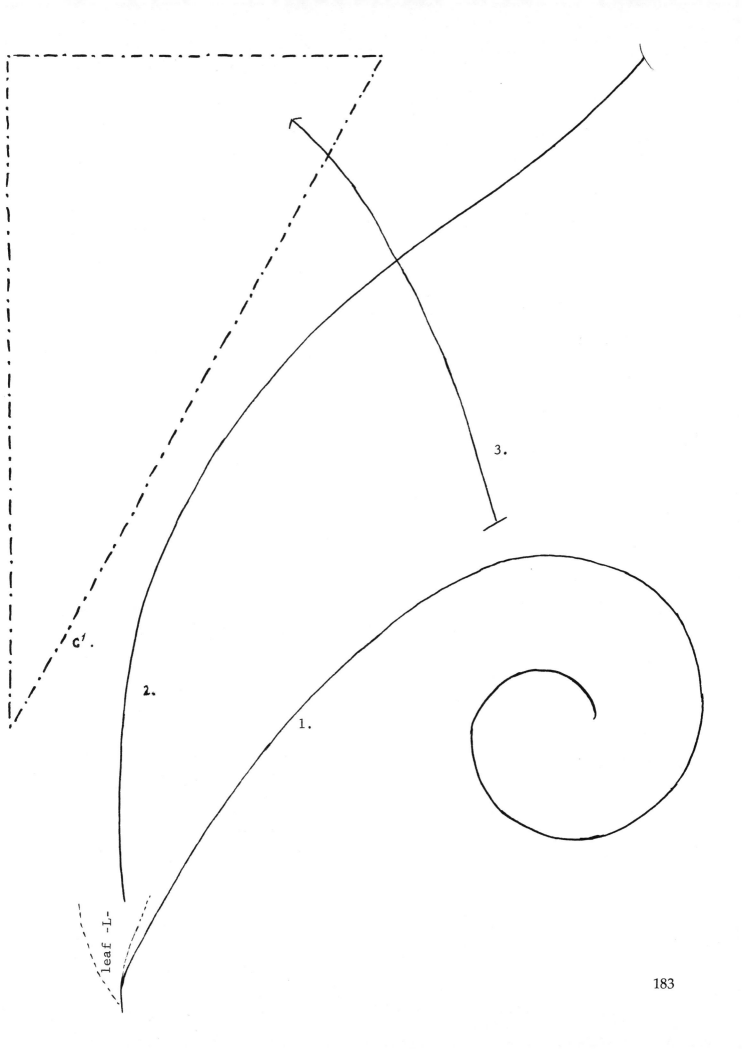

C¹.

2.

1.

3.

leaf -L-

183

I.

K.

J.

B.

H.

B.

C.

E.

First Recital—1977

Don't all little girls dream of being famous ballerinas? Well, even if they don't take lessons, they can have a quilt with five little ladies kicking up their heels in the spotlights.

The quilt in the drawing of the quilt top design is in twin bed size. The white background material of the original quilt is textured in a soft brocaded flower design, white on white. The borders are plain white of a matching shade. Be careful of this: There are many shades of white in materials. The center background must measure 36″ by 60″ (the swag border is positioned later and does not affect this measurement). Measure the cloth and place a pin in the exact center. Place four more pins, one in each corner, exactly 9½ inches from the nearest side edge and 15¾ inches from the top or bottom edge. These pins will mark the center of the tutu (skirt), which is also the center of each figure.

Each figure, in addition to the flesh tones of the face, arms, and legs, has its own hair color and style and one of five pastel colors with matching print for leotards, tutu and slippers. The leotard (body suit) should be cut from the matching print and the slippers and tutu from the plain pastel material in either blue, green, pink, yellow, or lavender. Place the child's favorite color on the center ballerina figure, which is also set off by facing the other way (reverse the cutting patterns) and, if you like, wearing eyeglass frames the same plain color as her costume. When the five girls have been appliquéd to the center, sew the four border strips, each 18 inches wide, to the center section. Use a plate for a pattern to obtain the round corners.

Use Ribbon Swag and Tassel Border, page 291 with ballet slippers at the ends of the strings rather than the tassels used with other quilt patterns. The two tips of the swag should be placed on the seam line between the border and center sections. Place the two bows found at the right and left tips of each swag on the center section and attach the laces and slippers on the borders. There will be four 3-loop and ten 2-loop bows in all. Cover the place where all these patterns come together with the round pattern representing the knot of the bows (pattern C on page 291). See the drawing of the quilt top design. The rings in the center quilting pattern are 12 inches across and can be drawn with a compass or a round cutting pattern.

Before beginning any work on this quilt, please read the General Directions (which begin on page 4), including Appliquéing a Block (page 16) and Directions for Embroidery, Fabric Paints, and Crayons (page 16). all sides.

First Recital Child's Quilt

187

189

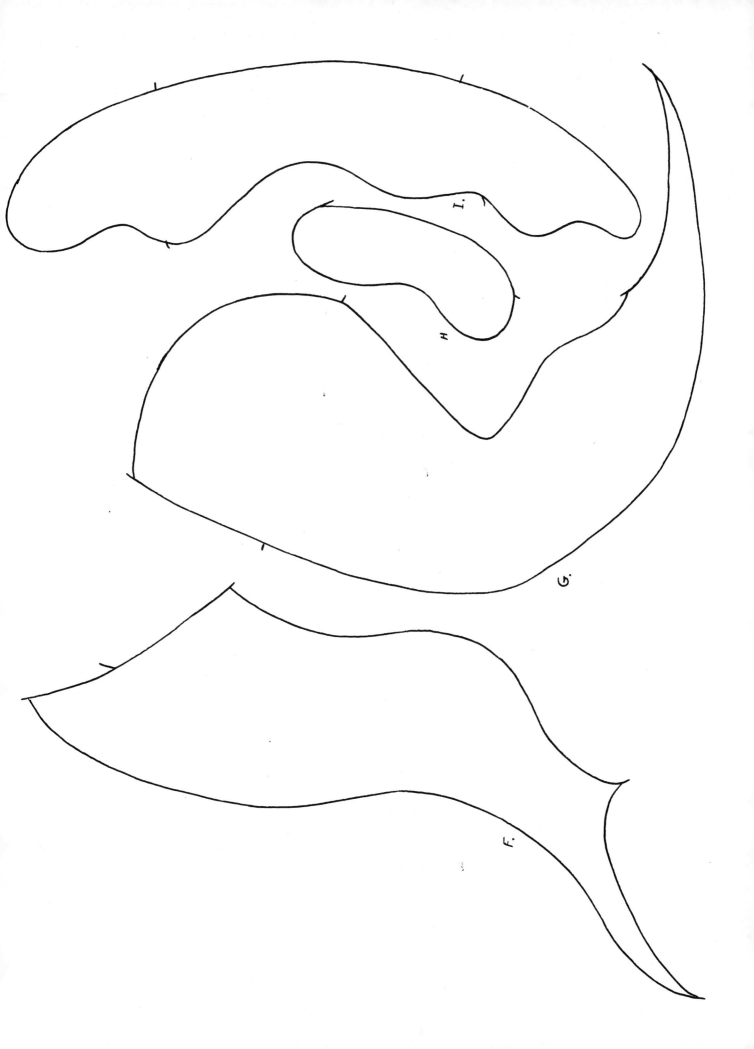

Cowboys 'n Indians—1981

Back around the turn of the century, Cowboys 'n Indians used to be strictly an American children's game. However, since then children all over the world have learned to wear their guns low on the hip and take pot-shots at one another with a toy gun or a stick. Both need an assisting shout of "Bang-Bang!" Remember the arguments? "I got you!"—"No you didn't, you missed!"—"No I didn't, I got you!" And the bumping run, which was augmented by slapping your hip. There were never better horses than those, because no matter where they were left, they were right at hand when needed again, even if the game was taken up again a month later and 100 miles away.

Watching the kids in my neighborhood, I don't think the rules have changed a bit. I think I could go out and join them right now and not miss a "Bang!"

So here are the patterns for Cowboy Bill, Sweet Sue, Mountain Lily, and Little Bear. The patterns are given in two sizes, the smaller of which should be done in embroidery, fabric paints, or crayons on 8-inch squares. They are given on pages 193 to 203. The larger patterns will fit 10-inch diagonal blocks or 12-inch straight blocks. These are given in outlines for embroidery, fabric paints, or crayons, and also in appliqué pieces. The blocks should be put together with 3-inch lattice strips and 3-inch corner blocks, which can be decorated with the horse-head design on page 195. Use the colors of your choice, but the repeat blocks of the same design should have different color schemes.

> Before beginning any work on this quilt, please read the General Directions (which begin on page 4), including Appliquéing a Block (page 16). All pattern pieces are finished size; add 1/4-inch seam allowance on All pattern pieces are finished size; add 1/4-inch seam allowance on all sides.

Cowboy Bill

12-in. blk.

193

A.

B.

hair

C.

E.

F.

D.

12-in. blk. appliqué

8-in. blk.

194

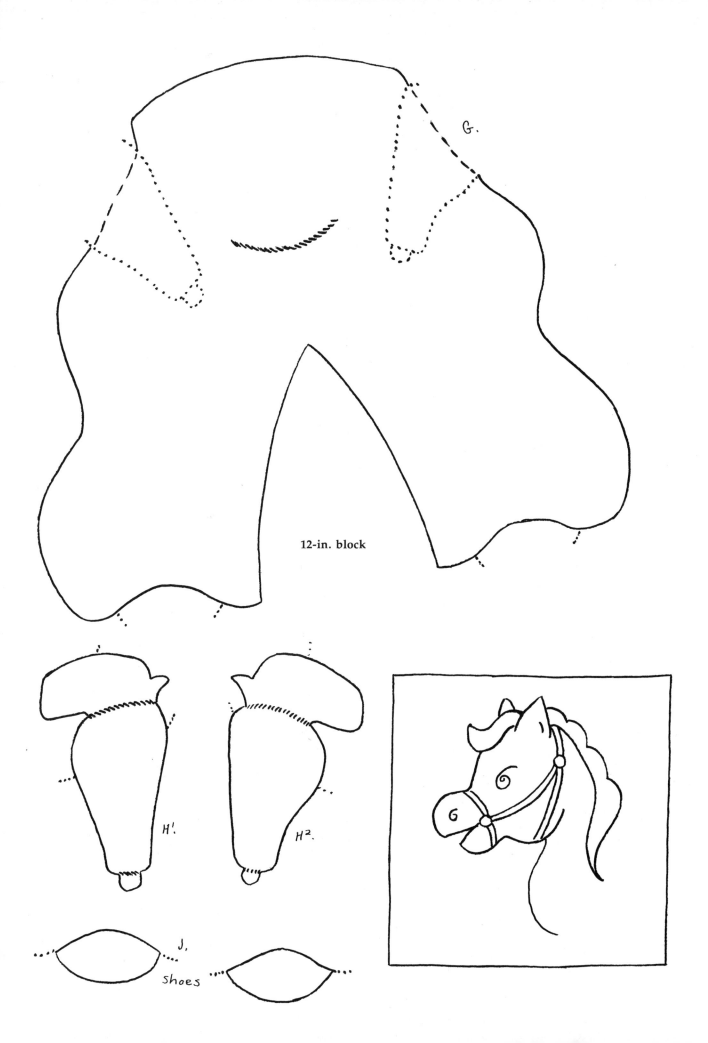

G.

12-in. block

H¹. H².

J,

shoes

G

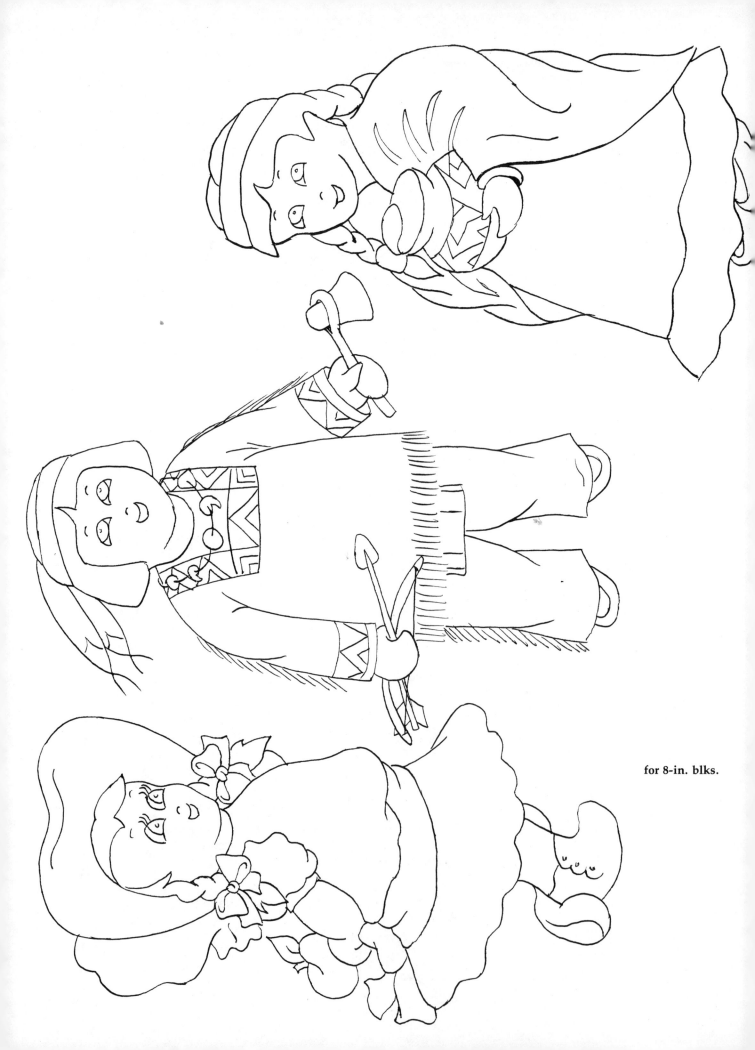

for 8-in. blks.

Sweet Sue

12-in. blk.

197

A.

B.

C¹

Hair

C³

C²

D¹

Hair Bows

D²

E.

F.

G¹

G²

K.

H. arm

J²

J¹

L. knees

M.

N.

12-in. blk. appliqué

198

Mountain Lily

12-in. blk.

199

A¹

B.

C.

A²
Hair

A³

D¹

Hands

D²

H. Shoes

E¹

F¹

F²

E²

Blanket

G.

12-in. blk. appliqué

Little Bear

12-in. blk.

201

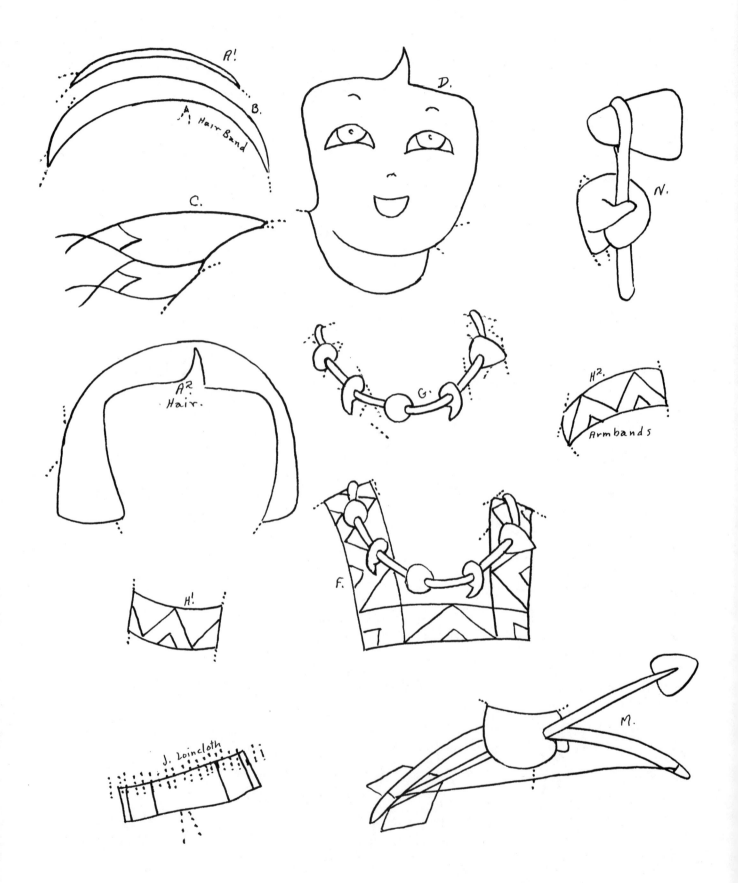

E.

K²

K¹.

Leggands

L¹. L².

Shoes

203

The Doll House Quilt

The Doll House Quilt—1967

A good friend who collects both dolls and doll houses challenged me to design a Doll House Quilt. It took me eight months of thought, but she lost her bet. Trying to keep my young son quiet when he had a cold gave me the beginnings of an idea: I decided to make the quilt something a child could play with quietly in bed. From this idea came two dolls and doll furniture; to keep the dolls and the furniture together, I had the idea of pockets—and there was the quilt. If you look carefully at the drawing of the quilt top, you will see dotted lines below the attic window and the kitchen table, as well as on the bed, chair, and car. These indicate the pockets.

This quilt was designed in the 1960's. It won several blue ribbons at shows and was shown in an interior decorator's studio in New York in the early 1970's. After that one of the better-known women's magazines, *House and Garden*, printed a picture of my quilt. Later, other designers made pocket quilts like the one with a farmer doll and farm machinery. Lately, several of the quilt pattern companies have also published patterns for pocket quilts, such as one with baby dolls and nursery furniture. Quilting is a folk art, and folk arts cannot be patented or copyrighted. Once shown, the ideas are open to anyone who wishes to copy them. I would, however, like it generally known that I originated the idea, and this design was, to my knowledge, the first pocket quilt. It pleases me that it has proved to be popular.

The finished quilt is youth-bed size, about 5' by 7'. The background of the quilt is composed of: six light blue rectangles, each 15" by 20"—plus two more oblongs of the same light blue material (described later)—for the sky; three oblongs (15" × 20") of a medium green floral print for grass; and four print oblongs (15" × 20") of colors chosen to look like different wallpapers in the bedroom, living room, garage, and kitchen for the house interior. If the print chosen for the garage is a mottled gray or tan or something similar, with flecks of stronger colors, it can be extended as shown to form the driveway as well. The two right triangles forming the attic are prominent red-and-white striped material. The roof and house outline is a plain red 1-inch-wide strip (add seam allowances). The base of the chimney is of the same material, as are the strips outlining the attic window.

To make the driveway, cut a 15" by 20" (plus seam allowance) oblong of the garage material. Then cut two wedges of the green print material for the lawn. These wedges should be 2¼ inches wide (plus seam) at the top and cut in a shallow curve to a point on the other end, as shown in the drawing of the quilt top. If you

fold a piece of the green material 20 inches long (plus seam allowances all around) and cut both pieces at once, you will have symmetrical right- and left-facing wedges. These are sewn or appliquéd to the two long sides of the driveway oblong. Consult the quilt top drawing.

Two more light blue oblongs must be cut for the sky over the house. Each of these should have a right triangle cut from the bottom of the oblong, one angled to the right and one angled to the left. (You should be able to line up the cut-out right triangles face up so that the 90° angles are back-to-back in the center.) These right triangles should be 14-½ inches on the short sides (high and wide) (to leave a seam allowance). The red-striped right triangles pieced to the sky oblongs for the attic should be 15 inches high and wide plus seam allowance. If you prefer, leave the two sky oblongs whole and appliqué the attic triangles to them.

The pocket for the attic should also be cut from the red-and-white striped material (see the pattern piece on page 219). Match the edges carefully, as shown. Finished, this pocket measures 4½" by 6". Finish the pocket sides and top by turning under the seam allowances and sewing them carefully in place. Sew the two sides to the background. The bottom will be sewn into the seam when the blocks are put together. The pocket top should be even with the top of the sill.

Following the top drawing for placement, appliqué the two bedposts, a 6-inch canopy eyelet frill, plus the headboard to the bedroom oblong, slipping the headboard edges under the posts. Cut a pocket 4½" by 6¼" (plus seam allowance) from white material and set two rows of ruffled eyelet to it. The eyelet ruffles should be 1 inch wider than the pocket at each side, and an inch higher and deeper than the pocket when they are both sewn to it. (If the eyelet edging is less than 6 inches wide, take out your appliqué stitches along the insides of the bedposts along the pocket and restitch so that the bedposts cover the edges of the pocket.) Appliqué the pocket in place, leaving its finished top open.

For the living room, the chair-arm of the appliquéd chair will form the top and right side of the pocket. Prepare the whole piece to be appliquéd. Appliqué the armchair to the background, leaving the top edge of the chair's arm open. Stitch down the left-hand dotted line to form the left pocket seam. You may want to reinforce the right pocket seam by stitching down the right-hand dotted line close to the appliqué stitches.

The garage pocket is the body of the car plus another piece of the background material cut to fit between the wheels (see the pattern on page 210). Piece the car body to the extra background piece; then appliqué to the background oblong, leaving the "dashboard" area open between the dotted lines. These dotted lines should be embroidered in a stem stitch to represent the sides of the car.

For the kitchen, a finished pocket 4½'' by 6¼'' should be matched to the background material. The tablecloth (white or contrasting fabric of the same weight as the rest of the quilt) is appliquéd over the pocket, except for the top edge, which is finished but left open. The table legs are pieced or appliquéd to a piece of background material of the appropriate size and shape (measure from the pattern pieces on page 208). If you piece the pocket to the legs, be sure to stitch the pocket to the background along the inside of the legs. If you appliqué the table legs over the pocket, be sure to cover the pocket seams.

Finish the chimney, clouds, sun and clouds, and flowers by appliquéing them in place. Join the quilt blocks, following the quilt top drawing and catching the lower ends of still-unfinished pockets in the seams. Finish the quilt by appliquéing the red 1-inch strips over the seams to form the outline of the house, the attic window and its panes. Extend the roof strips 6½ inches over the sides of the house to form eaves.

Cut two doll shapes for each doll, following the solid outlines on page 207. These may be from white or flesh-colored material. Embroider, crayon, or fabric-paint the features of the face, the underwear, and the shoes on the right side of the piece you choose as the front of each doll. Place right sides together and sew the two pieces of each, leaving a fairly large opening (an inch or two) in the mid-body seam to turn wrong sides in and stuff the doll. Clip V's in the seam allowances almost to the stitching line around all curves; trim the seam allowances all around to reduce their bulk. Turn the doll right side out and stuff lightly but evenly, using a foam filler, batting, or even old stockings that have been washed well. When the doll has been filled evenly, finish the open seam by catch-stitching it closed carefully.

Cut out the clothing for the dolls in any color or print fabric, following the dot-dash lines on the pattern pieces. Cut out two pieces of fabric for each of the three articles of clothing. Because the dolls are so soft and flexible, the clothing can be slipped over the dolls' feet and into position on their bodies after the seams have been closed, even though the dolls are stuffed. The right shoulder seam on each garment can be left open and finished with a snap if your child enjoys dressing and undressing dolls.

Place the two pieces of the girl's dress right sides of the fabric together. Sew the two side seams and one or both shoulder seams. Roll the seam allowances of the neck opening, sleeves, and hem. Decorate the dress with collar, buttons, and pockets in either embroidery, crayons, or fabric paints. These decorations should contrast in tone with the color of the fabric—dark if the fabric is light and light or white if the fabric is dark.

The boy's clothing is in two pieces: light or dark shirt and contrasting pants. The shirt may be sewn to the pants if the clothing is not to be removed, or else a shoulder seam may be closed with a snap if the clothing is to be removable. Close the side seams and one or both shoulder seams. Roll the remaining seam allowances for hems. The waist and leg openings of the pants must also have rolled and hemmed edges. Decorate the shirt and pants with collar, buttons, and pockets to match the decorations on the girl's clothing.

Embroidery floss or two-ply yarn can be used for the dolls' hair. Cut the strands long enough to reach from one side of the mouth to the other across the top of the head. Gather several strands and sew them in a bunch on the right side of the head at the cross line marked on the pattern pieces. The girl's hair should be even with her mouth on both sides; cut the boy's hair to about ½-inch long on the short side (the right side). Follow the sketch given with the pattern pieces. Lightly gather the hair on the other cross line and sew it loosely, so that the strands are not pulled tight to look like the part. Put a ribbon over the gathering stitches of the girl's hair, as shown in the sketch. Fasten the boy's hair on the long side (the left) at the gathering stitches and trim the strands close to the stitches.

Before beginning any work on this quilt, please read the General Directions (which begin on page 4), including Piecing a Block (page 15), Appliquéing a Block (page 16), and Directions for Embroidery, Fabric Paints, and Crayons (page 16). All patterns are finished size; add 1/4-inch seam allowance on all sides.

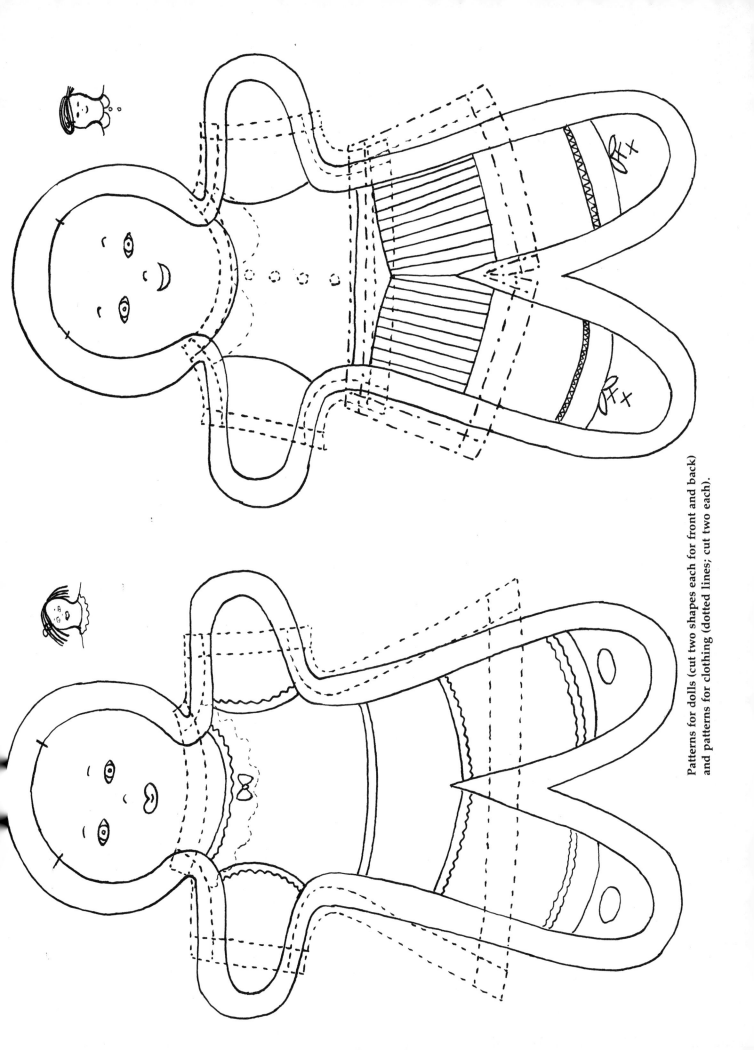

Patterns for dolls (cut two shapes each for front and back) and patterns for clothing (dotted lines; cut two each).

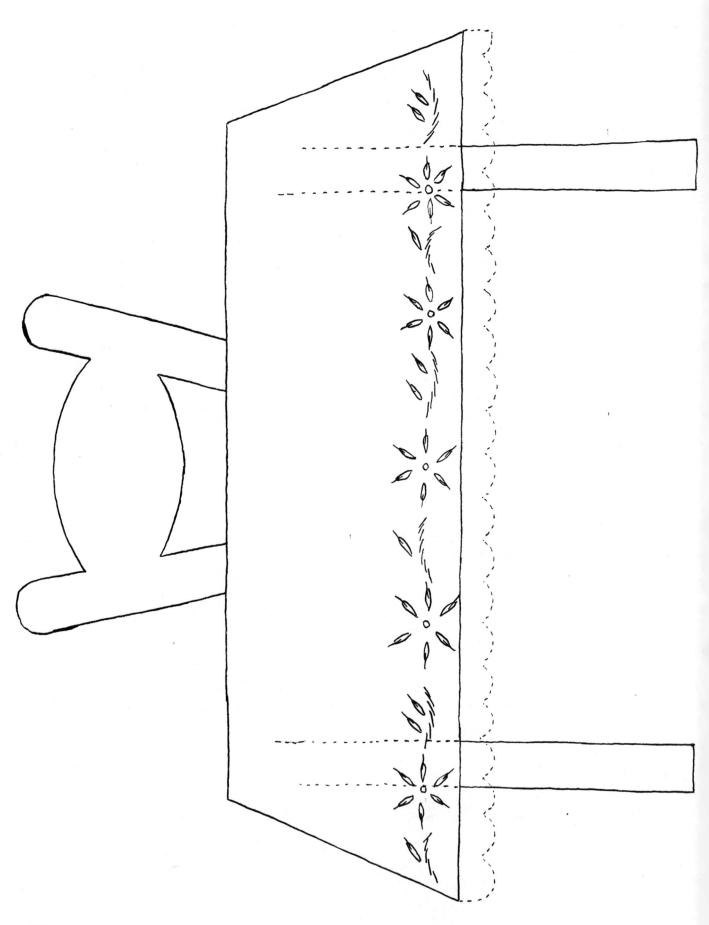

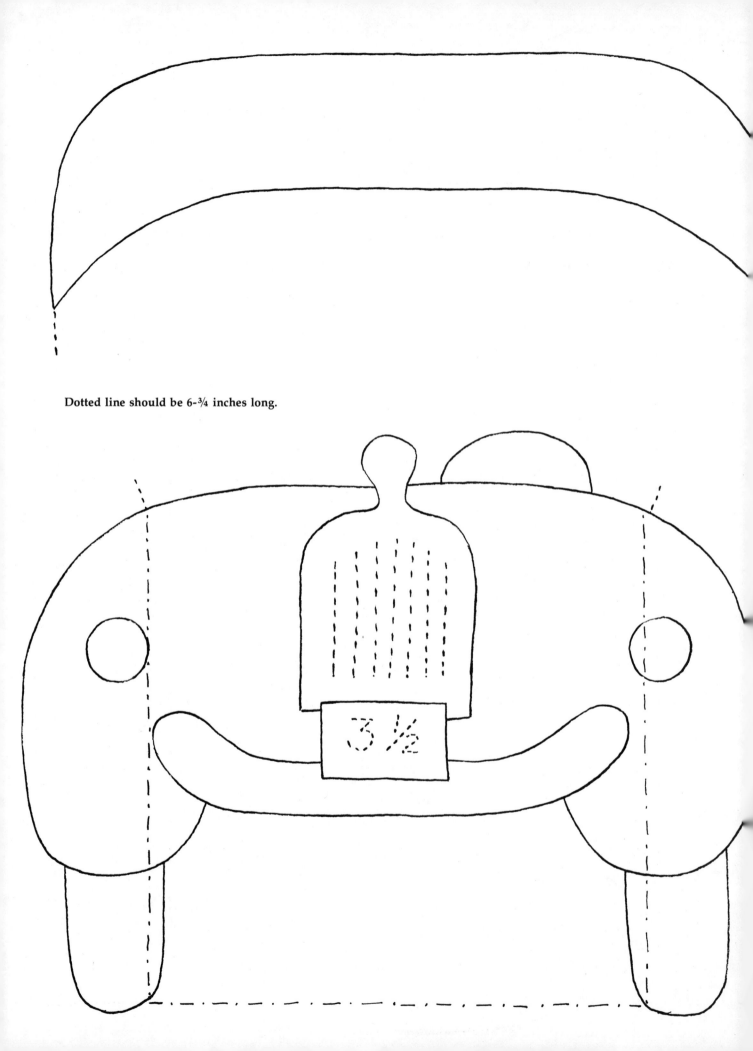

Dotted line should be 6-¾ inches long.

3 ½

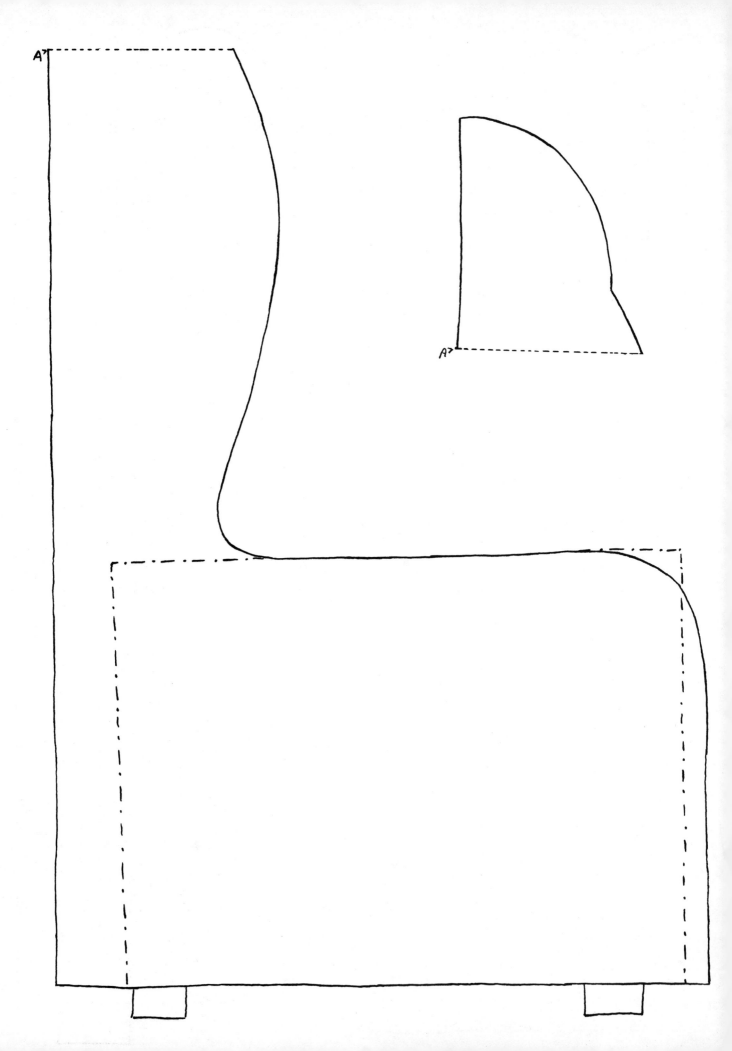

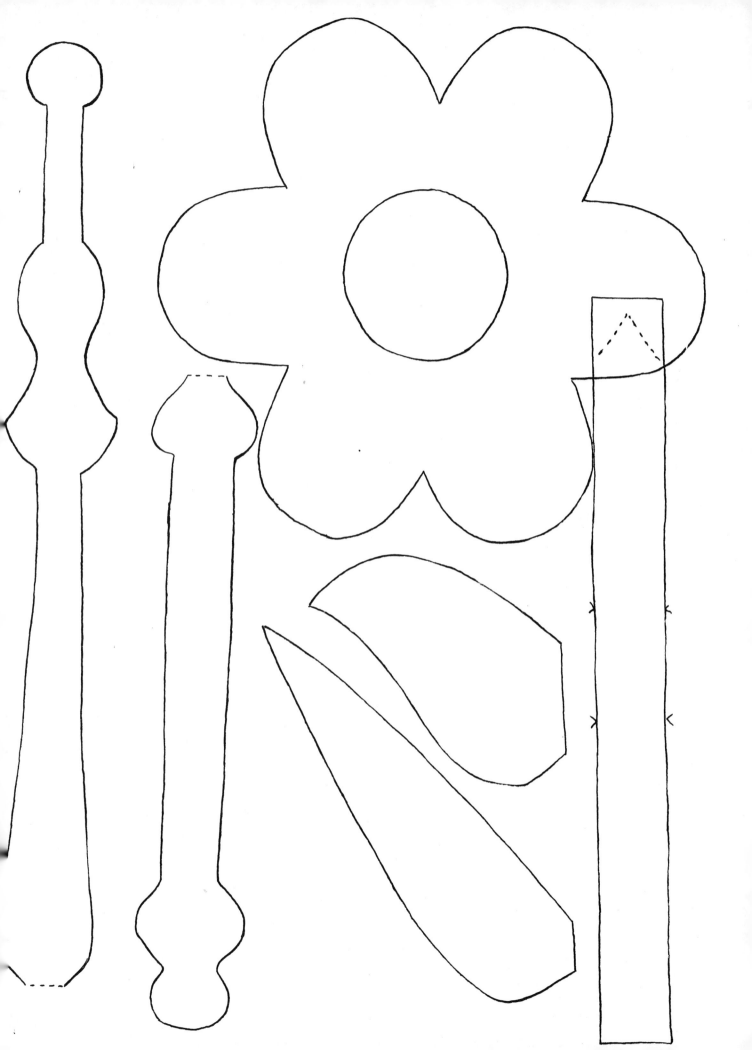

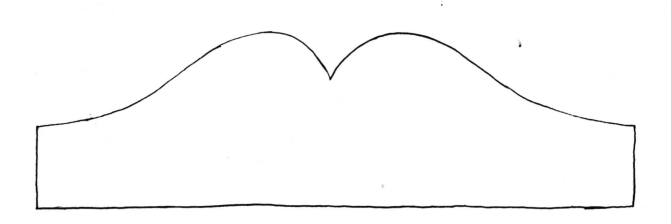

Chimney top

214

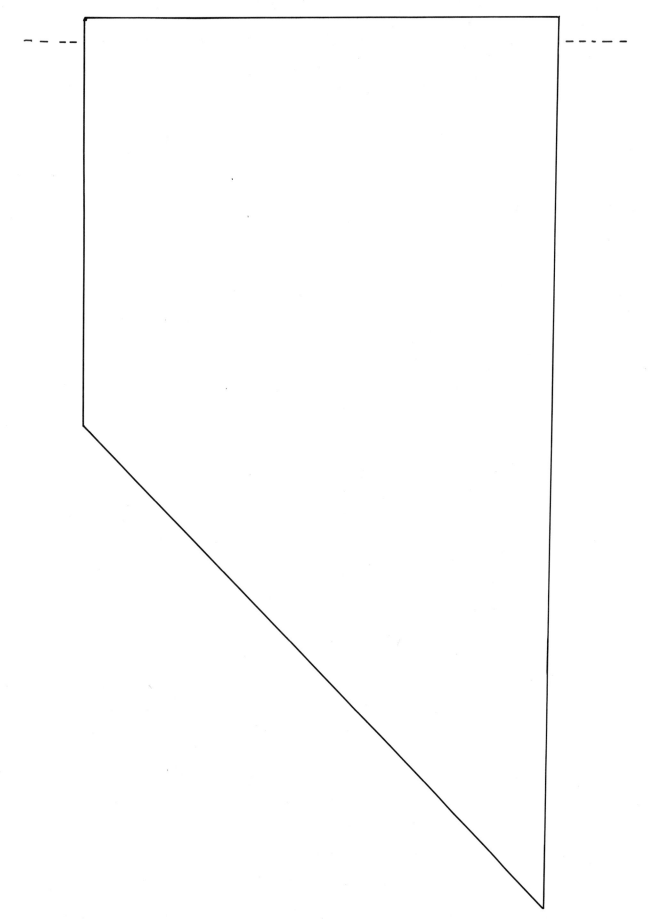

215

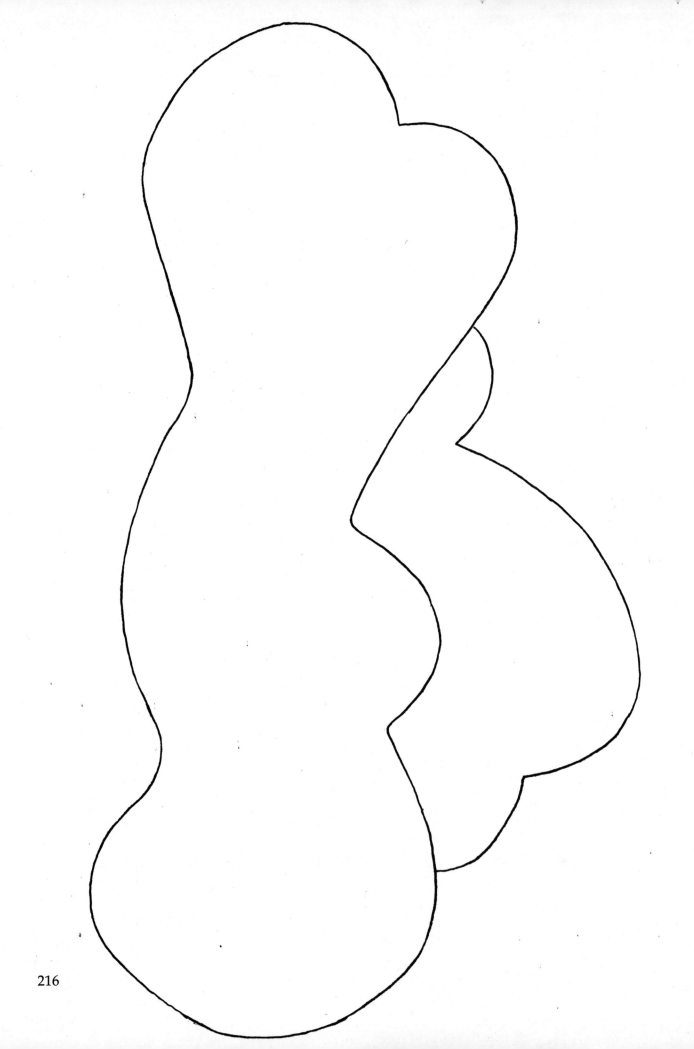

216

217

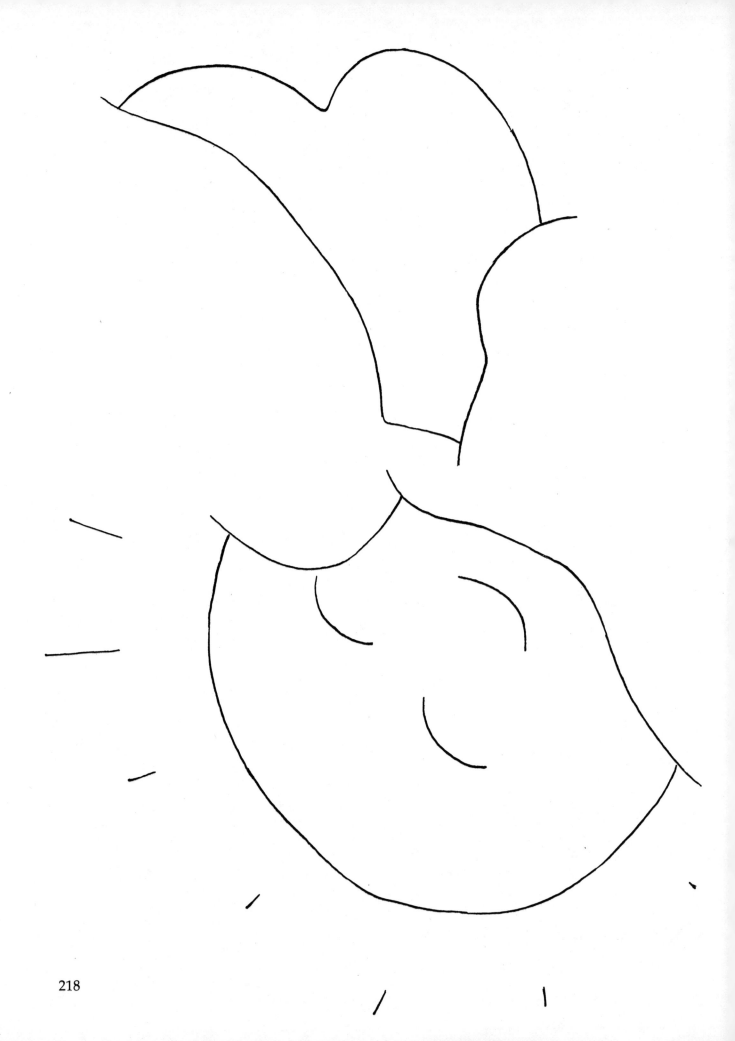

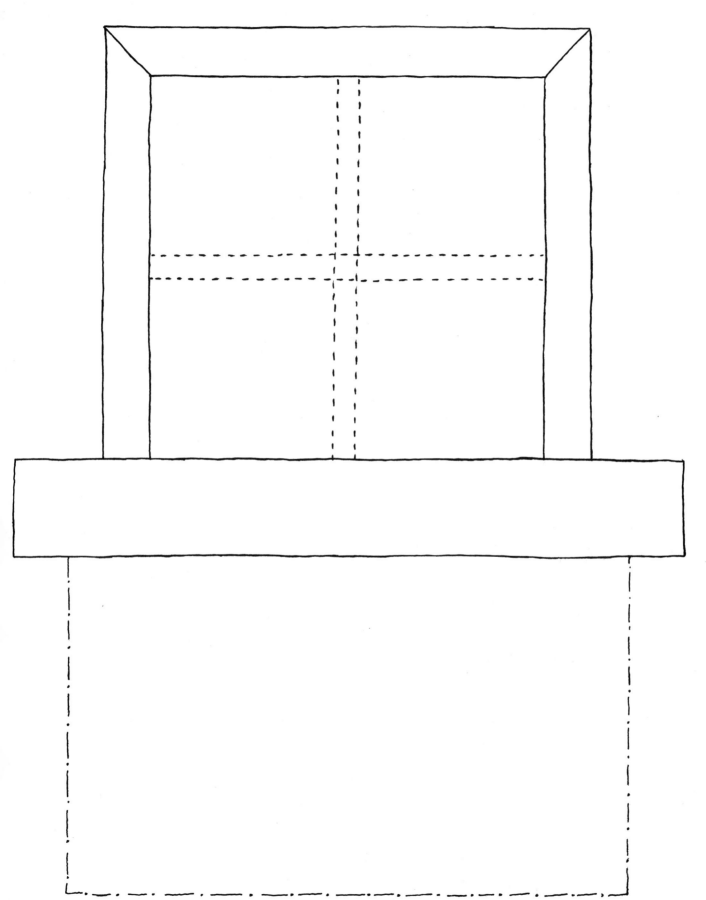

219

May Dance—1967

I designed this quilt for little girls several years ago. It has won three blue ribbons, and the pattern has been the one most asked for among those I have designed. I chose soft skin tones of peach, cream, tan, and brown to represent a schoolyard of little American girls dancing together. You may choose to make all of the little girls on the quilt the same color as the little girl who will own it, but I like the idea of the children of the world dancing together. In fact, for one month in 1974 this quilt was displayed in the U.N. Building in New York.

The four girls are cut together from one piece of cloth, pattern *a* (including the flower shapes). The hair can be the many shades of blond, brown, red, and black that appear on human heads. The hair of the cream, tan, and brown girls will, of course, be brown or black. The peach girls should all have different-color hair. The dresses should be individually cut from as many different scraps as are available. In the original quilt, there are only twelve pairs of little girls at opposite ends of the top that have the same print material in their dresses. Since the dress patterns are so small, this is a good place to get rid of those small scraps of material just a bit too large to throw away. The quilt border is a row of girls (*a*) with the flower chain (*d*) between them. The outlines of the hair ribbons and the dotted outlines on the flowers—plus their centers—should be embroidered in many bright colors, although they may also be fabric-painted. The girls should be appliquéd to a 10-inch block. This is not an easy pattern; it will take much time and care to complete the quilt, but it is well worth the effort.

Before beginning any work on this quilt, please read the General Directions (which begin on page 4), including Appliquéing a Block (page 16). All pattern pieces are finished size; add 1/4-inch seam allowance on all sides.

Block for May Dance Child's Quilt

221

fold

fold

fold

fold

fold

fold

a

b

c

d

Race to the Moon Quilt

Race to the Moon—1967

Do you have a little astronaut? I did. So I designed and made this quilt for him—and, incidentally, put a man on the moon two years before the U.S. Government did. The quilt has been shown in several arts and crafts fairs, in three quilt shows, and at two county fairs. By itself it has won five blue ribbons and two best of shows.

The colors are red, white, blue, green, and yellow. This is not an easy quilt to piece because of the pieced circles. There are eight astronaut blocks and twenty-eight rocket border blocks. The astronaut blocks (when finished) are pieced together in two rows of four blocks each. Around the joined center blocks is pieced a 3-inch-wide (plus seam allowances) plain green band. Piece eight rocket border blocks with the noses of the rockets pointed first to the right corner and then to the left corner to make them look as though they are on different courses. There are two of these strips of eight blocks and then, for the top and bottom borders, two strips of four blocks. Piece these strips to the edges of the green strips to go around the center clockwise. Add a 3-inch-wide green strip to each end of the pieced border-block strips, and sew the last four blocks into the corners. Bind the quilt in plain blue. A 1½-inch binding strip will result in a finished quilt 95 × 60 inches, not quite 8' × 5'.

The astronauts' faces and American flags may be embroidered, fabric-painted, or crayoned. Then appliqué the astronauts to the moons. Cut the moons in perfect circles 12 inches across. The circular curve on the inside of the A patterns is one quarter of a perfect circle and can be used as a pattern for the moons.

The corner pieces should be cut out as shown (remember to add seam allowances), except for A2. This piece is actually the entire triangle for the corner and should be cut from the pattern piece on page 227 (again, with seam allowances). A5 and A6 are yellow and red respectively. They are appliquéd to the A2 triangle. Then this triangle is pieced to the remainder of the corner. Using the B patterns, make the border rocket in the same manner.

Before beginning any work on this quilt, please read the General Directions (which begin on page 4), including Piecing a Block (page 15) and Appliquéing a Block (page 16). All pattern pieces are finished size; add 1/4-inch seam allowance on all sides.

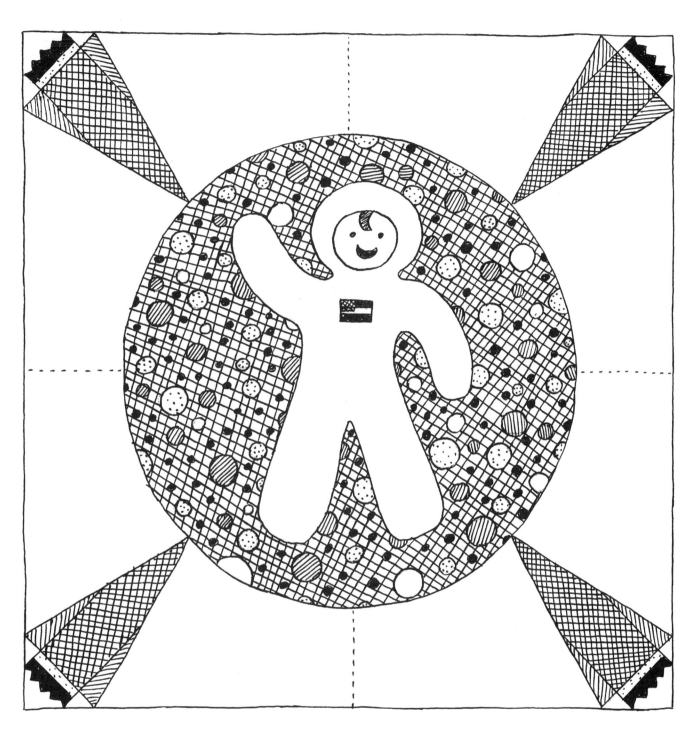

Block for Race to the Moon Child's Quilt

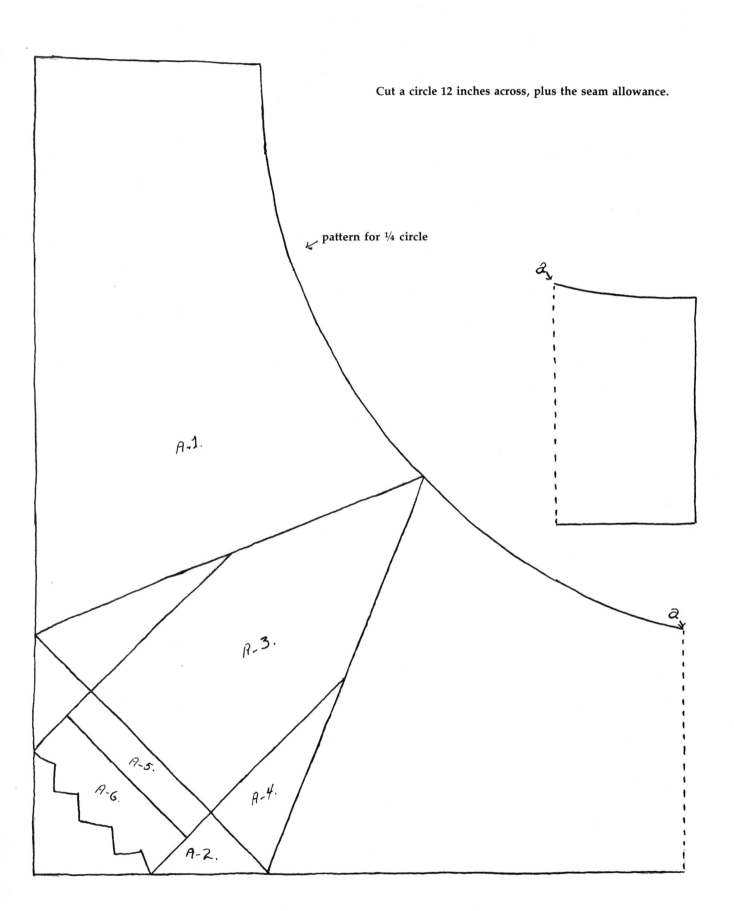

Cut a circle 12 inches across, plus the seam allowance.

pattern for ¼ circle

A-1.

A-3.

A-5.

A-6.

A-4.

A-2.

227

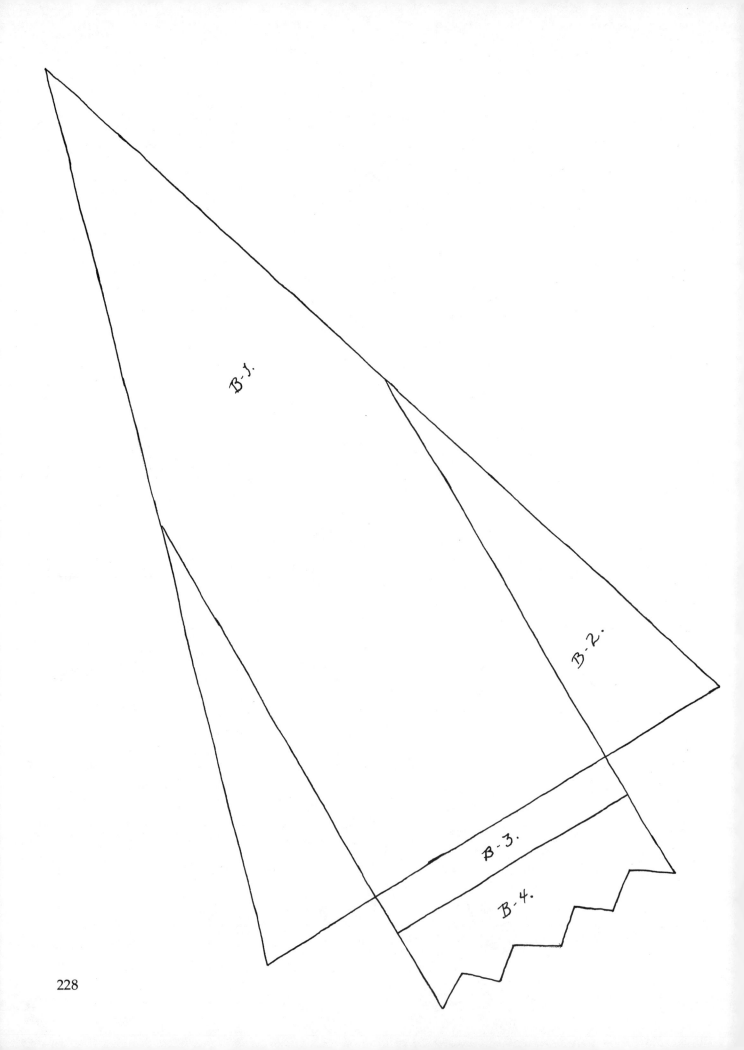

B-1.

B-2.

B-3.

B-4.

228

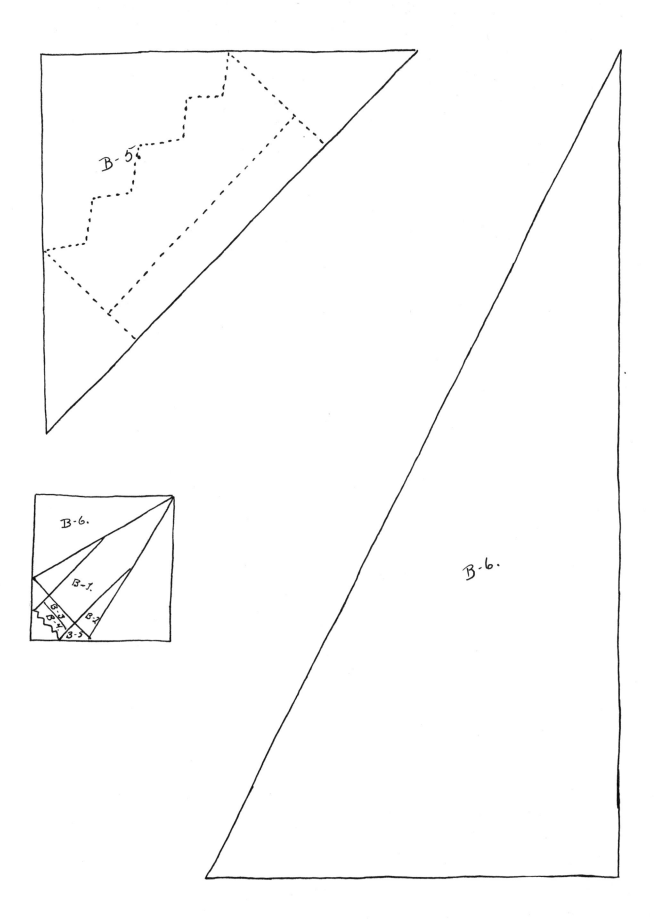

B-5.

B-6.

B-1.

B-3.
B-4.
3-5.
B-2.

B-6.

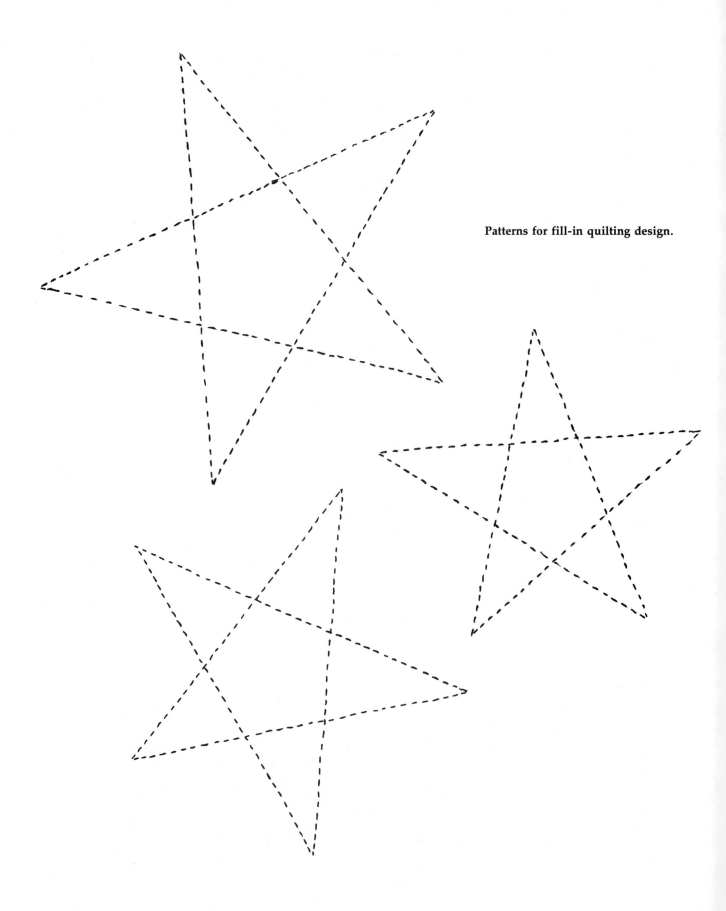

Patterns for fill-in quilting design.

Professional League Sports Child's Quilt

231

Professional League Sports—1977

This is probably the hardest quilt in the book. However, since both little and big boys like team sports, it seems imperative that this pattern be included. The patterns are given on graphs scaled to ¼-inch equaling 1 inch. Draw lines 1 inch apart in both directions to make the large graphs needed. For instance, the baseball player will require a graph paper 15″ wide by 29″ long, since the small graph uses this many numbered squares. Count off the squares in each row and carefully copy the lines of the figure shown in the small graph in the exactly corresponding squares on the large graph. When the figure has been finished on the large graph, it should look exactly like the figure on the small graph in this book. Enlarge all the pattern pieces in this way and cut them from the appropriate mate-rial, being careful to leave seam allowances. All of the pieces are large enough to be appliquéd easily. Trims may be embroidered, fabric-painted, or crayoned.

Cut a center from white material (it will probably have to have a seam down the center) 51″ wide by 75″ long. Make the center star by sewing red triangles to each side of the center pentagon (see patterns on page 233). Finish the letters in the center, then appliqué the star in the exact center of the white background mate-rial, as shown. Draw a line from each point of the star to the edge of the cloth, and finish it in the same manner as you choose for the letters. Position each figure and league symbol in the appropriate space. The borders can be either appliquéd or pieced (as you choose) after the patterns have been expanded to their proper size. Be sure to have the names of the quilt owner's favorite teams represented on the pennants.

Before beginning any work on this quilt, please read the General Direc-tions (which begin on page 4), including Piecing a Block (page 15), Appliquéing a Block (page 16), and Directions for Embroidery, Fabric Paints, and Crayons (page 16). All patterns are finished size; add 1/4-inch seam allowance on all sides.

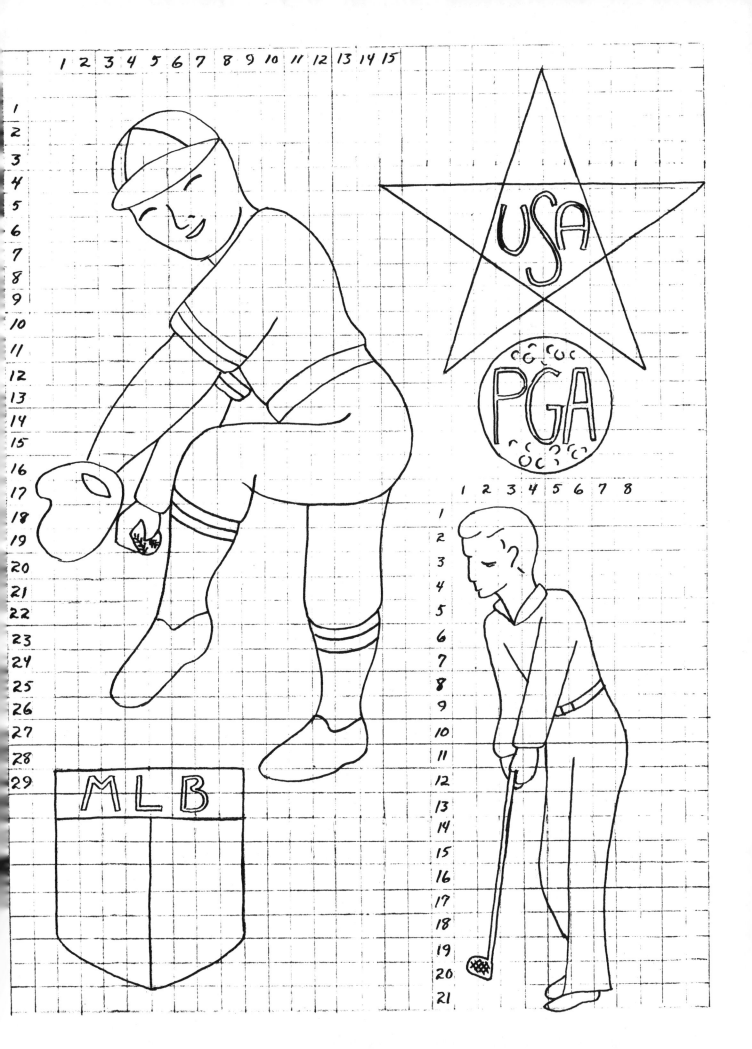

1 2 3 4 5 6 7 8 9 10 11 12 13 14 15

1
2
3
4
5
6
7
8
9
10
11
12
13
14
15
16
17
18
19
20
21
22
23
24
25
26
27
28
29
30

NFL

The Air Age—1928 to 1981

There are six designs in this group, each based on an American aircraft that advanced the science of aviation in this country. The designs are given in sizes that will allow them to be used singly or in groups on quilts. Some of the aircraft designs are very easy and some are very difficult. Only one is designed for appliqué, but if you choose to do one of the more difficult patterns, it is possible to piece the patterns composing the plane and appliqué these to a plain background block of the appropriate size. Any of the quilt top designs may be used with these patterns, although perhaps a more traditional type would be best for the older designs (pages 6 and 7).

Before beginning any work on this quilt, please read the General Directions (which begin on page 4), including Piecing a Block (page 15). All pattern pieces are finished size; add 1/4-inch seam allowance on all sides.

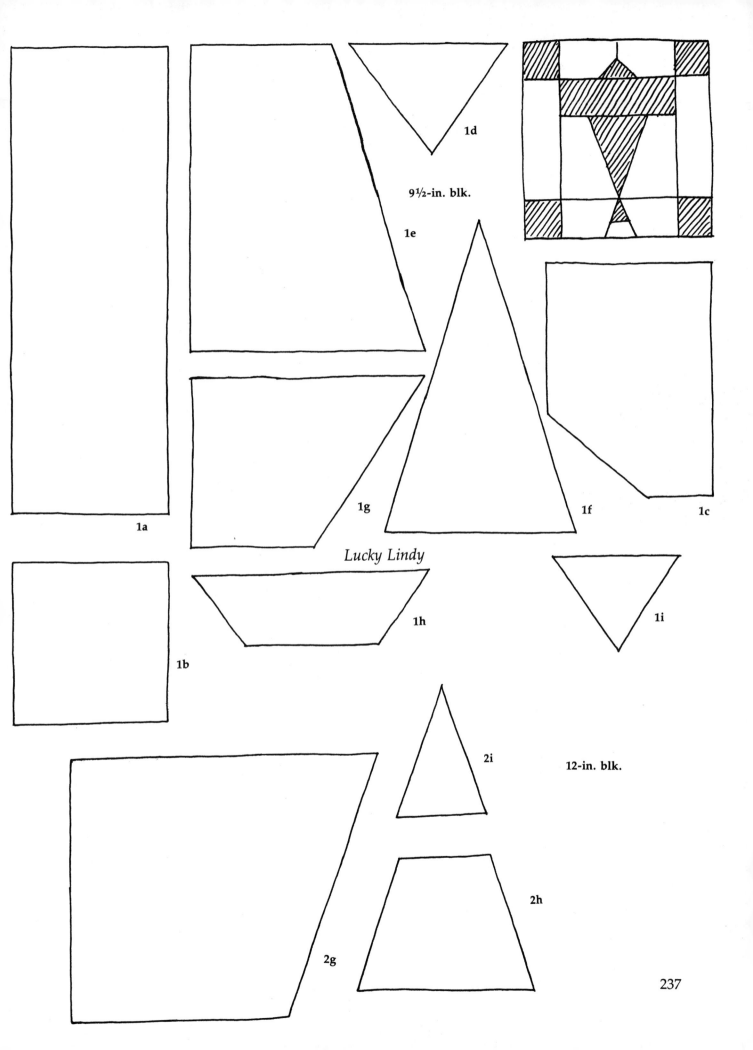

1a

1b

1e

1d

9½-in. blk.

1g

1f

1c

Lucky Lindy

1h

1i

2i

12-in. blk.

2g

2h

237

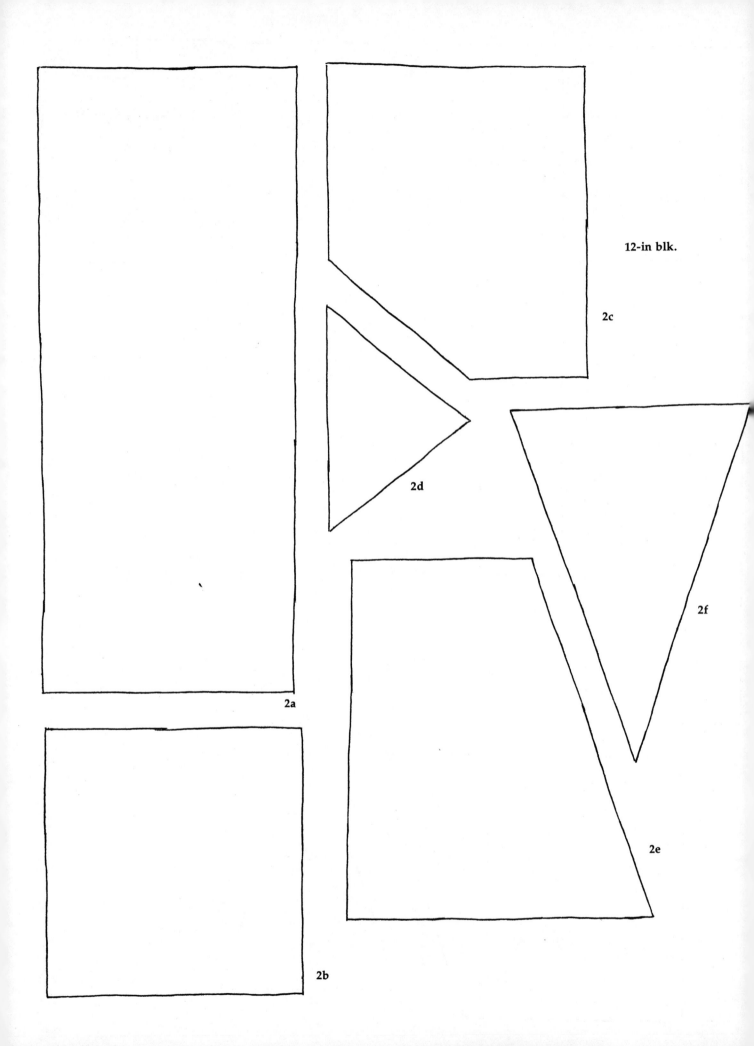

12-in blk.

2c

2d

2f

2a

2e

2b

Lucky Lindy—1928

The first airplane pattern in this group was designed after Lindbergh made his successful flight across the Atlantic Ocean in 1928. His airplane was called the *Spirit of St. Louis,* but the quilt patch is called Lucky Lindy. There are nine pattern pieces, Piece *a* is for the two sides and the wings; *b* is for the four corner squares; *c* and *d* are the plane nose and two side pieces. Pieces *e* and *f* are the body of the plane and the two side pieces. Pattern piece *i* is the tail of the plane, and *h* is the fill-in piece behind the tail. Piece *g* is for the two side pieces for that section. This pattern is given in two sizes. Pattern size 1 is for the 9½-inch-square block; size 2 is for a 12-inch-square block. This is not a hard pattern, but take care to make the seams even and the corners neat.

The Airplane—1930's

The second design, the Airplane, is only slightly later. It was designed in the 1930's and has been given a definite propeller. There are ten pattern pieces; those marked 1 in this pattern are for the 9½-inch block and those marked 2 are for the 12-inch block. Pattern 2f, the wing for the 12-inch block, is too long for the page. Draw the paper pattern twice this size with the middle of the pattern on the dotted line.

The Peace Plane—1941

The only appliqué design in this section on aviation was published in a women's magazine in 1941. It's name is the Peace Plane. It is given for a 12-inch-square block. The longer edge of the wing should be placed toward the front of the plane, and the stars are scattered around the plane to make a sky for it. This is the kind of airplane used for training flyers for the Air Corps during World War II. The U.S. entered the war just nine months after this pattern appeared.

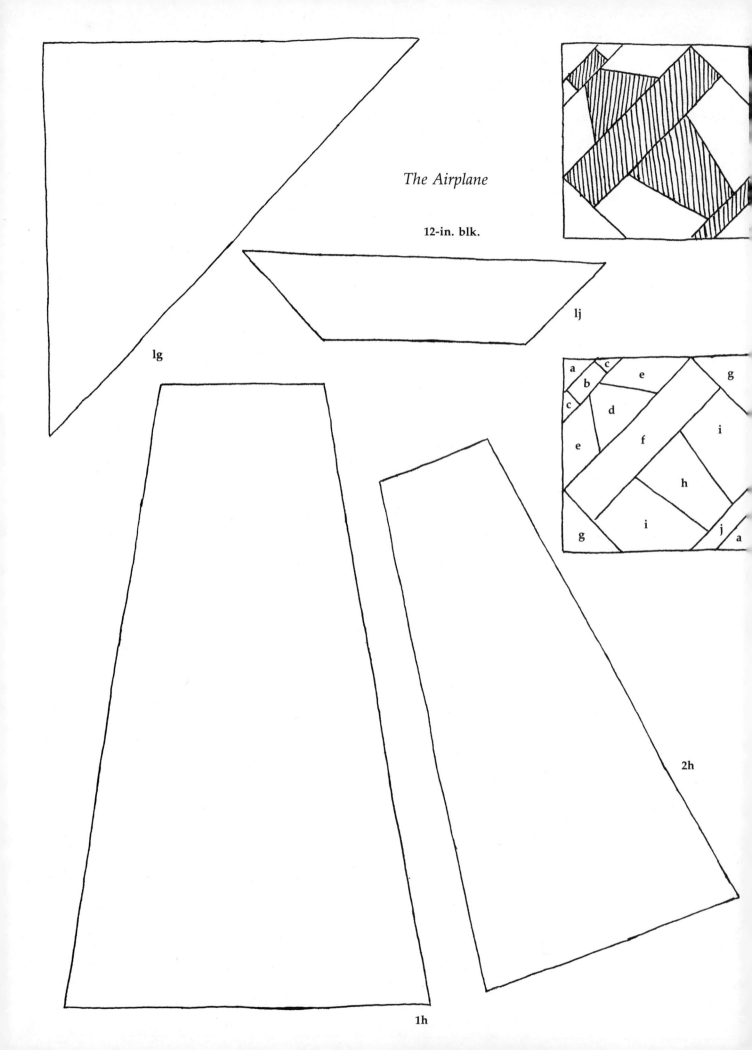

The Airplane

12-in. blk.

1g

1j

a b c e g
c d i
e f
h
g i j a

1h

2h

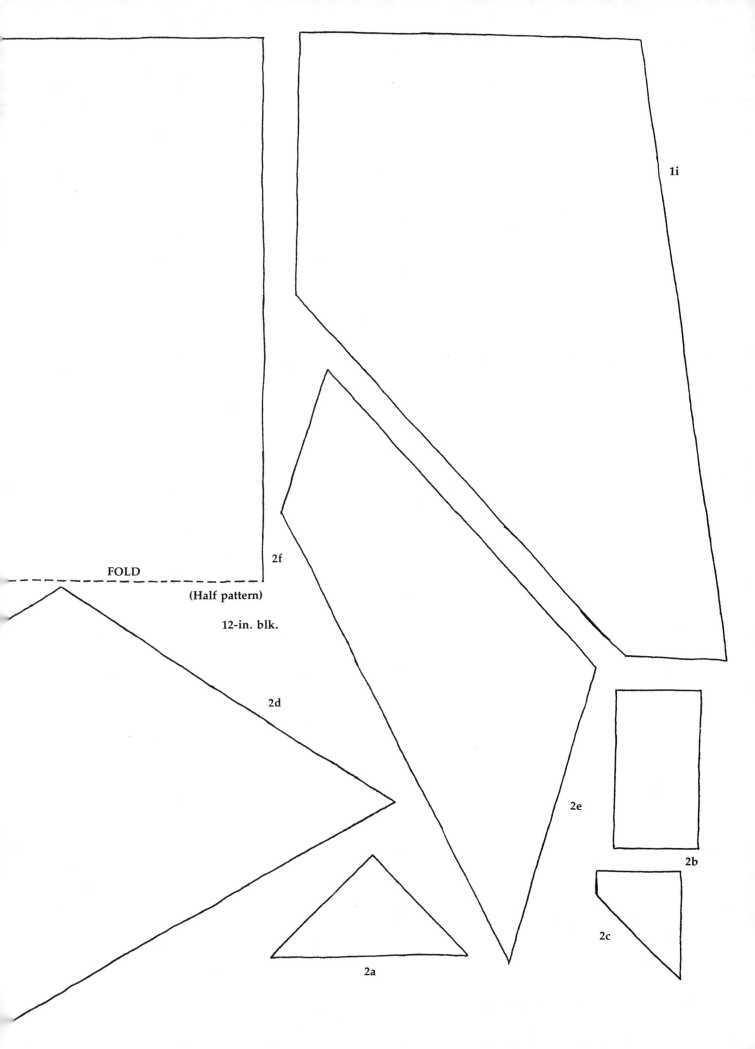

1i

2f

FOLD

(Half pattern)

12-in. blk.

2d

2e

2b

2c

2a

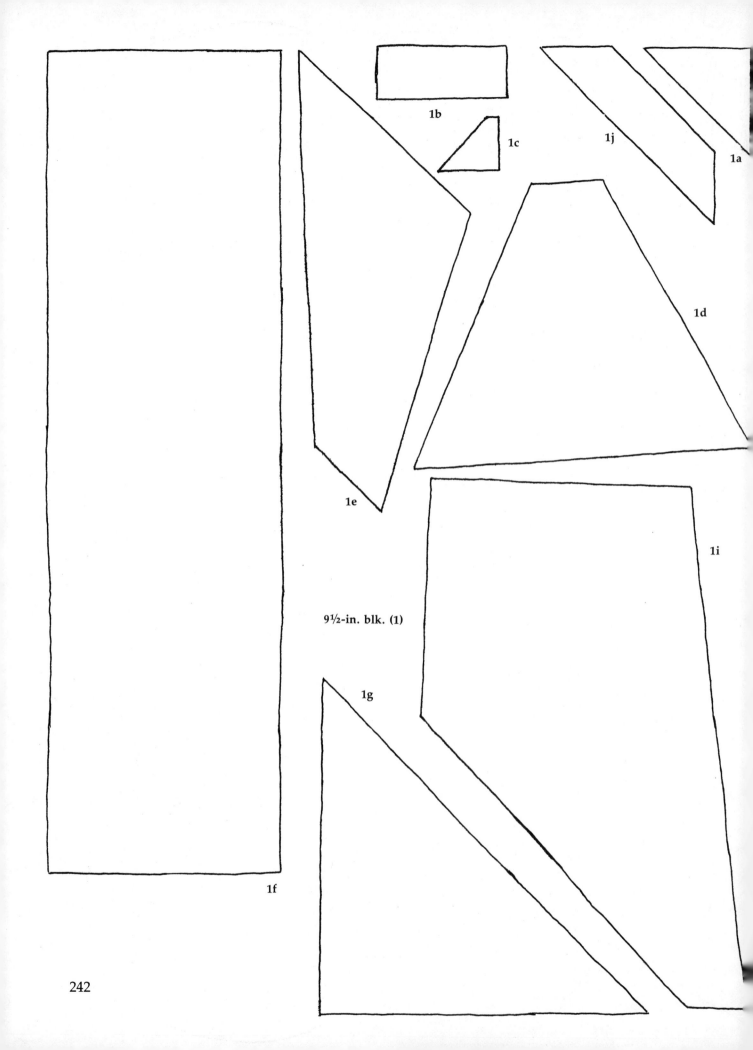

1b

1c

1j

1a

1d

1e

1i

9½-in. blk. (1)

1g

1f

242

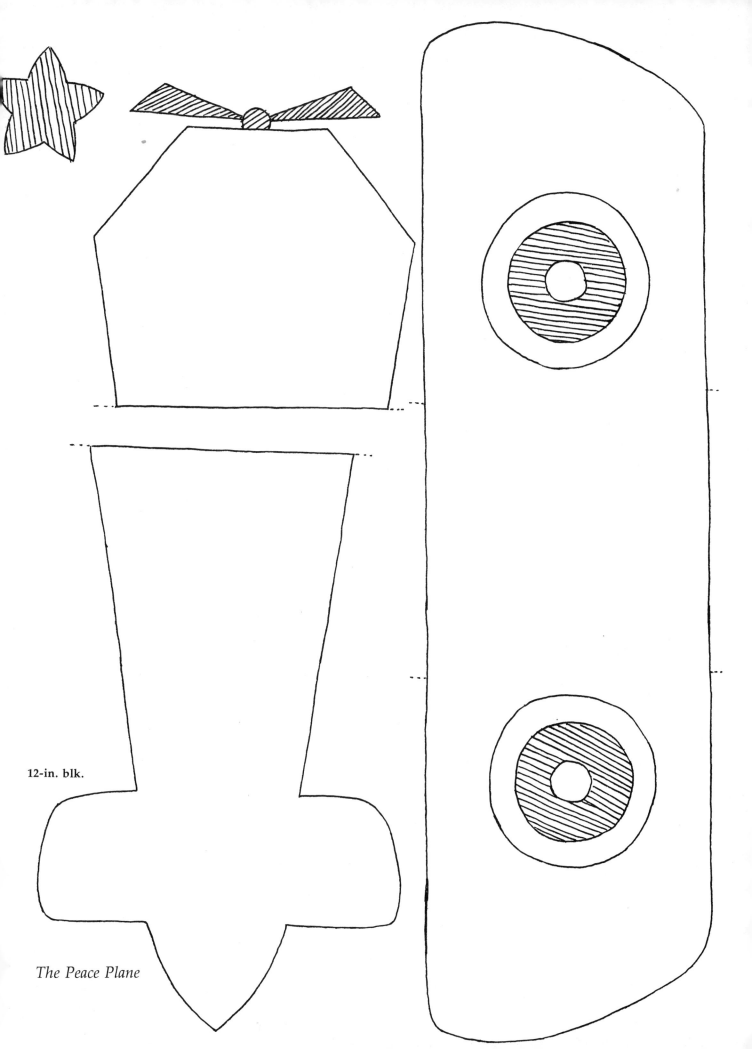

12-in. blk.

The Peace Plane

Jetliner—1981

The huge jets that crisscross the skies are as much a part of our modern landscape as the trees and clouds. It seems a wonder that they haven't been translated into a quilt pattern before this. Anyway, here is a Jetliner for your junior pilot's bed. If you are a beginner it might be best to choose the larger 12-inch block pattern rather than the smaller 9-inch block. If your child has a preference as to the airline he wants represented, you might add the insignia in embroidery to the jet. Some companies paint their planes in beautiful colors that would look lovely in the block's of a child's quilt. If you'd like the jet to look like aluminum, cut the pieces from white and the background from blue. It will look as though it is flying.

To make the pattern, sew a *b* to an *a* piece and add the second *a*. Then sew a *c* to a *d*; repeat this step. Lay these three squares aside. Sew an *e* piece to the front of the fuselage. Lay this aside. Sew two sets of the following: an *i* to a *j* and an *l* to another *j*. Sew the *m* triangle to the short side of the *l-j* pieces and a *k* to the long side. The *i-j* piece finishes the engine assembly.

Add pattern piece *h* to the *i-j* piece. Now add the *f* piece on one side and *n*, a wing, on the other. Lay these two sections aside. Sew the two *o* triangles to the *p* pieces.

The tail assembly is last. Sew a *q*, an *r*, and an *s* into a strip; then sew this strip first to the *p* and then to the *g* pieces. Add the other *q-r* section and the other *p*.

Sew the wing-engine sections to each side of the body, piece *g*. Finish with the three nose pieces, *a* through *d*. The pieces marked 1 are for the 9-inch block and those marked 2 are for the 12-inch block.

Before beginning any work on this quilt, please read the General Directions (which begin on page 4), including Piecing a Block (page 15). All pattern pieces are finished size; add 1/4-inch seam allowance on all sides.

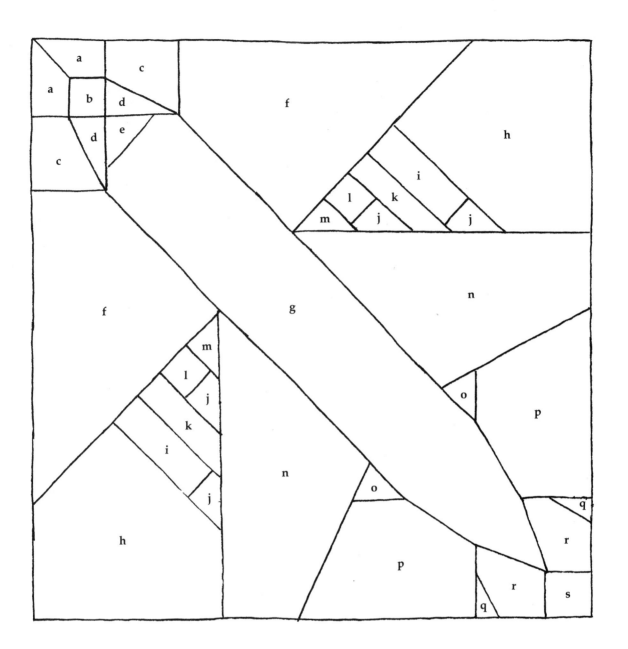

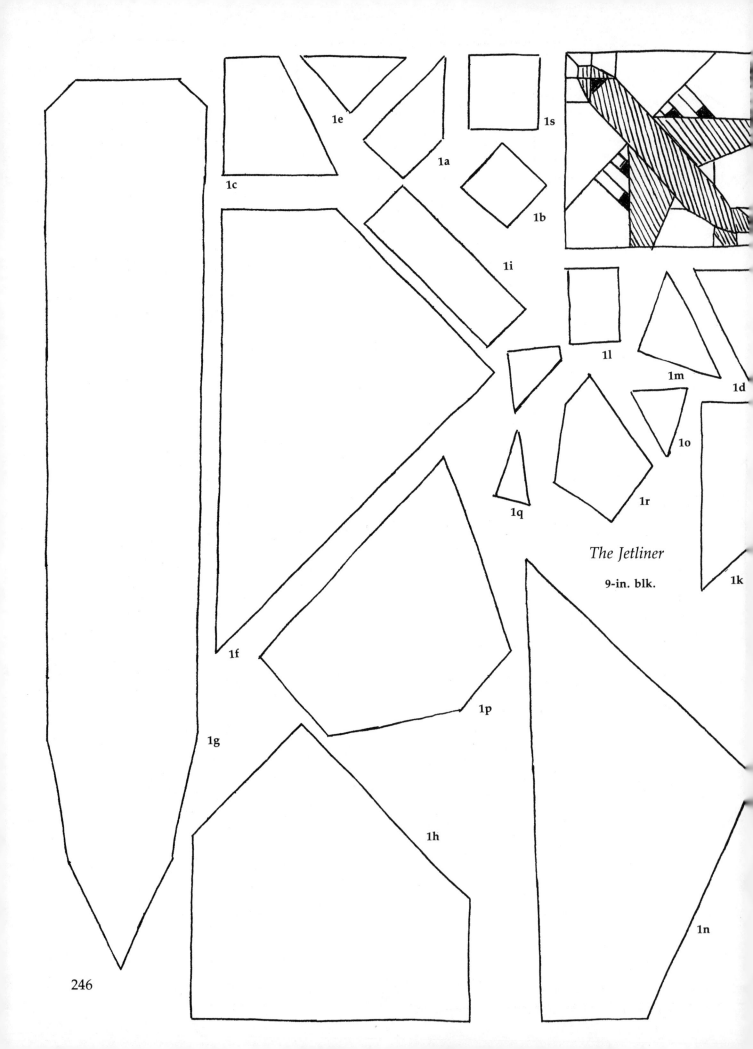

1e

1a

1s

1c

1b

1i

1l

1m

1d

1o

1q

1r

The Jetliner

9-in. blk.

1k

1f

1p

1g

1h

1n

246

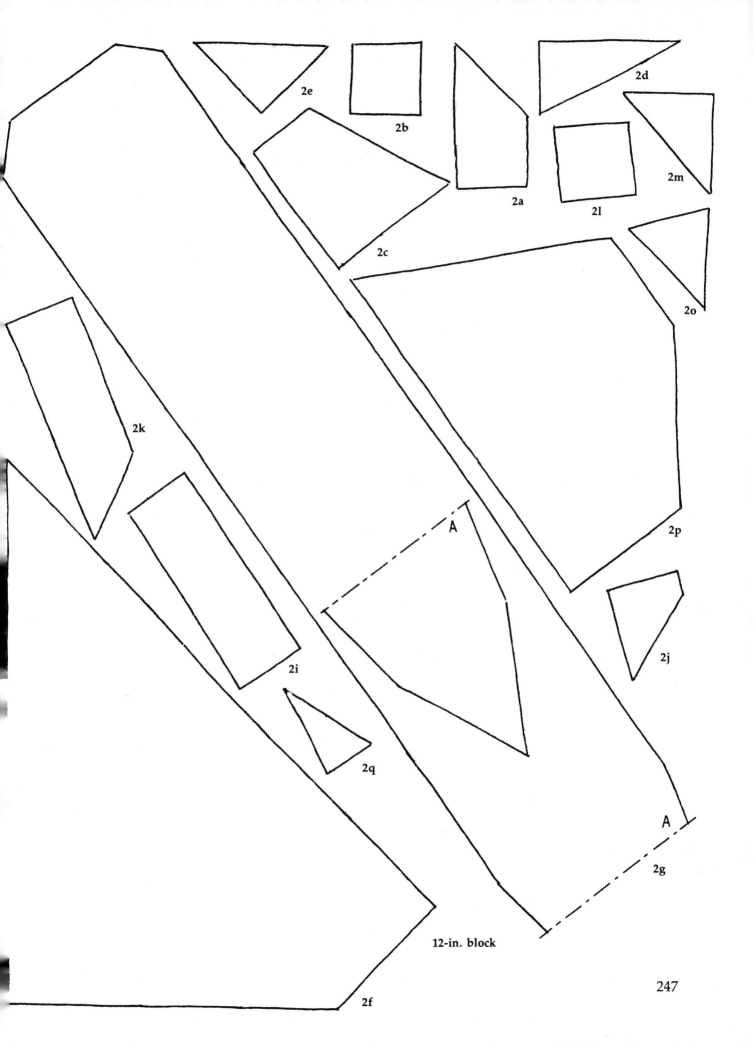

2e

2b

2d

2a

2m

2l

2c

2o

2k

2p

A

2i

2j

2q

A

2g

12-in. block

2f

247

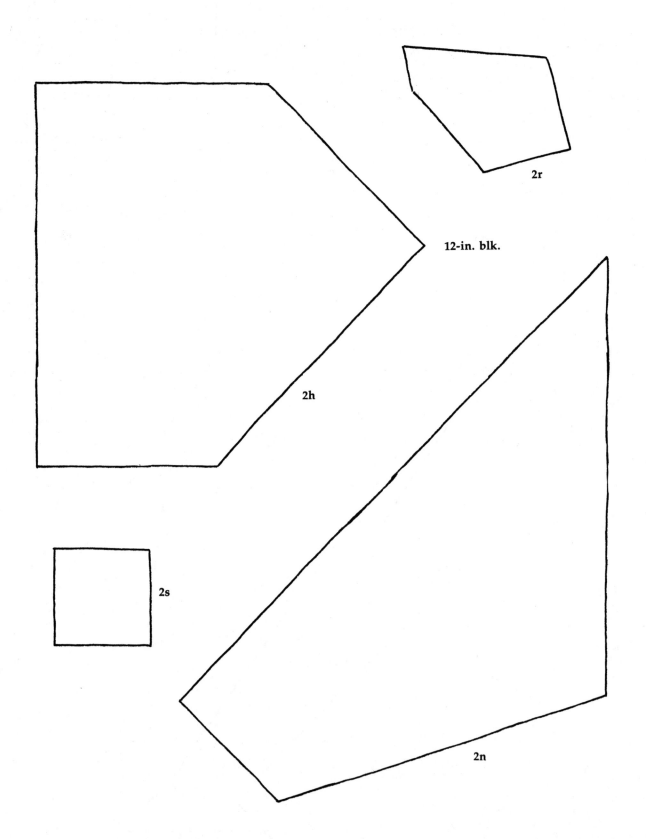

2r

12-in. blk.

2h

2s

2n

The Rocket—1968

This pattern was suggested by the author of an article on quilt patterns in one of the collector's magazines, *Spinning Wheel*. Some changes from the original design now make this a simple, colorful pattern that would be quite easy even for a beginner. This block would look best with lattice strips between the pieced squares. It is given in two sizes. The larger, 12-inch block is marked 1 and the smaller, 9½-inch block is marked 2.

To make the block, sew one pattern piece *e* on each side of the *f* triangle. Lay this strip aside. Now sew the *b* triangle to the smaller end of the *d* piece. Add a *c* triangle to each side of the *d* piece, and then add a *d* triangle to each side of this assembly. Finish the block with the *e-f-e* strip at the bottom.

Before beginning any work on this quilt, please read the General Directions (which begin on page 4), including Piecing a Block (page 15). All pattern pieces are finished size; add 1/4-inch seam allowance on all sides.

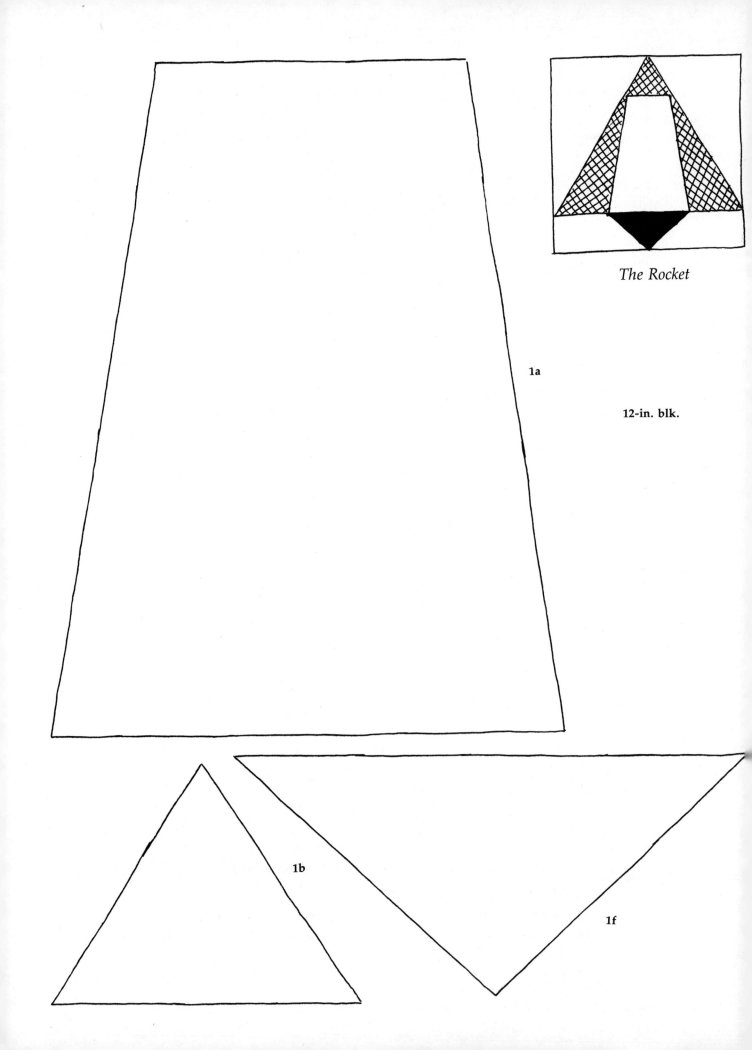

The Rocket

1a

12-in. blk.

1b

1f

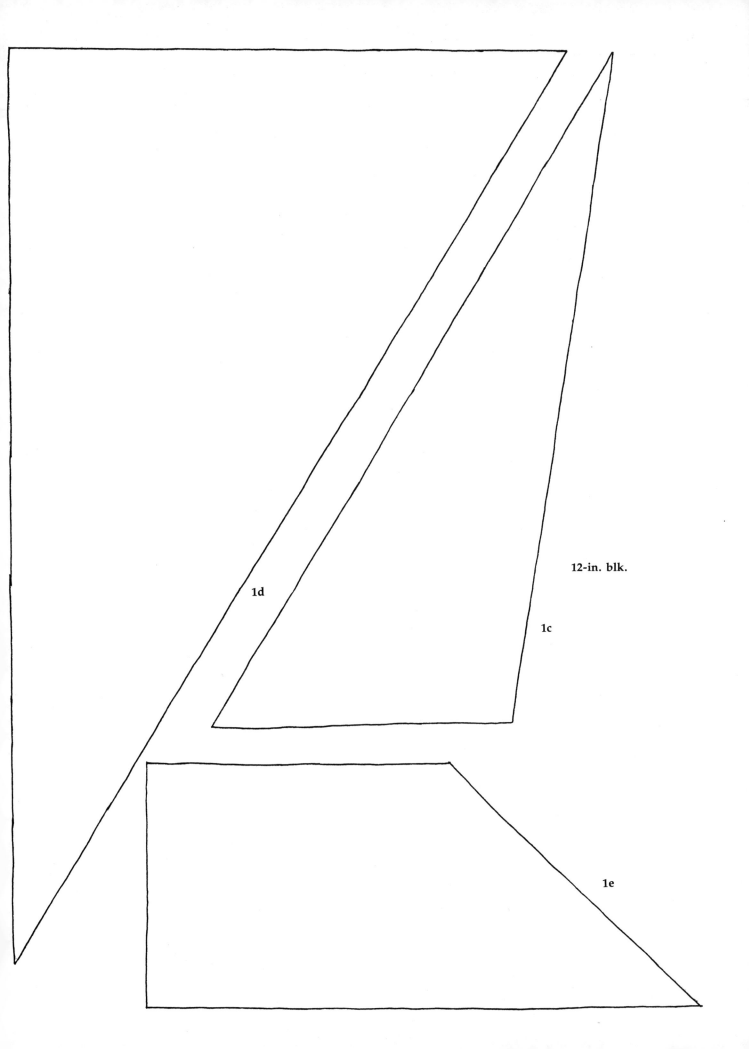

1d

12-in. blk.

1c

1e

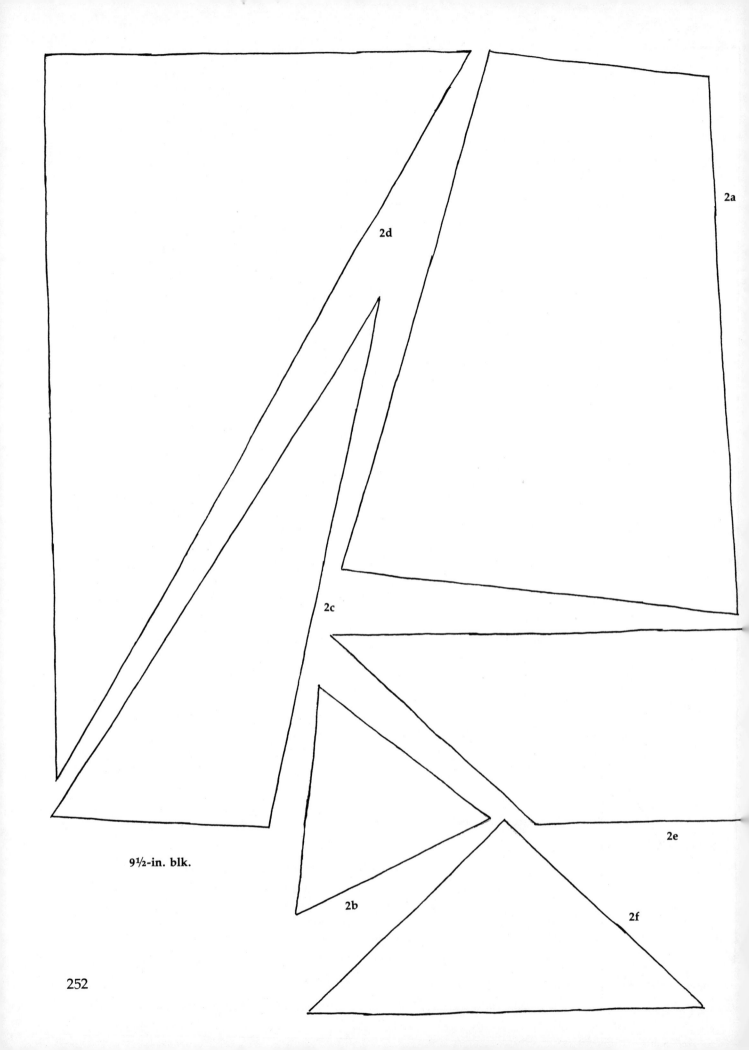

2a

2d

2c

2b

2e

2f

9½-in. blk.

252

The Space Shuttle—1981

In 1975 my family visited Redstone Arsenal in Huntsville, Alabama. Among the many interesting space exhibits there were models of the then-proposed Space Shuttle. There were about twenty design modules entered for consideration by engineers across the country. Also in the proposal stage at that time was a huge space telescope, now named Iris and in the final stage before launching. On another trip we visited Johnson Space Center near Houston, Texas. There, in 1977, we saw the progress that had been made on these two projects over two years.

We kept careful watch on TV and newspaper coverage, and got up at 5 A.M. on both April 10th and 12th, 1981, to see the Space Shuttle blast off for its first trip away from Earth into space. While we watched I sketched the shuttle, so that this new pattern could be included in this book. I hope your little astronauts like it.

This quilt is not for a beginner, but it could be sewn after two or three easier patterns have been made. The curved seam for the wings is the difficulty. Patterns for two sizes are given: 9-inch blocks use the pattern pieces marked 1, and 12-inch blocks use the series numbered 2.

Begin by piecing a c triangle on each side of the b oblong; then add the a triangle. Lay this corner aside. Sew the two e triangles to the two d shapes. Start at the seam between the d and e pieces on the left side, and sew the e piece to f (the body of the Shuttle). Return to the seam and sew the d piece to the f body. Repeat with the two pieces on the other side of f, and finish with

the seam between the two d pieces. Lay this assembly aside. Sew the h piece to the i wing. Embroider, fabric-paint, or crayon the flag and letters to the two i wings. Begin at the halfway point of the seam between the h-i section and g, and sew to one end. Return to the center and sew this seam the other way, easing the two pieces together carefully so they fit without puckering. Add the j corner triangles to these wing sections.

Sew the tail assembly together in this order: pattern piece r to piece p twice; q to o twice; n to o-q twice; n, o-q to p-r twice. Now using the technique for sewing curves described on page 16, add the k piece to l, twice. Sew the two l's to the n-o-p assembly, twice. Sew these two sections to either side of the m strip and add the s corner.

If you would rather appliqué the smaller pieces, sew the k, l, and m strip as shown above. Then appliqué the two o and p sections and the lower end of m to the t triangle.

Finish the block by sewing the two wing sections to either side of f, the body. Then add the tail section at the rear; add the nose to the front. The seams between the two d's and the b oblong must be treated as a curved seam. Start sewing at the seam between the d pieces and sew to the edge; then return to the center and sew to the other edge.

The pattern is given in two sizes. Those pieces marked 1 are for a 9-inch block and those marked 2 are for a 12-inch block. The Shuttle is black and white on a blue background, with red and blue trim on the wings. The trim patterns are marked A (the flag) and B (the USA insignia).

Before beginning any work on this quilt, please read the General Directions (which begin on page 4), including Piecing a Block (page 15) and Appliquéing a Block (page 16). All pattern pieces are finished size; add 1/4-inch seam allowance on all sides.

253

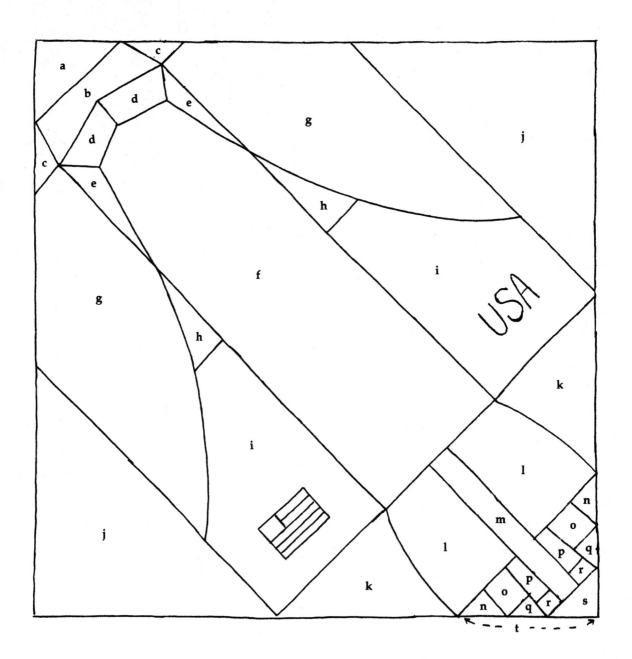

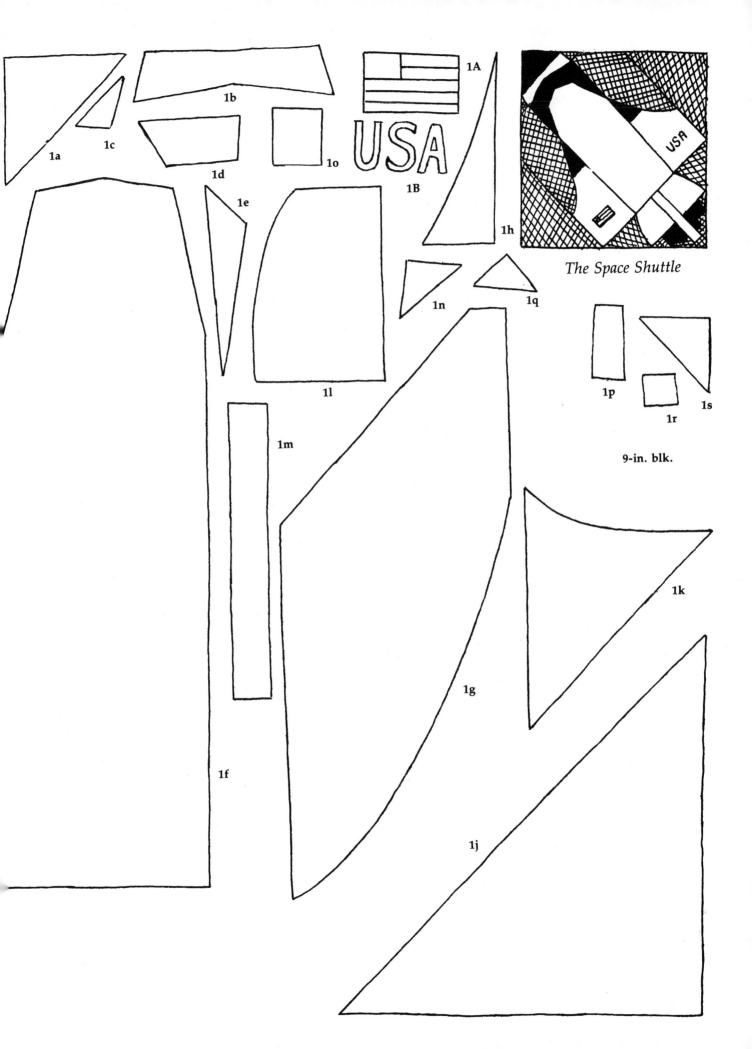

1a

1c

1b

1A

USA

1B

The Space Shuttle

1d

1e

1h

1o

1n

1q

1p

1s

1r

9-in. blk.

1l

1m

1k

1f

1g

1j

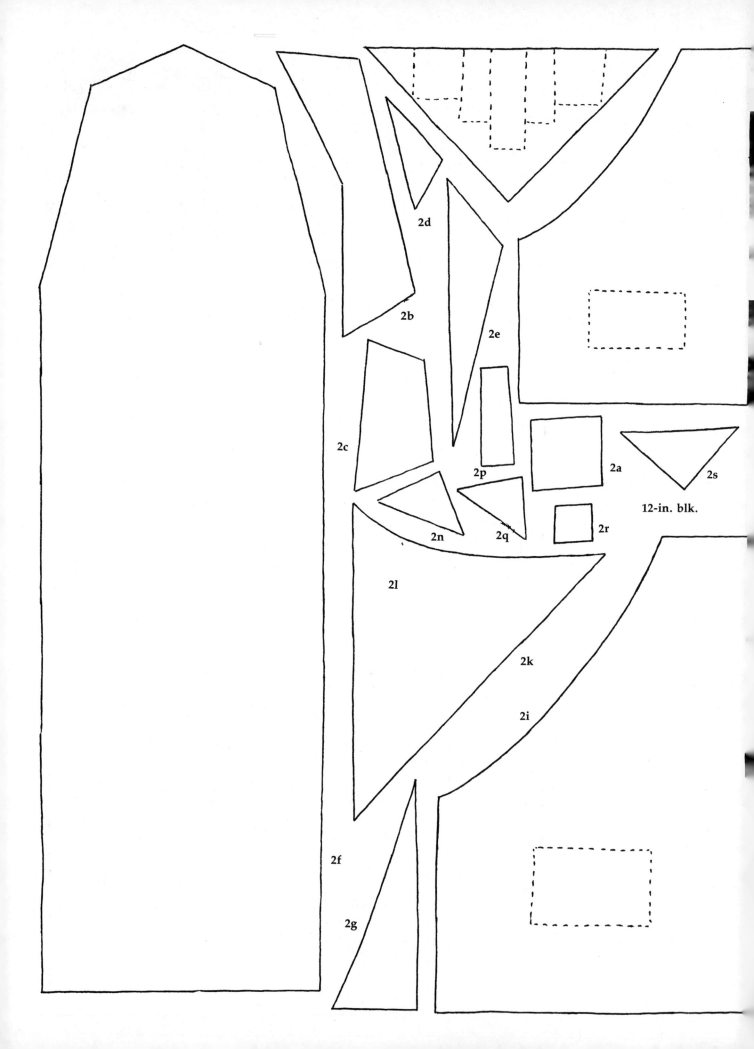

2d

2b

2e

2c

2a

2s

2p

12-in. blk.

2n

2q

2r

2l

2k

2i

2f

2g

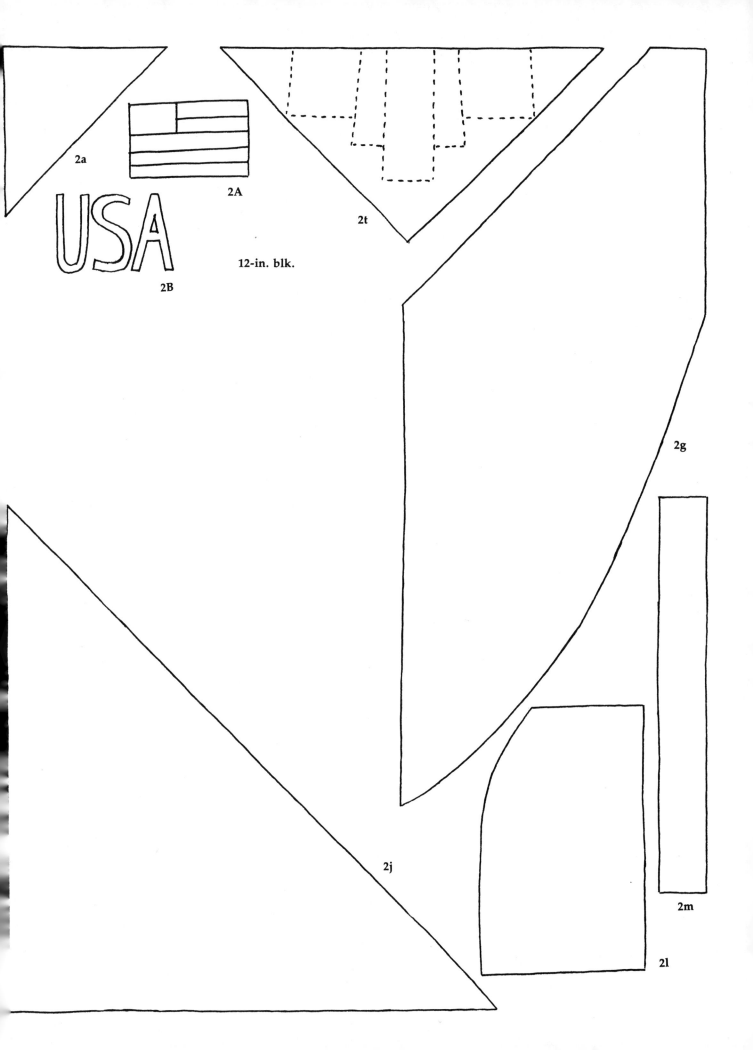

2a

2A

USA

2B

12-in. blk.

2t

2g

2j

2m

2l

The Sportsmen—1960's

A golfer, hunter, fisherman, and tennis player all have fun in this quilt pattern. The background blocks are 9-inch squares, half of which should be white or a light color and half a dark color. For a twin-bed-sized quilt—eight rows lengthwise of eleven blocks each—there should be forty-four light and forty-four dark blocks. Cut out twenty-two golfers and twenty-two tennis players from the light material and appliqué these to the forty-four dark squares. The hunter and fisherman should be cut from dark material and appliquéd to the light-colored squares. In the same order each time, and joining the bottom of one block to the top of the next, sew a row of blocks consisting of a golfer, fisherman, golfer, fisherman, golfer, fisherman, etc., until eleven blocks have been sewn together. The next row must be hunter, tennis player, hunter, etc. There are four eleven-block strips of each set of two blocks. Sew the rows together, alternating the two sets. Embroider the fisherman's line from hand to fish as well as the line from the end of his pole; embroider also the handle of the golfer's golf club and the strings of the tennis player's racket.

This pattern was sent to me several years ago by a very kind quilting friend. She drew it to make a quilt for her son. It should be well received by any sportsman, young or old. It is easy enough for even a beginning quilter.

Before beginning any work on this quilt, please read the General Directions (which begin on page 4), including Appliquéing a Block (page 16). All pattern pieces are finished size; add 1/4-inch seam allowance on all sides.

d

Flying a Kite—1968

Another of my quilting friends designed this pattern for her grandson. She got the idea from a child's coloring book and then simplified the pattern to achieve this appliqué and embroidery design.

All of the dash lines are for embroidery. The boy should be placed in the lower left of an 18-inch-square block and the kite in the upper right, with the string extended between the two motifs. The small patches of lines on the pattern of the kite tail indicate areas of satin-stitch embroidery. Blocks should be joined with 1-inch lattice strips between them.

In the original quilt the boy has on: blue jeans; plaid shirt; white shoes; pink face, hands, and ears; and a yellow hat. The kite is white with a red tail and brown crossed sticks. There are white, chain-stitched, curved lines in the upper right corner of the block for fleecy clouds. The background block is blue, and the lattice strips are red and white striped. With some curved lines indicating longer hair at the back of this figure's head, the design would serve just as well for a little girl flying a kite.

Before beginning any work on this quilt, please read the General Directions (which begin on page 4), including Appliquéing a Block (page 16) and Directions for Embroidery, Fabric Paints, and Crayons (page 16). All pattern pieces are finished size; add 1/4-inch seam allowance on all sides.

18-in. blk.

263

18-in. blk. appliqué

264

Bucking Bronc—1940's

A very good friend, ex-neighbor, and quilting pal from Tennessee was recently presented with her first grandchild. Among the presents we sent along for the new little cowboy were a pair of boots and blue jeans (size 6 months) and this pattern. His grandmother says that when he gets big enough for a twin bed the quilt will be all ready for him.

The cowboy and horse should be placed on the diagonal of the block, with the front feet of the horse much lower than the back. For fun, a few of the cowboys could be bareheaded—with their hats flying off over the backs of their horses. The smaller pattern is for a 10-inch-square block and the larger for a 14-inch-square block. The reins should be embroidered in a stem stitch and the horse's eye in satin stitch. Alternate the appliquéd blocks with plain blocks. If the appliquéd pieces are made from plain-colored cloth, it might look nice to have the blocks between the appliquéd ones cut from printed cloth with western motifs.

Before beginning any work on this quilt, please read the General Directions (which begin on page 4), including Appliquéing a Block (page 16). All pattern pieces are finished size; add 1/4-inch seam allowance on all sides.

10-in. blk.

(diagonal)

266

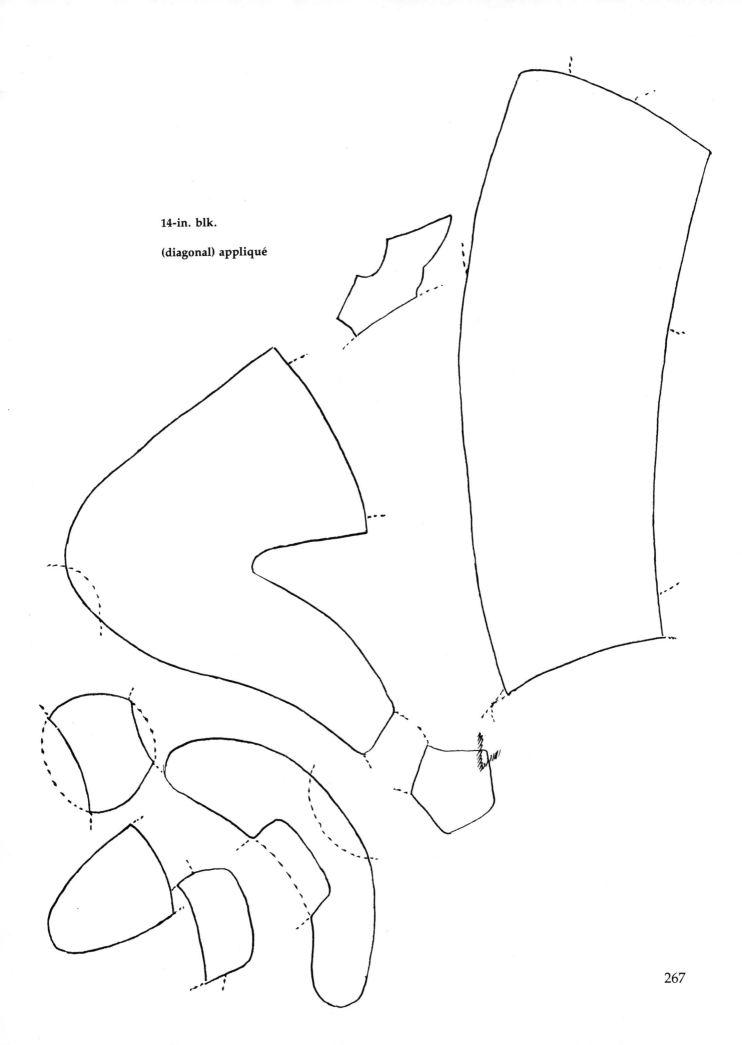

14-in. blk.

(diagonal) appliqué

267

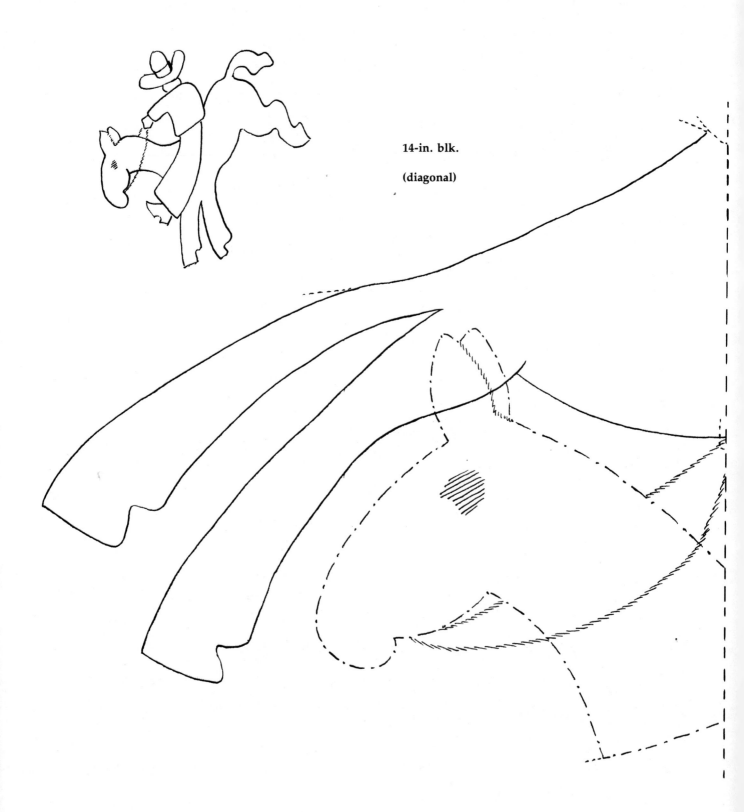

14-in. blk.

(diagonal)

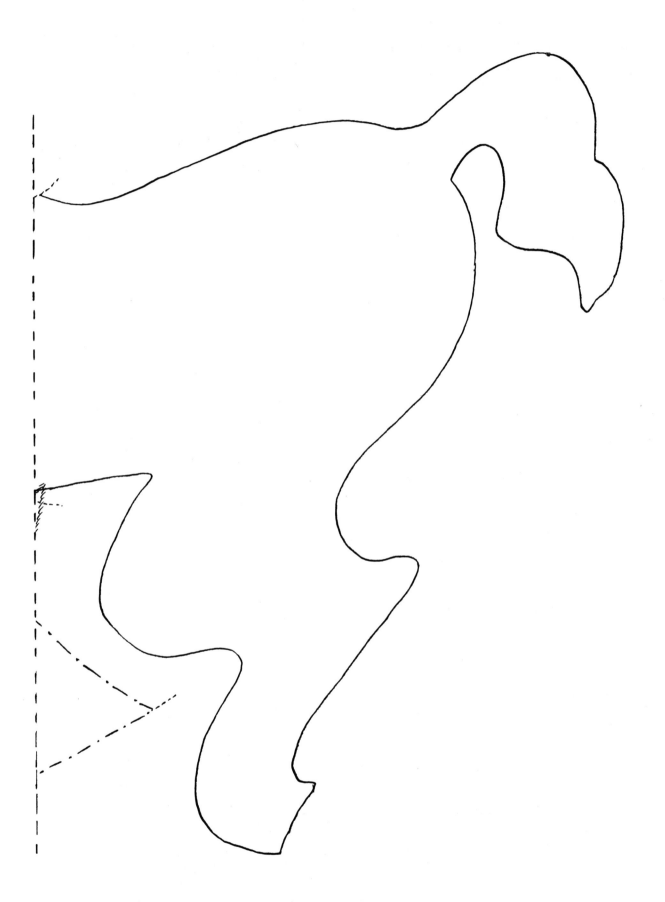

The Soldier Boy, World War I—circa 1918

This comical, geometrical fellow was published in one of the newspaper quilting columns back during World War I. He was to be made from khaki colored and white cloth with the features embroidered. The pattern is given in two sizes. The completed pattern shown in the drawing is for a 4½'' by 10'' block; the larger pattern pieces will make a block 6'' by 12''.

These are such odd-shaped blocks that I can envision them used in borders rather than in a top design. This soldier might look cute in the Baby Blocks border, page 287, or seeming to hold the swag from the Swag and Dot border given in the Humpty Dumpty quilt pattern, page 72.

By using another colored oblong between the figure's legs and devising a pieced hat in another shape, the soldier could have a girlfriend.

Before beginning any work on this quilt, please read the General Directions (which begin on page 4), including Piecing a Block (page 15). All pattern pieces are finished size; add 1/4-inch seam allowance on all sides.

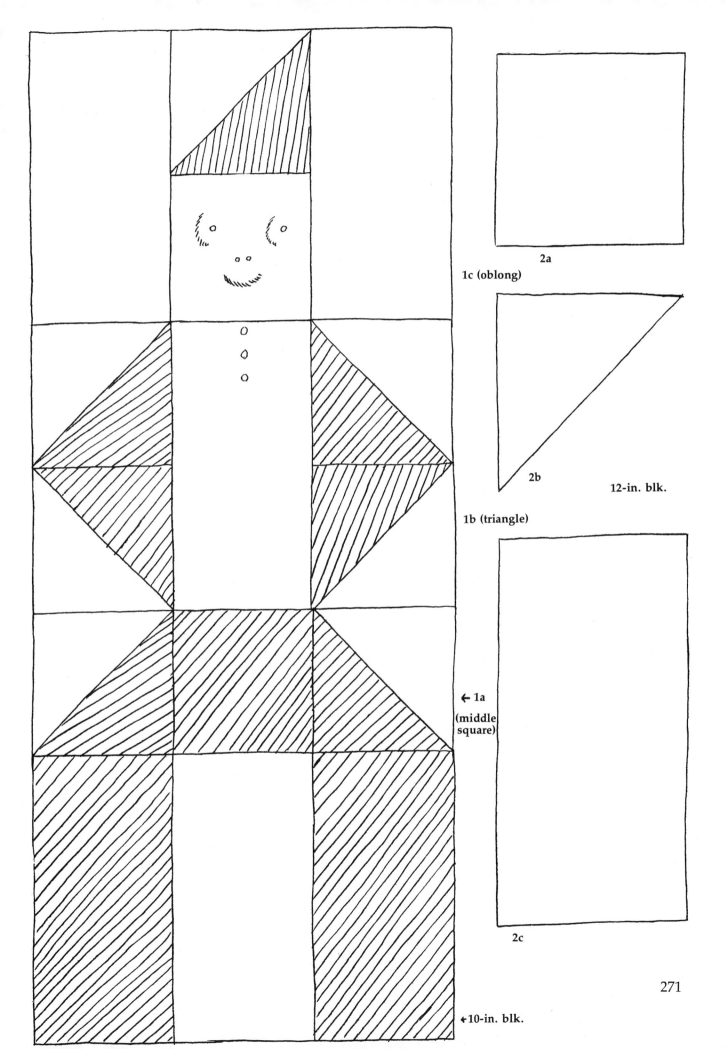

1c (oblong)

2a

1b (triangle)

2b

12-in. blk.

← 1a
(middle
square)

2c

271

←10-in. blk.

The Pieced Alphabet—circa 1900

This is a discontinued pattern from the Ladies Art Company, one of the United States' oldest needlework pattern companies. It was taken from a catalog printed in the first two decades of the nineteenth century. My copy is somewhat damaged, so some of the letter patterns were copied from the original and others had to be designed to look similar to the remaining original letter blocks. Pattern numbers 1a* and 2a are for the lattice strips and corner blocks used between the 5-inch-square letter blocks. There are twenty-five letter blocks. Twenty-four of these contain one letter each; the twenty-fifth has two letters, I and J. The quilt shown is a 5' by 5' crib quilt.

There are several ways to expand this design to make a larger quilt top. A plain border 2 feet wide at the top and bottom of the quilt and 1 foot wide on each side might be used. By careful calculation plain blocks might be inserted between the pieced blocks, but two more pieced blocks (perhaps with the child's name and the date) would be needed to fill out the number necessary to complete the design. Also there would need to be a plain band a few inches wide for the border. The blocks—with lattice strip added—are 9 inches square.

Because the pieces are small, this might be a little too hard to make for a first quilt. The block diagrams for each letter appear here as close to the pattern pieces needed for that letter as space allows. Trace off the pattern pieces for each letter on individual sheets of paper; use these sheets to check the cutting patterns before cutting the cloth with them. Several of the shapes are used in more than one letter.

*For this pattern, the individual pieces are designated by number rather than by letter. The pattern is for one block size only. Numbers do *not* indicate a difference in size, as they do elsewhere in this book.

Before beginning any work on this quilt, please read the General Directions (which begin on page 4), including Piecing a Block (page 15). All pattern pieces are finished size; add 1/4-inch seam allowance on all sides.

1a

Six pages of patterns follow.

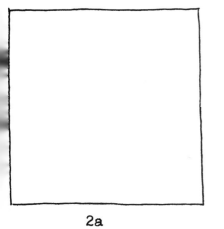

2a

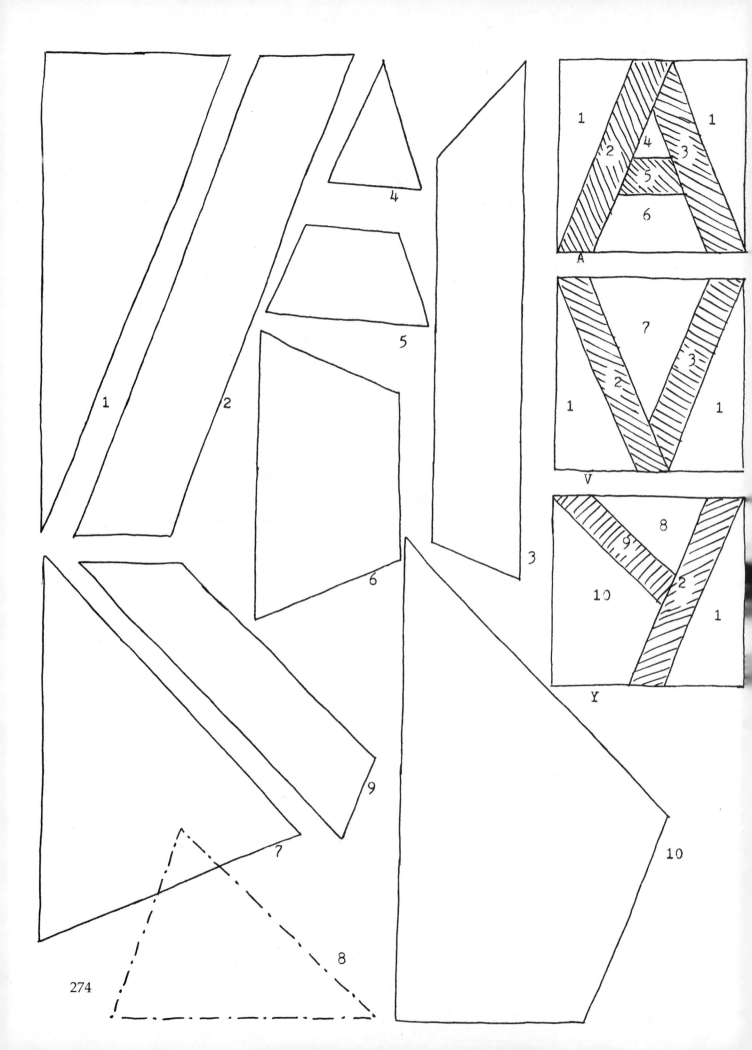

274

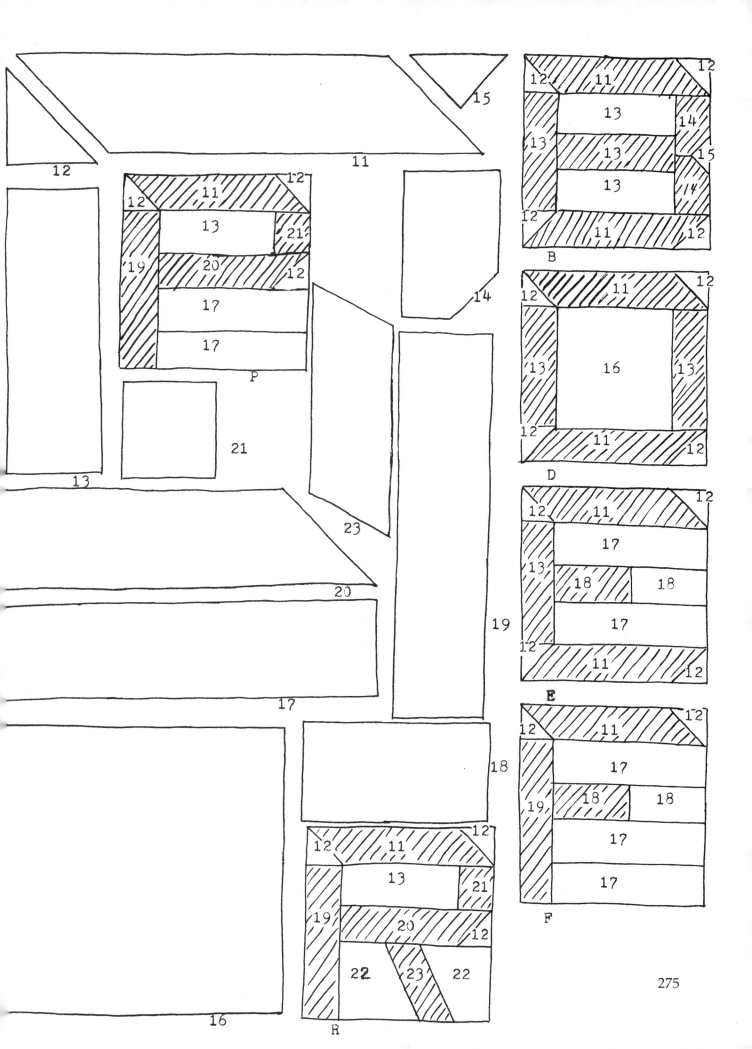

275

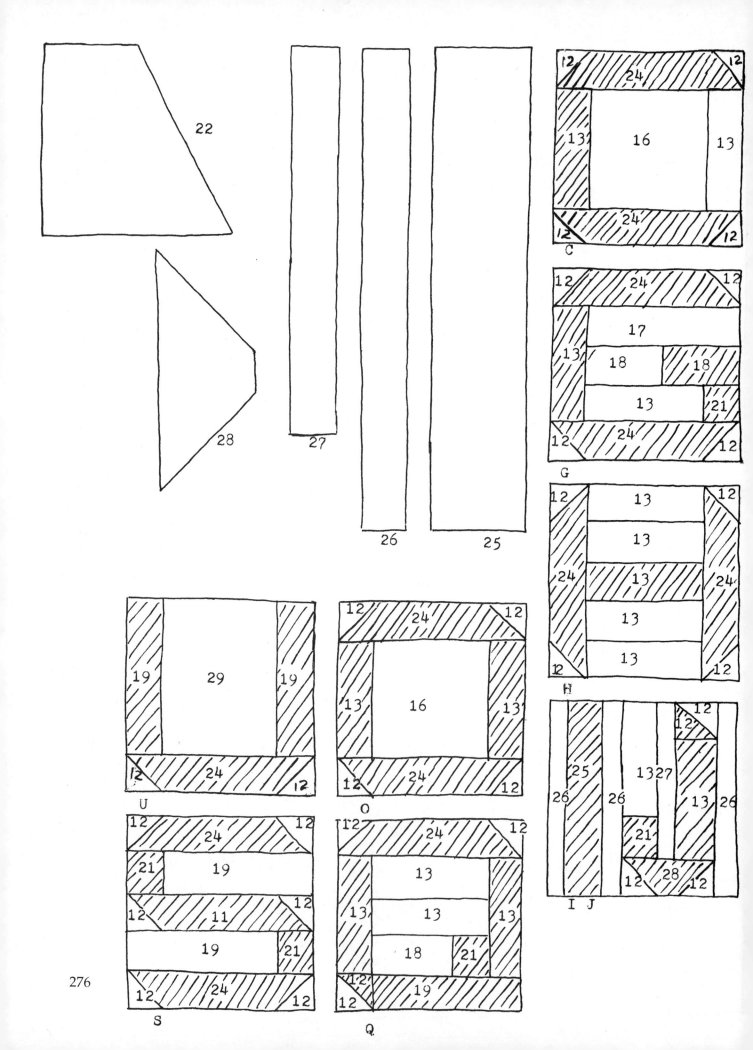

22

28

27

26

25

C
12   24   12
13   16   13
24
12   12

G
12   24   12
17
13   18   18
13   21
12   24   12

H
12   13   12
13
24   13   24
13
13
12   12

I J
25   12
12
13 27
26   26   13   26
21
12   28   12

U
19   29   19
12   24   12

O
12   24   12
13   16   13
12   24   12

276

S
12   24   12
21   19
12   12
12   11
19   21
12   24   12

Q
12   24   12
13
13   13   13
18   21
12
12   19

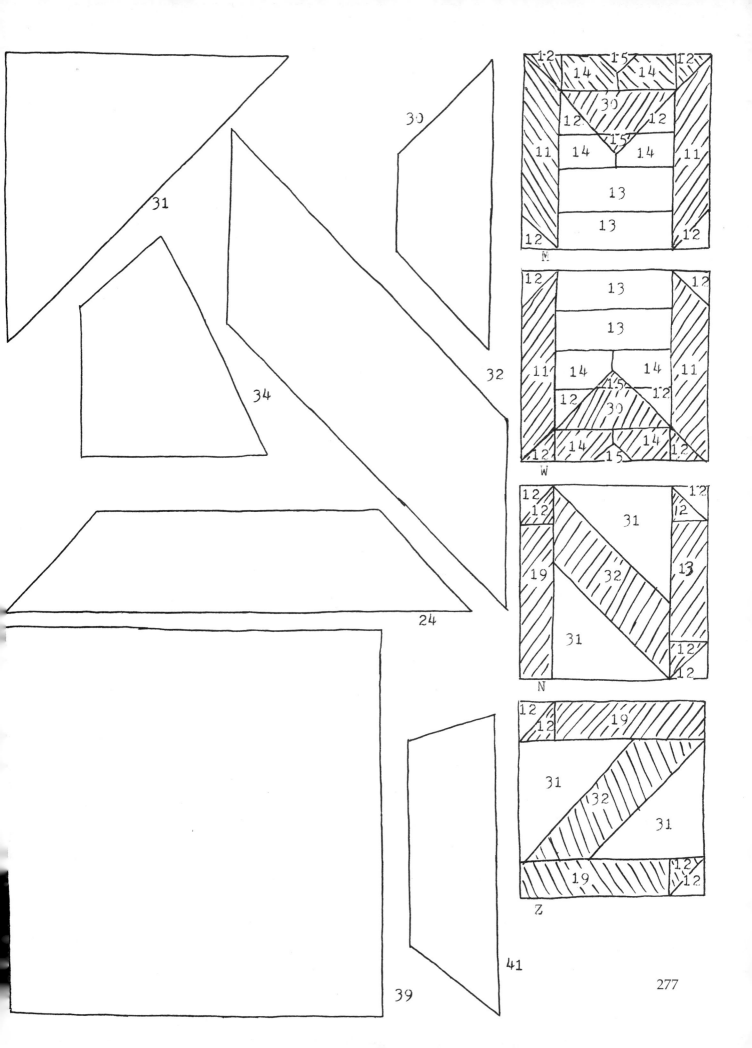

31

30

32

34

24

39

41

M
12 15 12
14   14
30
12   12
15
11 14 14 11
13
13
12   12

W
12 13 12
13
11 14 14 11
12 15 12
30
12 14 14 12
15

N
12 12
31
19 32 13
31 12
12

Z
12 12 19
31 32 31
19 12 12

277

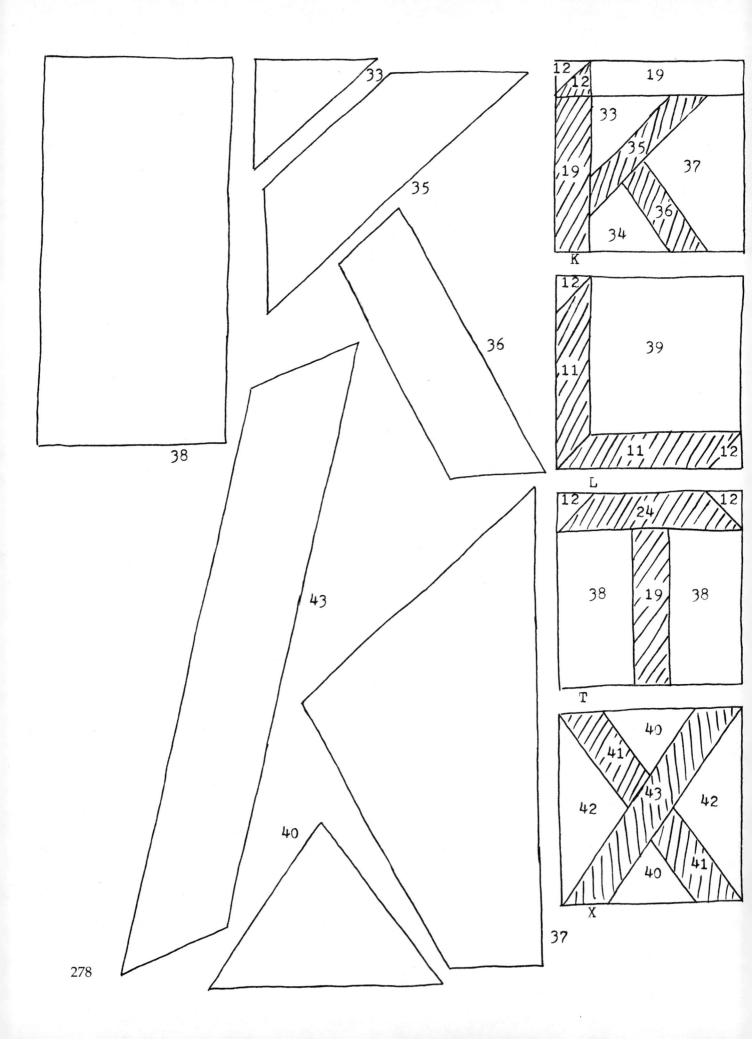

33

35

36

38

43

40

278

37

12
12
19
33
35
37
19
36
34
K

12
11
39
11
12
L

12
24
12
38
19
38
T

40
41
43
42
42
40
41
X

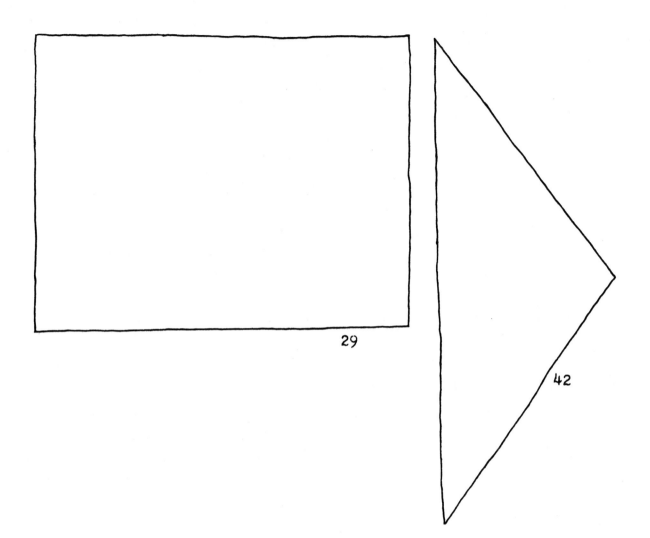

29

42

6

Take a Border

All of the border patterns for quilts in this book are not in this section; several are an integral part of the patterns they were designed to augment and appear with their quilts. This does not mean that they cannot be extracted from those patterns and used with other designs as well. All the borders are listed with their page numbers in the index. There are six appliqué patterns, five pieced patterns, five quilting-pattern borders, a pattern that uses both appliqué and piecing, one that uses either technique, and a lattice-strip pattern in appliqué which can be also used for a border. These patterns range from narrow to quite wide and so can be used to adjust the size of the quilt top to almost any desired width. It is also possible to use two or more borders, one inside the other, in the same or in different techniques, to adjust the size or enhance the look of your quilt.

The first border in this section, Peony and Grapevine, is an early nineteenth-century pattern. It is illustrated in the Frontispiece and its history is given with the Peony Wreath block design, page 46. This border is one of the earliest solutions to a swag pattern. The main motifs are floral patterns. The corners are peony sprays (these are given in exact size and placement on the 8-inch block). Stems are embroidered, and leaves, flower, and buds are appliquéd. In the original the pattern pieces are laid out on the background strips and the vines or stems are drawn in to suit the arrangement. This accounts for the varied placement in the different sections of the border. Try this method; you might find an arrangement that you like better than that in the original border. Or, you might prefer to repeat one of the arrangements all the way around the border. The original was red and green on white. Suit your color scheme to your own taste.

Peony Spray Corner

(circa 1850)

Grapevine and Peony Border

(circa 1850)

Peony from Border

Flower Face

(see page 287)

283

The pattern pieces for the next four borders are given in Chapter 3, on page 29. By varying the size of the squares used and the width of the plain strips a wide selection of sizes can be achieved.

Naughts and Crosses is a pieced border that needs only two colors—a dark and a light. The two plain strips are the same width as the squares, so this border will be 10½ inches wide if the square size is 1½ inches.

Hit Or Miss and All Mixed Up are two borders constructed in the same way as the quilts in the third chapter. They are essentially scrap border patterns and are most effective when combined with an appliqué center. The colors in the squares should complement or echo those in the appliquéd center. In these borders the plain bands are twice the width of the squares; thus, if the squares are 1½ inches, the border will measure 12 inches across.

The Baby Blocks border (see page 287) is another variant of the same kind of border, again using squares for the pattern. In this case, a plain square alternates with a pieced oblong of the same height; the oblong is made up of twenty small squares in four rows of five. The bottom row of the oblong is made up of five print squares. The second row is a plain square, three print squares, and a plain square. The third row is two plain squares, a print square, and two plain squares; and the last row is five plain squares. Center the printed motifs in some of these squares, as shown in the drawing.

There are many spot motifs scattered throughout the book. Pick some of these that appeal to you or are compatible with the center of the quilt; piece, appliqué, embroider, fabric-paint, or crayon these in the plain large squares, as shown. Again, the plain bands are the same width as the squares, so a 1½-inch square will make a 9-inch-wide border. The plain large squares will be 6 inches on a side.

The Sawtooth border, in all its variations, was one of the most popular nineteenth-century quilt designs. It became so popular in the 1870's and 1880's that it now almost symbolizes the quilts of that era. If a line of triangle points surrounded a block or plain bands, lattice strips, and so forth, they were always called Sawtooth: however, if the same line of triangle points surrounded a pieced pattern forming a star, triangle, diamond, or other shape, then that part of the pattern was said to be "feathered."

Because turning a Sawtooth corner is difficult, there are four corner treatments given. It is not always possible to have all four corners match. Do not be surprised if the two corners on the right are different from the two corners on the left of your border. They can also (if the measurements are just right) match across the diagonal of the quilt. For all four corners to match, all four sides must be the same length. However, Sawtooth patterns are so complicated and busy in themselves that most people do not notice the mismatching unless their attention is called to it. These borders are not at all hard to do; just be careful to keep your seams straight and the points in line. The patterns for this border are marked A1 and A2 on page 290.

We have recently gone through a bit of minor madness called the U.S. Bicentennial. It's fun to have an excuse to "wave the flag" once in a while, and I think that American quilters had more fun than anyone else while our two-year-long birthday party lasted. But we don't really need a national movement as an excuse for a good flag quilt. The Stars and Stripes is a border for a future patriot's quilt that will bring a cheery red, white, and blue note to any child's bedroom. The blue squares are 9 inches on a side. Appliqué the five stars in place as shown on each blue square. There must be exactly this number of squares in each border, no matter what size the quilt. (If you count the stars, you will see that there are exactly 50—as there should be.) When the blue squares have been arranged, measure the spaces between. This measurement will give the length needed for the striped sections. (Remember to add the seam allowances to these measurements.) The patterns are marked B1 and B2 on page 290.

The Ribbon Swag border is taken from the First Recital quilt pattern. The drawing of the border and directions are given with the quilt (see page 187). The ballet slipper patterns *f* and *g*, are for use as tassels in the above quilt. You can use the same directions to make a Ribbon Swag and Tassel border, which could be used with almost any quilt pattern. The tassel is used at the end of pattern *d* at line A.

In the next section—on quilting—there are several more border patterns for use in quilting. Several of these could be traced for cutting patterns and then appliquéd, rather than quilted, if you wish. The border patterns in the quilting section are A, B, C1 and C2, E, and U1 and U2.

Before beginning work on any quilt, please read the General Directions (which begin on page 4), including Piecing a Block (page 15) and Embroidery, Fabric Paints, and Crayons (page 16). All pattern pieces are finished size; add 1/4-inch seam allowance on all sides.

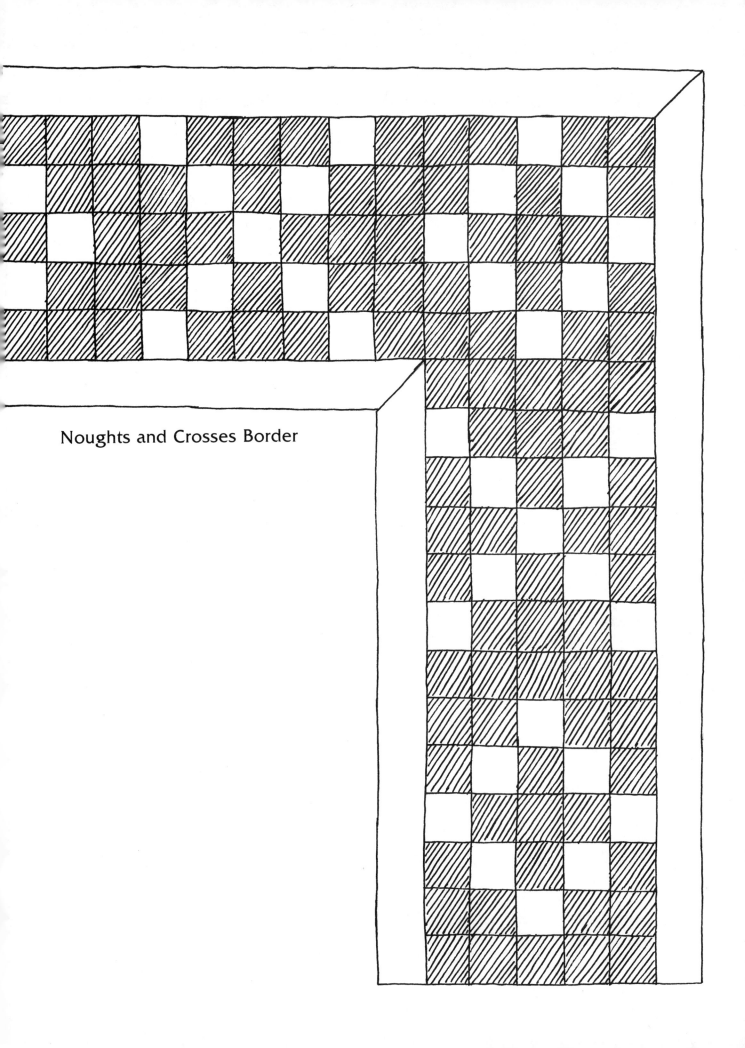

Noughts and Crosses Border

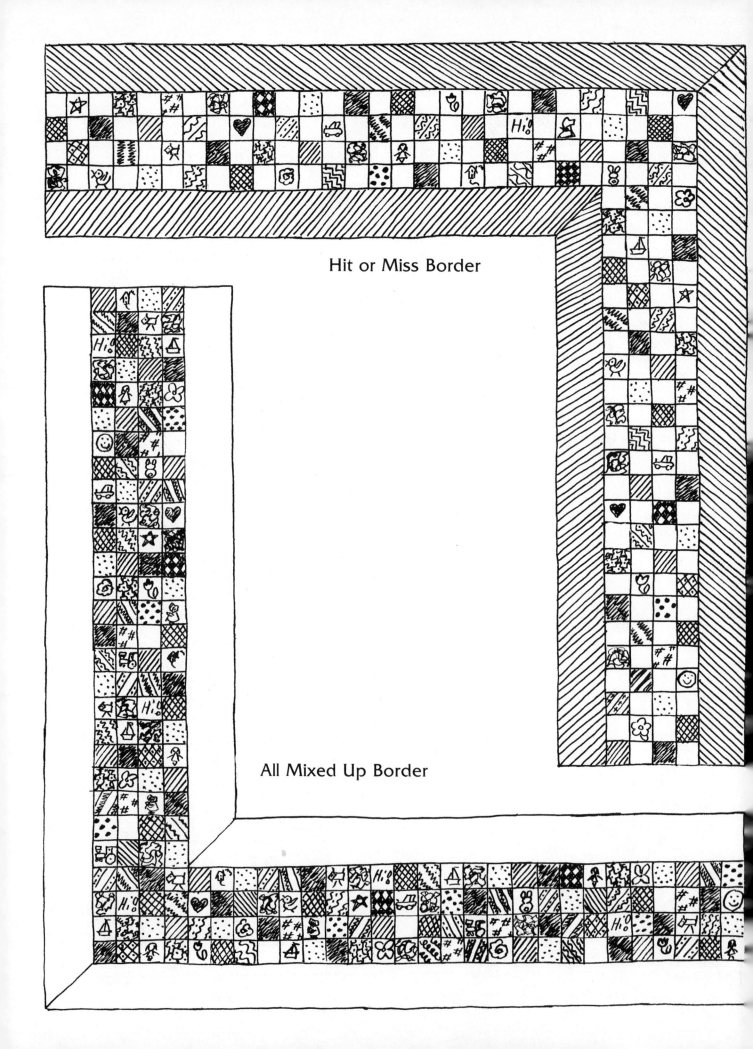

Hit or Miss Border

All Mixed Up Border

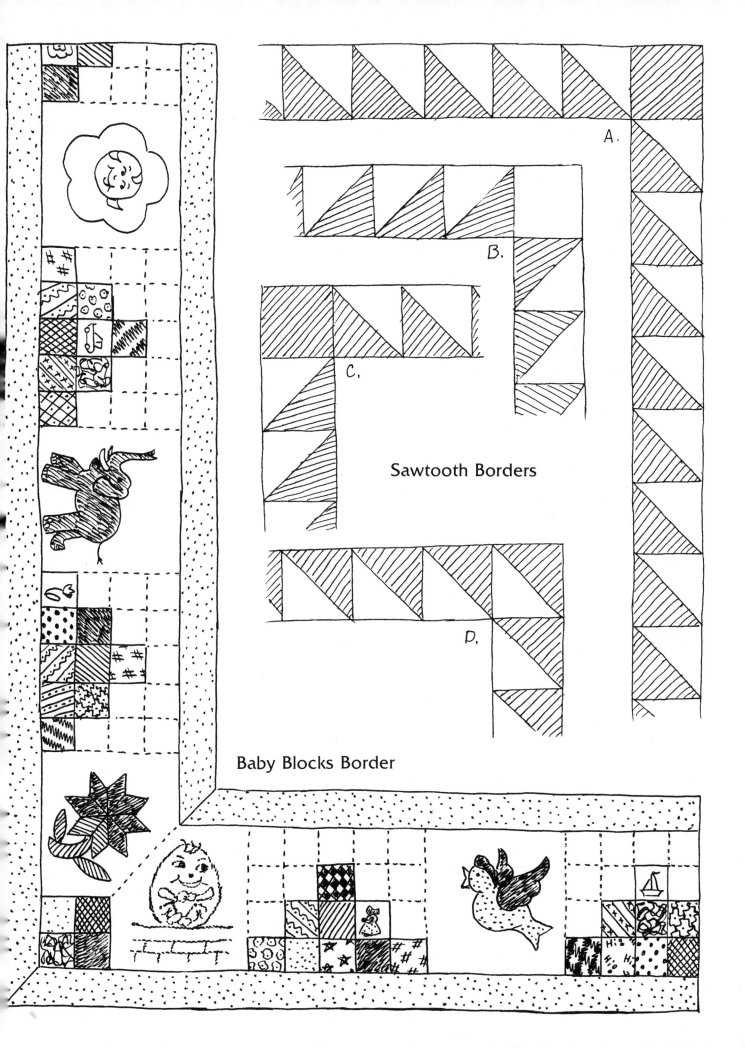

A.

B.

C.

Sawtooth Borders

D.

Baby Blocks Border

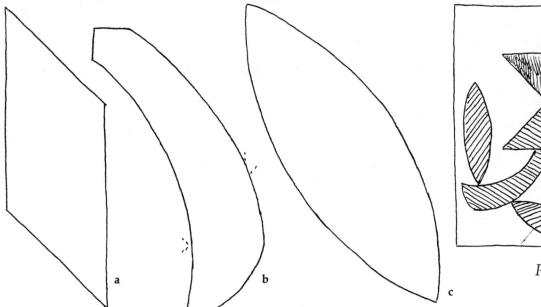

a   b   c

Pieced Peony

8-in. blk.

Humpty Dumpty

6-in. blk.

The Stars and Stripes Border

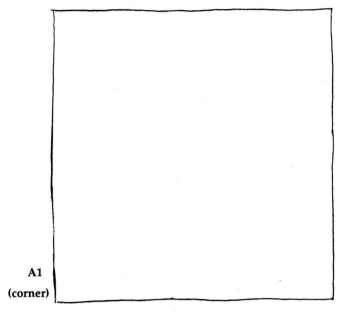

A1
(corner)

Two pattern pieces for Sawtooth Border

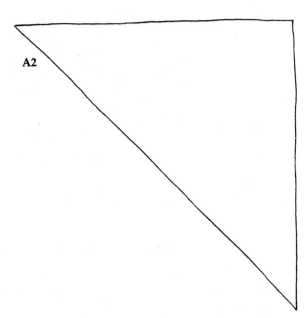

A2

Two pattern pieces for Stars and Stripes Border

B1

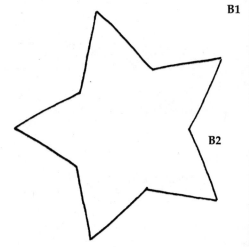

B2

290

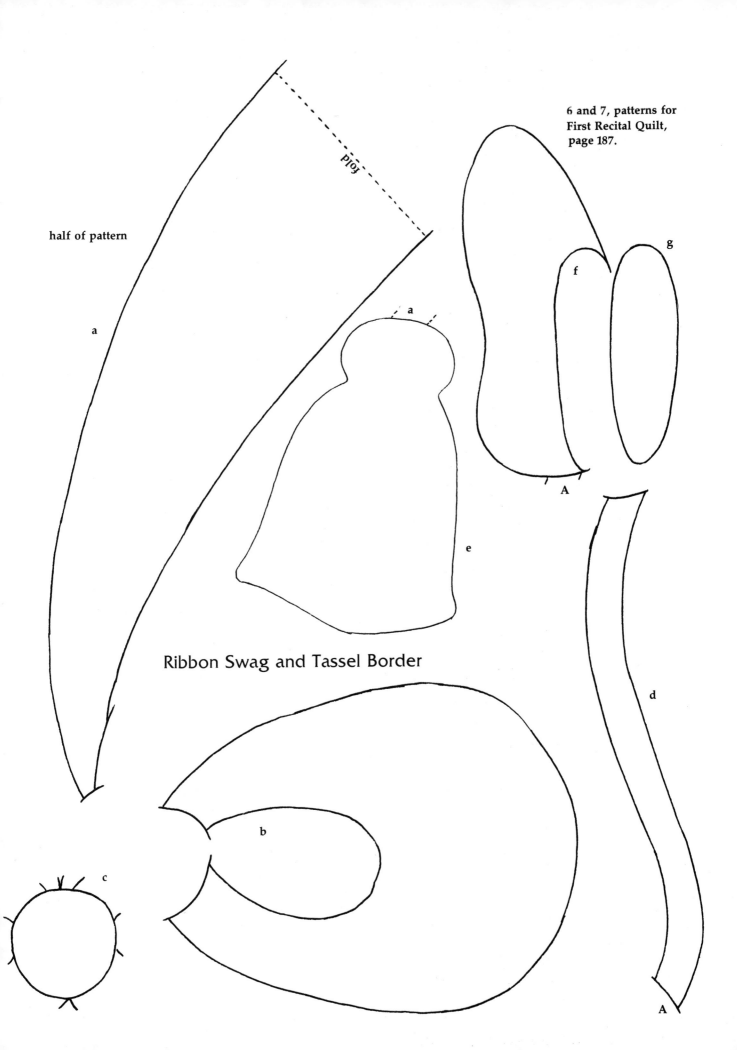

half of pattern

fold

a

6 and 7, patterns for
First Recital Quilt,
page 187.

g

f

a

A

e

d

Ribbon Swag and Tassel Border

b

c

A

7

Take a Quilting Pattern

Border and fill-in quilting motifs in various sizes and shapes are given here. Two designs, Hearts and Flowers (C1 and C2, pages 294–296) and Tulip and Leaves (W1 and W2, page 307) fill a large triangular area and can be used either for corner fill-ins or for unusual borders. Each of these patterns is too large for these pages; they have therefore been divided by dotted lines and given on more than one page. Another motif, called Paisley, is given in two sizes: for areas just larger than 4½ inches square and for areas just larger than 8 inches square. The two designs are shown inside square shapes, but they can be fitted inside circles or other shapes as well (pages 299 and 300).

In addition, there are many small spot motifs—some *very* small. In eighteenth- and very early nineteenth-century quilts, the filler was loose and needed to be quilted very closely to hold it in place. If there were small places left in the quilting designs that were really too large to be left unquilted, small random designs would be quilted in. They did not necessarily have anything to do with the main patterns but are quite charming because they show some of the things that interested the quilters. I have given some of these spot fill-in designs, such as the leaves, fruit, and birds on page 302. Modern quilts need fewer than half the quilting stitches the early quilts did to hold the filler in place, but, since quilting enhances the looks of the finished quilt, these spot-fillers should still come in handy. They may also be enlarged to any size by using the graph method described in the pattern for the Professional League Sports quilt, pages 232 and 233.

Many beginning quilters do not realize that almost all patterns (except those for piecing) can be used interchangeably as methods of quilting, appliqué, embroidery, fabric-painting, and crayoning. All of the designs in this section would look well executed in any of these other methods mentioned. Also, most of the animal, figure, and flower motifs in the other sections would look good as quilting designs. An all-white quilt designed from the nursery rhyme figures or perhaps with the small animal figures from Noah's Ark scattered among fancy floral designs could be lovely—and all your own: an original, one-of-a-kind quilt for a one-of-a-kind child.

Before beginning work on any quilt, please read the General Directions (which begin on page 4), including Quilting (page 18)

A.

Spiral Border

B.

Interwoven Border

C1.

X.

Z

Hearts and Flowers, Corner

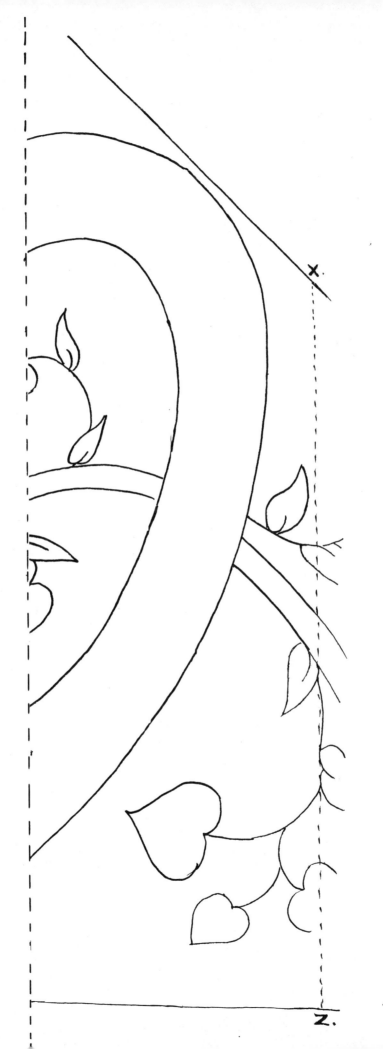

X

Z.

295

Hearts and Flowers. Corner of border

C2

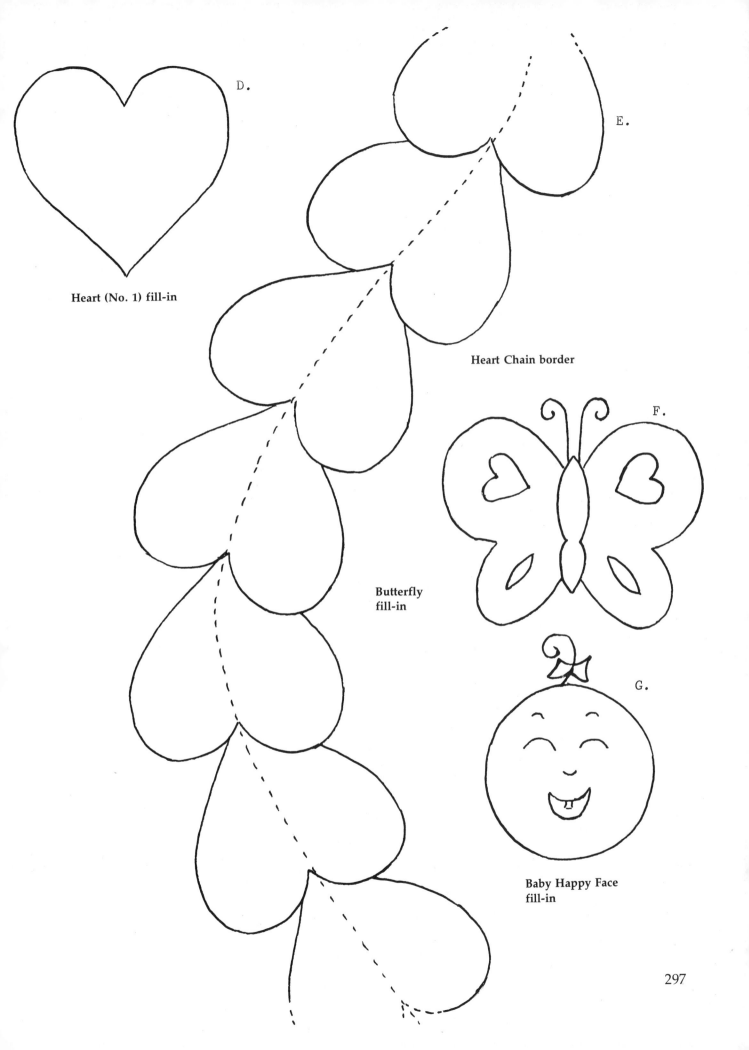

Heart (No. 1) fill-in

D.

E.

Heart Chain border

F.

Butterfly
fill-in

G.

Baby Happy Face
fill-in

H.

Flower Medallion

Folk Flowers

Paisley (no. 1)

Paisley (no. 2)

Heart Flower
(no. 1)

L

M

Basic Flower Shape

N

P

Heart (no. 2) fill-in

*letter O not used

Heart Flower
(no. 2)

301

Odd Fill-in Patterns

R2.

R1.

R3.

T1.

S1.

S2.

Q1.

Q3.

Q4.

T2.

Q2.

R4.

S3.

All-White Quilt

There are four separate patterns in this set. The arrangement of motifs into a top is shown in E in the Frontispiece. Cut a piece of plain-colored cloth—either white or one of the pastel shades. The backing can be a soft white cloth, or it can be of the same material and color as the top. For the quilt shown, use a square 48 inches on each side. If the cloth must be pieced, cut a square for the center and piece four strips around this. The border quilting pattern needs a strip 8 inches wide. To hide the seams in the pattern, cut the center square 32 inches on a side and add the 8-inch-wide borders to this. The corners of the border can be mitered; an 8-inch square might be placed in each corner to avoid having to figure the angle of the miter, or the border strips could each be cut 40 inches long. These strips could then be sewn across the corners in the manner of a Log Cabin pattern. See diagrams A, B, and C, pages 6 and 7.

When the cloth square for the top is finished, read the directions for making a quilting pattern on page 18 of the General Directions. Place the patterns on the material, being very careful to measure the placement so it is absolutely correct before you begin to mark the cloth.

The Star pattern in the center and the Folk Flower pattern (page 306) are not confusing. Study the Tulip and Leaves pattern—which has to be drawn in two sections—very carefully before making the cutting pattern for it. The leaves are angled out at the bottom of the flower, right and left as shown by the dotted lines (marked c). Once the leaves are drawn on a large-enough paper, you will see that the shape fills a corner triangle. The Princess Feather border is also divided onto two pages with a dotted line (d) to show where the ends are joined to the center. This center "feather" is also divided by a dotted line marked *fold*. This is half of the center pattern. The Feathers will fill the border strip from corner to corner.

U, Star Pattern

304

U, Star Pattern

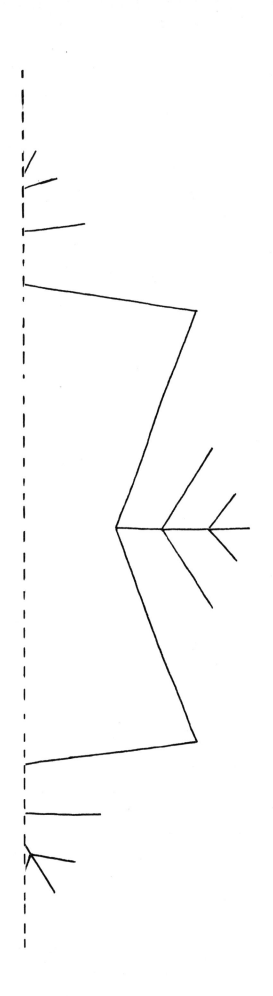

a

a'

b

b'

a

a'

b

b'

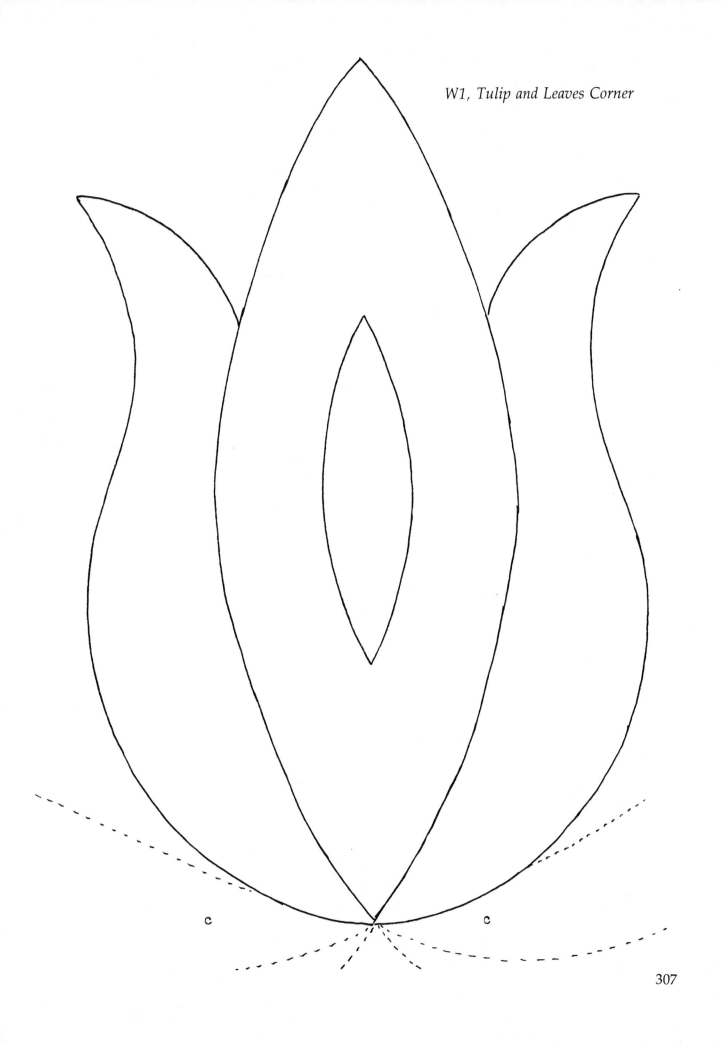

W1, Tulip and Leaves Corner

c

c

307

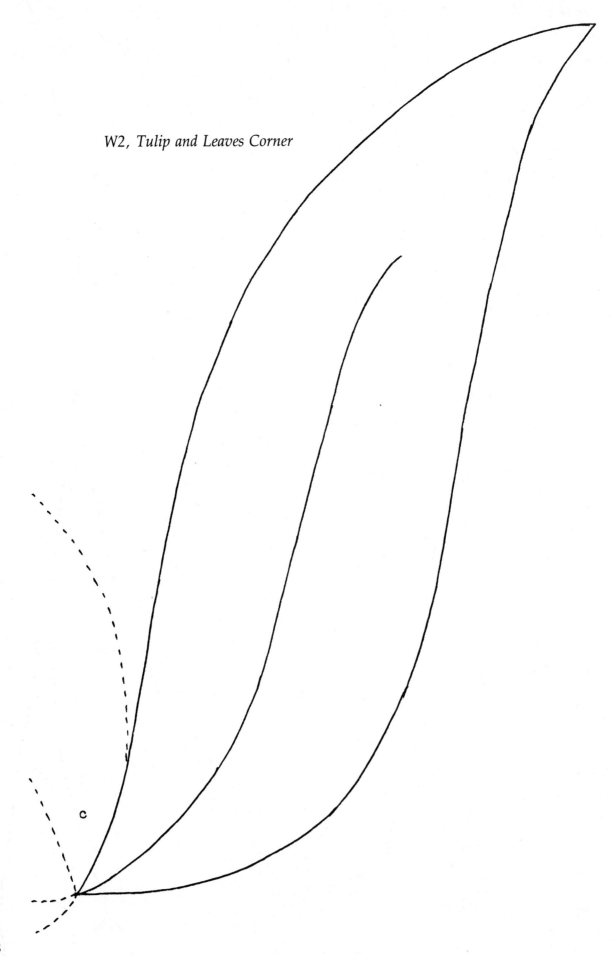

W2, Tulip and Leaves Corner

c

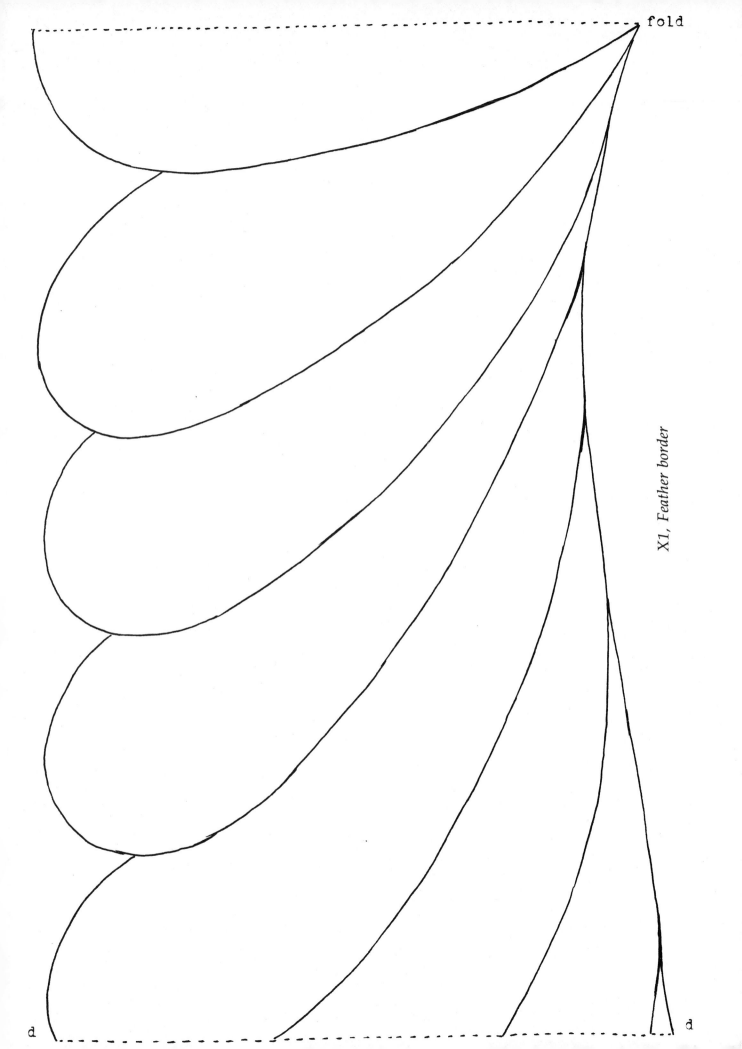

fold

X1, Feather border

d

d

d   d

X2, Feather border

INDEX